The Vanished Cities of Arabia

"Anyone coming from Europe with so much interest centring in the Middle Ages has to accustom the eyes to a new focus. It is as if he were to come from a well-kept garden to life in mid-ocean, stretching the eyes over a waste of waters. Everything is so old in the East; and being so old, is apt to be fragmentary. Civilizations come and go; nations have their rise, their period of prosperity, and then they disappear..."

THE DEAD SEA FROM THE MOUNT OF OLIVES: SUNRISE

THE VANISHED CITIES OF ARABIA

Mrs Steuart Erskine

Routledge
Taylor & Francis Group
LONDON AND NEW YORK

Published 2014 by Routledge

First published in 2004 by
Kegan Paul Limited

This edition first published in 2009 by
Routledge
2 Park Square, Milton Park, Abingdon, Oxfordshire OX14 4RN

Simultaneously published in the USA and Canada
by Routledge
711 Third Avenue, New York, NY 10017

First issued in paperback 2014

Routledge is an imprint of the Taylor & Francis Group, an informa business

© Kegan Paul, 2004

All rights reserved. No part of this book may be reprinted or reproduced or utilised in any form or by any electronic, mechanical, or other means, now known or hereafter invented, including photocopying and recording, or in any information storage or retrieval system, without permission in writing from the publishers.

British Library Cataloguing in Publication Data
A catalogue record for this book is available from the British Library

ISBN 978-0-710-30984-6 (hbk)

ISBN 978-1-138-86969-1 (pbk)

Publisher's Note
The publisher has gone to great lengths to ensure the quality of this reprint but points out that some imperfections in the original copies may be apparent. The publisher has made every effort to contact original copyright holders and would welcome correspondence from those they have been unable to trace.

CONTENTS

CHAPTER		PAGE
I.	Sunrise	9
II.	Petra	21
III.	The Nabatæan City	33
IV.	The Khazne Fur'un	45
V.	Pre-Roman Petra	57
VI.	Roman Petra	67
VII.	The Crusaders' Castle	75
VIII.	Kerak	85
IX.	A Feudal Castle	97
X.	Kerak Besieged	107
XI.	The Cities of the Plain	119
XII.	Aroer and Machærus	131
XIII.	The Desert	143
XIV.	Madeba	155
XV.	Rabboth Ammon	167
XVI.	Philadelphia	175
XVII.	The Decapolis	187
XVIII.	The Citadel	199
XIX.	Ptolemy Philadelphus II and the Greek Theatre	209
XX.	The Nabatæans Again	221
XXI.	Jerash	233
XXII.	The Story of Gerasa	243
XXIII.	The Temple of Artemis	255
XXIV.	The Theatre	265
XXV.	The Silver Age	279
XXVI.	The Neo-Platonists	293
XXVII.	Arab Geographers and Christian Pilgrims	307
XXVIII.	Sunset	317

LIST OF ILLUSTRATIONS

THE DEAD SEA FROM THE MOUNT OF OLIVES: SUNRISE	*Frontispiece*
	FACING PAGE
THE WADI MUSA AND THE ARABAH	12
THE KHAZNE FUR'UN FROM THE SIQ, PETRA	22
THE TRIPLE GATE, PETRA	28
STEPPED TOMBS, PETRA	34
ROCK-CUT ENTRANCE TO THE "TOMB OF THE KINGS," JERUSALEM	38
THE KHAZNE FUR'UN, PETRA	46
ABSALOM'S TOMB, JERUSALEM	50
THE THEATRE, PETRA, AND THE ENTRANCE TO THE SIQ	58
THE CORINTHIAN TOMB AND THE TOMB WITH THREE STORIES, PETRA	62
THE TEMPLE OF THE URN, PETRA	68
VIEW FROM THE COLONNADE OF THE TEMPLE OF THE URN, PETRA	70
THE DEIR, PETRA	76
THE APPROACH TO KERAK	86
ANCIENT ROCK-CUT ENTRANCE TO KERAK	90
KERAK CASTLE, OVERLOOKING THE DEAD SEA	98
THE GATE OF KERAK	108

LIST OF ILLUSTRATIONS—*Continued*

	FACING PAGE
THE GATE OF THE ARNON	120
THE DEAD SEA	132
IN THE DESERT—ON THE PILGRIM'S WAY TO MECCA	144
THE LITTLE RUIN OF THE MARKET	156
PORTRAIT OF KING HUSSEIN OF THE HIJAZ	168
ROMAN RUINS AT AMMAN	170
THE GREAT THEATRE, AMMAN	176
SPRINGTIME IN THE VALLEY OF THE UPPER ZERKA	180
ROMAN VAULTING OVER THE RIVER, AMMAN	188
THE SASANIAN BUILDING, AMMAN	200
INTERIOR OF THE SASANIAN BUILDING, AMMAN	204
THE EMPEROR'S BOX, AMMAN THEATRE	210
THE KASR EN-NUEIJIS	216
VIEW IN THE MOUNTAINS NEAR AMMAN	222
THE TRIUMPHAL GATE, JERASH	234
STREET OF COLUMNS, JERASH	238
AT THE CROSS ROADS, JERASH	244
THE PORTICO OF THE TEMPLE OF ARTEMIS, JERASH	256
COLUMNS OF THE IONIC ORDER IN THE FORUM, JERASH	266
THE ROMAN BATHS, JERASH	280
THE FORUM, WITH VIEW OF THE BEIT ET-TEI, JERASH	294
THE FORUM, JERASH	310
THE END OF THE DAY	318

THE VANISHED CITIES OF ARABIA

CHAPTER I

Sunrise.

WHAT is there in a sunrise that appeals to the imagination so strongly? It is usually less striking in effect than a sunset, the sun often hides behind fleecy clouds with mock modesty and you are not aware of his presence before you see him riding insolently up aloft. But the appeal is there, perhaps because, apart from the placid beauty of the scene, it suggests so much. We see in imagination the morning of the world, of the Universe, of life itself; it symbolizes the beginning of things and so is peculiarly suitable to the beginning of a journey. It is more than ever suitable when that journey is to the site of vanished cities whose history goes back into the dim ages.

One of the most lovely sunrises that I remember to have seen occurred on the morning when we were waiting on the heights before riding down to Petra. Just as Petra comes slowly out of the mists of time in history, so the topmost peaks of the rock city were touched with fire by the rising sun, which gradually penetrated into the blue mists below, and lit up the mass of Mount Hor and the distant Idumæan hills and all the rainbow colours in the vast sweep of the Ghor. The colours were so delicate, the air so pure, the whole panorama so unearthly that one could hardly believe that it was not some illusion of the senses.

The scene stretched out before us is one of

historical interest. To westward lies Petra enclosed in a great wedge of red sandstone, only the topmost of her fantastic peaks showing above the mass; beyond is the fine outline of the Jebel Harun, the Mount Hor up which Aaron went to die and where he was buried. Behind Petra stretches the desert of Sin, where the Children of Israel wandered and where they murmured against Moses, who struck the rock—was it really the entrance to the Siq, according to tradition? (!) —and the water flowed out. Dr. Alois Musil, whose long studies of all this region entitle him to hold an original view, thinks that the Kadesh round about which the Israelites spent the thirty-eight years of their exile in the wilderness was no other than Petra. And it was somewhere in this region that, in an earlier age, Esau came after that affair of the mess of pottage, dispossessing the Horites who were the first people living in Petra of whom we have any knowledge. It was from Petra that he went out with four hundred men to meet Jacob, passing by with his wives and his servants and his flocks, anxious to propitiate the brother whom he had cheated out of his birthright.

Anyone coming from Europe with so much interest centring in the Middle Ages has to accustom the eyes to a new focus. It is as if he were to come from a well-kept garden to life in mid-ocean, stretching the eyes over a waste of waters. Everything is so old in the East; and being so old, is apt to be fragmentary. Civilizations come and go; nations have their rise, their period of prosperity, and then they disappear, like those cities the vestiges of which we have come so far to see.

Before going down to Petra it is almost necessary, at the risk of being tedious, to endeavour to conjure up a picture of the times in which she rose to greatness, fell into a decline and vanished from human ken.

We must go back into the dawn of history. About four thousand years before Christ the Summerian empire extended from the Red Sea to Mount Taurus,

Sunrise

the Armenian mountains and Turkistan, from the Levant to the Persian Ocean and the Indian Ocean. What were the boundaries of the empire of Amurru? It was of vast extent and comprised a small, insignificant tract of land running down by the Mediterranean Sea which we now know as Palestine. Palestine first comes into history when the Hyskos were expelled from Egypt in 1700 B.C., and proceeded to conquer Syria; it appears fitfully in the Tell-el-Amarna tablets in the fifteenth century B.C., it formed part of the Hittite and Egyptian empires. Under Egypt it remained for about four centuries, it paid fealty to Assyria and Babylon and Persia, was conquered by Alexander the Great, after he crossed the Hellespont in 333 B.C. and passed over to Syria to dispossess the Persians. The rival Greek dynasties of Seleucids and Ptolemies fought over Palestine until Antiochus the Great defeated Ptolemy at Paneon in 198, and in 135 the Maccabees came into power, to be followed by the Romans, who annexed Syria as a Roman province in the spring of 63 B.C. For six hundred years Rome was overlord, and then Persia once more took possession of the country, to be ousted soon after by the Moslem uprising. Farther than that we need not go for the present, and indeed it is confusing enough to follow the varying fortunes of Palestine for so long. It is like shaking a kaleidoscope and watching the little bits of coloured glass arrange and rearrange themselves in ever varying patterns.

Not only did Palestine pass from the suzerainty of one great power to another, but the nations of the north and the south marched up and down their land, which was like a causeway between north and south, to settle their accounts with each other. Whether for war or commerce, the route between the principal centres of power or commerce had to pass that way; owing to the formation of the land, the armies marched more often down western Palestine, fighting often in the great plain of Esdraelon for choice, while the caravans chose the eastern route. As the formation of the land had much to do with the separate histories of western and eastern Palestine, we must take a bird's-eye view of it as a whole.

Palestine has always been a land of tribes, its boundaries have altered, its very names have changed with its overlords, its various component parts have stretched out and shrunk into themselves like so many pieces of elastic; but one great natural division has always remained to separate one part of the country from the rest, to act as a spiritual as well as a physical barrier. That barrier is, of course, that extraordinary Ghor, which is a fault in the earth's surface and which dips down as low as twelve hundred and ninety-two feet below sea level at the shore of the Dead Sea, the bottom of which is, in places, thirteen hundred feet lower still. The Rift (as the Arabs call it) is one hundred and sixty miles long; it starts at the foot of Hermon and in its bed are contained the lakes of Huleh and Tiberias, the river Jordan, the Down-runner, to use an expressive word, which rushes down until its unquiet waters with their zigzag current lose themselves in the Dead Sea, and the Dead Sea itself. This strange hollow, unique in the world, leaves the Dead Sea, rising as it goes along, and we have just seen it as it sweeps round beyond and beneath Petra on its way to the Gulf of Akaba.

The character of the land east and west of the Rift is quite different one to another. The story of western Palestine has been told over and over again by those competent to do so and will always be of intense interest to humanity. The cradle of our religion is to be found among its arid mountains and its placid valleys; Jerusalem is the shrine of the world. But comparatively little has been written about eastern Palestine except by scientists, and its story is not so much bound up with religious as with political upheavals.

The strip of land that stretches from Mount Hermon

THE WADI MUSA AND THE ARABAH

on the north to the Gulf of Akaba on the south has the Rift for a boundary to the west and is merged in the great Arabian desert in the east. The natural divisions of eastern Palestine are made by three great rivers, the Yarmuk, the Jabbok and the Mojib, which cut deep fissures through the rocky plateau; they have not always answered to the political divisions, but it is impossible to follow all the changes that, from time to time, altered the boundaries of the dominant tribes. Speaking roughly, the land north of Yarmuk is the ancient Bashan, included in the district known from time immemorial as the Hauran; a land of rich alluvial soil and volcanic deposit that is the granary of Syria. Between Yarmuk and Jabbok is Gilead, a land of mountains and of fertile plains that produced grazing land and all manner of fruit and spice; south of Jabbok and as far south as the further end of the Dead Sea are Ammon and Moab, and farther south again is Edom. Moab is a high, rocky plateau, varying from about two thousand feet above sea level to two thousand five hundred; here also is good grazing land, but the desert begins to encroach more and more until, in Edom, we have more bare rock and waste of sand than anything else.

Like western Palestine the names change with the different masters of the country, even that name of Palestine has come to mean something quite different to what it meant at first. To Moses it meant the strip of coast-land known as Philistia, of which it is a corruption; the Arabs keep the original name and still call their country "Filistin." When Moses sang his song of triumph to the Lord, he used Palestina in its restricted sense and called the whole country Canaan.

"The people shall hear and be afraid; sorrow shall take hold on the inhabitants of Palestina.

"Then the dukes of Edom shall be amazed; the mighty men of Moab, trembling shall take hold upon them; all the inhabitants of Canaan shall melt away."

In the days of Christ the country between Yarmuk and Mojib was called Peræa, a name given by the Greeks who called the whole peninsula Arabia and the whole of eastern Palestine Cœle-Syria. The Persians divided the country into Satrapies, the Romans shook the kaleidoscope vigorously and re-arranged their new province according to their own ideas. There was then Palestina Prima, including Judæa and Samaria, Palestina Secunda, with Galilee and east of Jordan, and Palestina Tertia, having Edom and Moab. Later still the Crusaders made eastern Palestine into the fief of "Oultre Jourdain." But we are getting too far away from the sunrise and the morning of history.

In prehistoric ages a Megalithic people lived in eastern Palestine, as the dolmens, menhirs, circles and rock-cut cisterns to be found there freely testify. In the dawn of history there were cave dwellers who were to be found at quite a late date inhabiting certain parts of the country. The Horites who lived in the apparently inaccessible caves in Petra were troglodytes, and no doubt the natural hiding places were both economical and safe. At a time when any settler was at the mercy of nomad tribes intent on booty, these eyries were not to be despised; at a later date whole cities, such as that of which we now have the remains at Deraa, were built underground for safety's sake.

Whether or no Arabia was the cradle of the Semitic race, it has been the home of the Semitic world for thousands of years. The Arabs base their descent from Shem, the son of Noah, and the Bedawin claim a special descent from that wild man Ishmael, son of Abram and Hagar; whether they are Semites or whether they come from a pre-Semitic stock does not seem to be satisfactorily proved. Whatever their origin the Arabs appear to have had a very early civilization, although it varied very much in different parts of the country.

Arabia, like Palestine, had a natural barrier that

divided the country into two parts, only this time it was not a river but a wild waste of desert called the " Solitary Quarter." El-Yemen (" the Right "), or Arabia Felix, as that part of the country was called, was very fertile, and enjoyed sub-tropical vegetation. It was a rich soil producing two crops a year of cereals, as well as trees and bushes from which spice and balm were taken ; the riches of this part of Arabia became famous, and excited the cupidity of nations from far off. In this district were two tribes that arrived at the supreme power successively—the Sabæans and the Himyarites. King Solomon ordered gold and precious stones for the decoration of the Temple from Saba, and the Queen of Saba, who was "inquisitive unto philosophy," went in state to visit him on a celebrated occasion. She took with her camels laden with jewels and gold, with myrrh and nard, and a root of balsam that is said to have provided the parent stock for the balm of Gilead. Although the Queen was accustomed to barbaric splendour she was frankly astonished at the luxury of the palace of the wise King ; she admired the order with which his service was conducted, the magnificence of his daily table, and the advanced stage of civilization that he had reached. No doubt when she returned to Saba she instituted all sorts of reforms ; but the fact remains that the Sabæans had already a considerable amount of culture. The earliest records that we have in Arabia are contained in the Sabæan inscriptions, and the Sabæan empire stretched from the Red Sea to the Persian Gulf. The Himyarites, who succeeded them as dominant power in that part of Arabia, were never so great, though they had some distinguished men among their rulers. The Sabæans and the Himyarites spoke South Arabic, which differs considerably from the Arabic of the north. They were peaceful people, contrasting strongly with the northern Arabs of the Hijaz, those nomads living in " houses of hair," even as they do at the present time, who were of those who claimed descent from Ishmael. When the caravan routes were changed from land to water, the South Arabians lost their commercial advantages and gradually declined, until the Himyarites, long after the fall of the Sabæans, were conquered by the Abyssinians and vanished from the scene.

The true sons of the desert had no use for civilization in those early times any more than they have at this day. They have been described by one who lived amongst them as being divided into two groups—the real Arabs, who do not use the word "Bedawin," but the more generic term Arab, and the half-Arabs; the rest of the population are called by them fellaheen. The true Arab is the noble of the desert; he is a camel breeder, while the half-Arab, who is also a nomad, is a breeder of goats and sheep. The latter moves less freely and is more apt to settle down and cultivate a piece of land, thus forming a link with the despised fellah, who exists only to provide the Arab with corn that he has not sown and pasture for his camels that he does not own. The Bedawy cannot be forced to obey nowadays any more than he could when the world was young, for if he be pursued he drives his camels into some waterless desert where his enemies, mounted on horses, cannot follow. If they do persist he has all sorts of pleasant devices calculated to stop them, such as filling the wells with a camel load of locusts. The great laws of the desert were probably much the same then as they are now—regard for hospitality, for protection of the clan and for revenge of any insult. The presence of these tribes, pitching their camps wherever they chose, striking them at a moment's notice, raiding the settled part of the population, has always constituted the danger of eastern Palestine, which is totally unprotected towards the Arabian desert.

Besides the comparatively cultivated Sabæans and Himyarites and the unruly sons of Ishmael, there existed a tribe of Arabs, called the Nabatæans, that arrived at a great position, achieved almost unexampled prosperity and then went the way of other nations, leaving only the indifferent Bedawin to pitch their tents on the ruins of former glory.

"Frail houses of hair, they were here four thousand years ago ere civilization had left the Nile and the Euphrates, and they flowed in again upon the decay of one of her most powerful bulwarks. For the Arabs have been like the wild ocean, barred off for a time, yet prevailing at last over the patience and virtue of great empires."

CHAPTER II
Petra

CHAPTER II
Petra

A HALT made before plunging down into the valley two thousand feet below is good, because it enables you not only to enjoy the vast panoramic view, but it also makes plain the majestic and isolated position of this unique rock city. It gives you leisure to think over the romantic story of Petra's greatness, her fall and her extinction.

We are in the heart of Arabia Petræa, in that Edom which was so often heartily cursed by the Prophets. The Mount of Esau had a reputation for evil, wisdom and secrecy; the descendants of Esau were powerful people governed by Dukes. Why did they abandon their eyrie? Diodorus Siculus says that they moved out of Petra when the Babylonian Captivity gave them an opportunity of taking some of the Israelites' possessions. On the face of it this seems likely, as the Edomites and the Israelites were always enemies ever since, or possibly before, Moses and the children of Israel were forbidden to " cross their border "; but the Prophet Malachi says that the Lord hated Esau and laid his mountains and his heritage waste for the dragons of the wilderness. Which looks as if there had been a fight rather than a peaceful evacuation.

Accounts differ as to the first arrival of the Nabatæans at Petra; it is sometimes said that their first stronghold was Kerak—the other Stone of the Desert. They probably came to Petra in the sixth or fifth century before Christ, but the earliest notice we have of them in secular history is in 312 B.C., when the forces of Antigonus I unsuccessfully attacked the city. They are mentioned in the Bible and are spoken of as " they of the south " who were to inherit the

Mountain of Esau; they figure in the cylinder of Asshur Bani Pal in the seventh century B.C.; although doubt has been thrown on this attribution, it seems certain that the Nabatæans were indicated. They are connected with the Sabæans by commerce and must have absorbed what culture they had from the same source. They had colonies in the land of the Minoans and were probably of the same race. Diodorus says that they were " pre-eminent among nomad Arabs," but they do not seem to have been altogether nomads, even in early times, for we hear of their cities that were without walls because they were peace-loving folk. Which, by the way, does not sound as if they were the descendants of Nebajoth, the first-born of Ishmael, that wild man whose hand was against every man's.

We are not surprised to hear that the Nabatæan culture was connected with Palmyra, as, although the importance of Palmyra was not so great as that of Petra, as long as the latter was the centre of the great caravan routes, still the two cities were connected by these and Palmyra and Damascus were near neighbours. The Nabatæans spoke Arabic but used Aramaic, which was the *lingua franca* of the Persian empire, for their inscriptions, in the text of which are allusions to princes, elders, horsemen, scholars, doctors, and bards. They are said to have possessed a considerable literature, but I do not know on what authority; the " Nabatæan book of Agriculture," supposed to have been translated from the Chaldean, is, I believe, not authentic.

These people rose from obscure traders to be the possessors of an empire that stretched, at one time, from the Red Sea to Damascus; like the piece of elastic, its length varied as circumstances extended or contracted their dominions. The period of greatest prosperity began about one hundred years before Christ and continued until 106 A.D., when it was annexed by Rome. The Romans kept up the trade and the importance of Petra for a long time, but it was already declining, owing

THE KHAZNE FUR'UN FROM THE SIQ, PETRA

to the change of the trade routes and the growing importance of Palmyra, when Rome fell and with it Romanised Petra. After the rise of Islam in the seventh century a veil falls over Petra, which is only partially lifted during the twelfth century by the advent of the Crusaders. In 1265 A.D. the Mameluk Sultan Beybars visited Petra after taking Kerak ; he climbed up to see the Crusaders' fort and found it very strong and the architecture admirable. After that the veil falls so completely that Petra vanished as if she had never been.

The centuries pass, heavy with the destinies of mankind, but the once busy metropolis is as silent as the tombs that are honeycombed in her walls. She becomes a legend, a city that may have once existed or that may even be a myth. Only the students still keep a desire to re-discover the rock city, and they are kept away because the part of Arabia Petræa in which it is supposed to be situated, is infested by war-like Arabs who resent any intrusion. In the case of Petra, that they guarded so jealously, it was accentuated by a tradition that some of the great riches that had once been kept there were still hidden among the caves.

In 1812, nearly six hundred years since Petra had vanished from our ken, a bold explorer resolved to do a daring deed. He spent three years learning Arabic, living among the Arabs as one of themselves and his disguise as Sheikh Ibrahim was complete ; yet he took his life in his hand when he ventured into Petra under the guidance of an Arab who had his suspicions. Burckhardt spent only comparatively few hours in Petra, but he came to the conclusion that it must be the Petra of history because there was no other place at all like it in Arabia Petræa. He must have felt a thrill when he stood at the classic spot where every visitor to Petra has stood since, but his words are sober in the extreme. " On the side of the perpendicular rock " he writes, " directly opposite to the issue of the main valley, an excavated mausoleum came in view, the situation and beauty of which are calculated to make an extraordinary impression upon the traveller."

Since Burckhardt, there have been a limited number of archæologists and scientists and a still more limited number of casual visitors to the ancient city of the Nabatæans; Dr. Musil was the first to make a scientific study of the tombs; the latest are Mr. Philby, the late British adviser to the Trans-Jordan Government, and Sir Alexander Kennedy, whose books on the subject are eagerly looked for by the increasing number of people who take an interest in Petra. It is to be hoped that a systematic excavation will soon be undertaken, without which the secrets of the city, throwing back as far as Esau or perhaps the Horites before him, to say nothing of the Nabatæans, will be for ever buried in the thick red sand that covers the successive cities that have stood in the Valley of Moses.

But the sun is up and it is time to ride down to Petra.

About an hour and a half's ride brings you down to the region of red sandstone; the way is often precipitous and sometimes slippery, but the small, sure-footed horses negotiate any difficulty if left to pick out their own way among the rocks. As you near the entrance to the Siq, the scenery gets wilder and more unlike anything else on earth. Great masses of sandstone tower above, almost meeting over your head; after the Bab-es-Siq—the Gate of the Siq—the gorge narrows and the cliffs get more and more precipitous. It is like the entrance to a robber's cave: sombre and mysterious. Curiously enough, Rome, the civilizer of the ends of the earth, has set her mark here before we even enter the Nabatæans' stronghold. We are riding over what was once a paved road, like any of those to be found in a Roman city, only now it is broken up and overgrown by weeds and scrub. By it runs a brook in winter, but it is dried up by the beginning of springtime. The

Siq is well described by Irby and Mangles in their
" Travels in Egypt and Syria " :—

" There is, however, one frightful chasm for the
passage of this stream, which furnishes, as it did
anciently, the only access to Petra on this side. It is
impossible to conceive anything more awful or sublime
than such an approach ; the width is not more than just
sufficient for the passage of two horsemen abreast, the
sides are in all parts perpendicular, varying from four
hundred to seven hundred feet in height, and they often
overhang to such a degree that, without their absolutely
meeting, the sky is intercepted and completely shut out
for one hundred yards together, and there is little more
light than in a cavern.

" The screaming of the eagles, hawks, and owls, who
were soaring above our heads in considerable numbers,
seemingly annoyed at anyone approaching their lonely
habitation, added much to the singularity of the scene.
The tamarisk, the wild fig, and the oleander grow
luxuriantly about the road, rendering the passages often
difficult ; in some places they hang down most beautifully
from the cliffs and crevices where they have taken root ;
the caper plant was also in luxuriant growth, the
continued shade furnishing it with moisture. . . .

" The brook has disappeared beneath the soil
from the dryness of the season, but the manner
in which its occasional overflowings have broken
up the antique pavement and the slippery passes
which the running of the water has made, by
polishing the rock where it had been cut away
to form the road, sufficiently prove the necessity
of providing another course for its waters. A trough,
carried along near the foot of the precipice upon the left-
hand side, was destined to confine the water and to
convey it upon a raised level to the city. At a considerable distance down the ravine this watercourse crosses
over to the opposite side ; and towards its extremity may
be traced, passing along at a great height, in earthen

pipes, bedded and secured with mortar, in horizontal grooves cut in the face of the rock and even across the architectural fronts of some of the tombs, which makes it probable that it is of later date."

As you ride along this winding ravine, you have plenty of time to look about you for, owing to the roughness of the ground, it is all a matter of going at foot's pace. Occasional tombs there are, but none of any special interest, although you may halt at one that has a low portico with columns of the Doric order standing on an excavated square space. If you be wise you will push on, for time is precious in Petra, where few have more than three or four quite inadequate days to spend within her magic circle.

The steep sides of the gorge are so near that you could almost touch them with your outstretched hands; they are deep red, violet, almost sable, although, even in shadow, there is a lurking flame which gives warmth; a sudden shaft of sunlight sends a brilliant zigzag of rose colour on to the sombre rock, and then a turn in the ravine shows you the unforgettable picture of the Treasure House of Pharaoh framed in the dark gorge of the Siq. It is a picture that everyone that has gone to Petra has tried to express by pen or pencil, but I can point to the fine sketches of Major Benton Fletcher, instead of attempting to describe it in words. He has taken one unconventional view, seen from within, neither framed by the gorge nor taken from exactly opposite; the great charm of the view from the gorge consists in the wonderful colour, more flame than rose, of the sandstone which is reflected by the sun's rays, and the contrast between Nature in one of her most wild and rugged moods and Art in one of her most graceful manifestations. I cannot think of the Khazne Fur'un—the Treasure House of Pharaoh—as of a late Roman work; Syria was Hellenised long before the Romans came, and it was surely under that influence that the clever Nabatæan architects carved this temple out of the living rock.

Passing on to take a general view of Petra, you come at once into a street of tombs that widens out until you get to a theatre excavated out of the rock, from which you have an extraordinary view of the basin of the Wadi Musa, where successive towns have stood, but which is now a mass of masonry covered by scrub and a tangle of oleander. On all sides the gaunt red cliffs stand, honeycombed by rock dwellings and tombs, with here and there a pseudo classic façade or one that reminds you of Assyria or Egypt; immense headlands stand up against a sapphire sky. It is all new, strange and indescribably old; which may sound paradoxical, but which is strictly true.

By degrees the principal features of Petra impress themselves on a newcomer. The chief street of the Roman town ran, as usual, along the bank of the river, which was also, according to almost invariable custom, vaulted over for a considerable space. The remains of the Temple and part of the Triple Gate are the only built monuments still standing. They belong to a late period, after the Roman annexation.

The huge mass called El-Habis by the Arabs is a bold promontory of rock which has one of the High Places of Sacrifice on one of its plateaux; the equally imposing Zebb 'Atuf has the most finished of these ancient sacrificial places on its summit. Both of these commanding heights have the remains of a fort which once guarded Petra and provided a post of observation for those who defended the almost impregnable city.

The two principal rock walls containing tombs of interest are the north-east wall where some of the finest of the classical tombs are situated—the Urn tomb, the Corinthian tomb and the tomb of the Governor to name the most famous; and the south-east wall where some of the older and more interesting Nabatæan tombs are found. The High Places are approached by climbing up ravines in which, from time to time, steps have been cut in the rock for the use of worshippers—another climb of this description leads up to the Deir, the so-called Convent, from which magnificent views can be obtained. The walks may be rough but the air is so invigorating and the country so picturesque that you are well repaid for the effort.

To ascend the Zebb 'Atuf, or Obelisk Mount, as it is sometimes called, you have to follow a gorge to the left as you leave the Siq, mounting up a rock-hewn path, with stairs cut at intervals. They are the stairs up which the Nabatæans climbed to worship Dusares, and one wonders whether they mounted up so high every day or whether they offered frankincense and myrrh on the roofs of their houses in preference. As they had their own little high places there, it is possible that they only climbed up to the lofty summit of the Zebb 'Atuf on great occasions. On the summit are two obelisks and places of sacrifice; higher up is the fort and, higher again, the great Place of Sacrifice which is well described by Sir Alexander Kennedy in a lecture delivered before the Royal Geographical Society in January, 1924 :—

" On the other side—that is, the north side—of the shelf, past the ruined tower of the fort and at the highest level and narrowest part of the ridge, lies the often described "holy place" of Zebb'Atuf, the largest and most complete and least weathered of all the Sacella of Petra. The sacrificial basin, itself perhaps an altar also, stands beside a central altar, on the one side of a great cleared and levelled rectangle, like a gigantic triclinium, about fifty by twenty-two feet. It is clear that if there were animal sacrifices or burnt offerings of any kind here, the animals must have been small enough to be somehow carried up, whether dead or alive, for walking up would be impossible. A good deal has been written about the probable functions of the altar, tank, and seats, but I fear that what has been written amounts to little beyond guesswork. It is very singular that in this notable place of worship, although there is plenty of room for cele-

THE TRIPLE GATE, PETRA

brants, there is absolutely no room, on account of the narrowness of the ridge and its steep sides, for other worshippers."

So it is probable after all, that only the Priests performed their sacrificial rites up on this eminence and that the worshippers were content to follow them from a lower level. The supreme god of the Nabatæans was Dusares or Dhu-Shara, the god of the mountain district of Spara, the biblical Se'ir. He was a form of Ba'al connected with the springs and his natural shrine would seem to be in some grove, watered by a stream that fertilized a desert oasis. The Nabatæans are also said to have worshipped the Sun, and Dusares has been later indentified with Dionysius, so that we can only conjecture what their form of religion was. Dusares was symbolized by a black rectangular stone that may have represented his throne. Who were the first people to worship up here? The altars, lavers and other sacrificial objects are pure Semitic and might even have been used by Esau, though they were probably hewn out of the rock at a much later date.

The Nabatæans, although their supreme god took precedence over all, had a hierarchy of their own, in which were two principal goddesses, Lat or Allat, the mother of the gods, and Chaabon, the virgin mother of Dusares. These were possibly Sun goddesses.

Strabo tells us that they were very punctilious in performing their daily rites; we know that they believed in evil spirits and had curious theories about the external soul, and were superstitious regarding shadows. Their Kings consulted diviners and their women were skilful in making both love potions and poisons.

The sacrifices of the Nabatæans are said to have been an act of communion with the god, not an offering to appease him. The worship of Ba'al was, of course, local and differed in different places. The Ba'al was not supposed to be omnipotent, his power was, more or less, restricted to his own shrine and its neighbourhood, where he was all powerful. He was a tribal god, the head of his human family; he was linked with nature, not outside it, and he was naturally the god of fertility and the god of agriculture. That Dusares, the god of the fresh springs, should ever have become connected with Bacchus and should have taken on his attributes, and that the Nabatæan feasts would have become orgiastic, was, I suppose, just a sign of the advance of civilization!

The South Arabic inscriptions contain many allusions to Sun goddesses; if they were worshipped here what a magnificent place the Obelisk ridge would have been for catching the first and last rays of the sun; and when the moon rose and flooded the whole plateau with white light, perhaps the Moon god walked there and looked down on Petra sleeping under the Syrian stars, the busy hive of bees almost as silent then as it is now under the same softening and all-pervading radiance.

CHAPTER III
THE NABATÆAN CITY

CHAPTER III
THE NABATÆAN CITY

NO vestige remains of the Nabatæan city to tell us how they lived when they deserted the caves and occupied those sumptuous stone houses that Strabo talks about. They were probably built of the prevailing sandstone, but may have been covered with stucco and painted, following the Egyptian fashion. As we have seen, they had little high places on their roofs where they made daily oblations to the sun or to Dusares, burning frankincense and myrrh before his symbol, the square rectangular block that represented his throne.

The Nabatæans were, before all things, merchants; although they do not seem to have settled in Petra so early, I am told by Professor Musil, whom I must quote once more, that they controlled the world trade at the beginning of the first millennium before Christ, proof of which he has found in every oasis along every trade route in Arabia. The trade of the world was at that time centred in south-western Arabia, and the long caravans carrying gold and silver and precious stones, as well as spice and balsam and strange animals, such as apes and peacocks, with dyes and draperies, and the necessaries of life like corn and oil, went to and fro unceasingly. In each stopping place the Nabatæans, who, in spite of their peaceful tendencies, kept a standing army, had a picket to protect their own merchandise and that of others who paid tribute in return for a safe conduct over the Nabatæan dominions. It is evident that after they took up their abode in Petra, so conveniently situated just where two trade routes crossed, they must have given shelter to the caravans and they must have had vast storehouses to receive the goods.

The key to success in commerce in those days lay in command of the trade routes. In the annals of the Assyrians it is related that they got possession of the northern part of the north-west road between Phœnicia and Egypt; they flourished accordingly, and their troops punished any attempts to rob the caravans under their protection. In the same annals we find that the tribe of Nabaiti camped east of Petra in the seventh century B.C., in the neighbourhood of their remote kindred, the Edomites. In this district were two roads crossing one another; one went from the Persian Gulf to Phœnicia, the other united Egypt with Babylon. After King Assurbanipal conquered the Kedar tribe, these Nabaiti became the most powerful people in northern Arabia. They overran the land of the Edomites, whose power had been destroyed in the sixth century B.C., and became the masters of the coveted trade routes, as well as acquiring grazing lands for their flocks. Petra thus became a great commercial centre, and ended, in the last century before Christ and the first of our era, by monopolizing nearly the whole of the world trade. The Nabatæans obtained an ascendancy in the Sinaitic Peninsula, they got possession of Damascus, they held the important oasis of Adumu, the modern Jauf, where two roads met, one leading to Babylonia, the other to the Persian Gulf. They founded important colonies in the state of the Minoans which were connected to Petra by roads over which they had control.

What a busy scene Petra must have presented when a caravan arrived! The clerks and the customs officers hurried out to meet the long string of heavily loaded camels outside the town, to take stock of their merchandise. To the merchants and drivers it must have seemed like arriving at a gay metropolis after their toilsome march across the desert waste from one oasis to another. And when they had unloaded the camels and refreshed themselves with wine made from the date palm, perhaps they walked about the crowded streets

STEPPED TOMBS, PETRA

The Nabatæan City

among a throng of people of many races ; nomads from the interior of Arabia, Egyptians, Jews, Syrians, Nubians, Nabatæan citizens and guards. It was not all an affair of housing goods that were on their way elsewhere ; the Nabatæans bought purple stuff from Tyre although they supplied some dyes themselves ; they bought brass, iron, styrax, saffron and white cinnamon, besides having a fancy for pictures and statues. There was, no doubt, buying and selling going on in Petra when a well-supplied caravan arrived, and the Wadi Musa must have hummed with life. How different to the absolute desolation of the Petra of to-day, with her rifled tombs and her ruins covered with weeds and scrub ! How different from these streets that were crowded with the living are the empty tombs where the footfall is noiseless on the fine, heaped-up red sand, seeming as if the past had been swept away so remorselessly that the present cannot even wake up an echo.

Although the Nabatæans lived principally in houses in the valley, they must have also occupied many of the caves that have been called tombs ; Sir Alexander Kennedy points out that this was the case, and he mentions a large room carved out of the rock not far from the theatre which must have been used as a storehouse for merchandise. It is divided into thirteen or fourteen large recesses, each more than six feet by three high by eight feet deep ; it is obvious that the greater safety of such a room, excavated out of the rock and with only one entrance, would appeal to a people who were still more or less cave dwellers.

Although a commercial people owning a city that was one of the most important of the caravanserai that were used for storing merchandise, the Nabatæans had a standing army and could bring ten thousand men or more into the field. Their form of government was monarchical but far from tyrannical ; their laws were just and their lives were simple. What their houses were we can but guess, for all that remains to-day is a quantity of excavated tombs or temples, beside those rock chambers that have no architectural features.

The Nabatæan tombs are the most interesting monuments in Petra. They have been described at length by Brunnow and Domaszewski in their monumental work " Die Provincia Arabia," by Dr. Gustav Dalman, Burckhardt, Doughty, Dr. Musil in " Arabia Petræa," Jaussen and Savignac in " Mission Archeologique en Arabie " and others. By borrowing from these authoritative works, we may endeavour to get a clear idea of the several styles that distinguish the different periods during which the tombs and chambers were laboriously carved out of the living rock.

Brunnow and Domaszewski divide these tombs into six classes; the Pylon, the stepped tomb, the Protoheger, the Heger, the purely foreign and the Temple style. Dalman substitutes three classes : the Nabatæan, simple stepped tombs with a battlement, dating from the third and second centuries before Christ, the Hellenistic, marked by the employment of new motives and by the invention of the distinctive Nabatæan capital and the Roman style with a pediment, dating from 106 A.D. Sir Alexander Kennedy also divides the tombs into three classes, but before doing so he makes an interesting distinction between those that were connected with some form of religious rite and those that were not. His three classes are the Assyrian, the Egyptian and the Classical.

The earliest of these tombs that derive from Assyria have a plain façade with crow-step gables rising over a straight groove. There is no decoration over the plain doorway, the gables are generally five in number ; a very few of a later date have an architrave over the door. As the style develops, or the architects come under a new influence, there is sometimes a double line of crow steps, occasionally even a classical pediment over the door.

The second style is the Egyptian, in which the

The Nabatæan City

peculiar feature is the heavy cornice, the cavetto, sometimes doubled, and the huge crow steps, few in number, that surmount the cavetto. Into this severe and massive style classic influences crept gradually, here in a pilaster, there in a decoration. In some arched tombs there is a suggestion of Syrian influence.

The Egyptians were, of course, great tomb builders; the Pyramid tombs alone stand as monuments of the first ten dynasties of their Kings. They have plain rock-cut tombs in the Valley of Kings, but they decorated them inside with paintings that have made the whole epoch live again before our eyes. Their domestic buildings, of which no important specimen remains, can be reconstructed from these paintings as well as their costumes and their customs. What a pity that the Nabatæans did not, however roughly, paint the insides of their tombs so that we might see them as they were!

From the Pyramid builders the Arabians got the obelisk and the form of tomb, following another kind frequently seen in Egypt, a square building decorated with a truncated pyramid. It can be easily understood that during the four hundred years or more that Egypt was predominant, the fashion of Egyptian architecture should have been followed by a people who were intimately connected with them by trade. The men who took spices and balsams from Arabia Felix and bitumen from the Dead Sea to the land of the Pharaohs, had plenty of opportunities of studying the manners and customs of the Egyptians, the houses they lived in and the tombs that they erected for their dead. Perhaps they brought back with them some Egyptian architect to modify the style of architecture that they had received from the Assyrians, for the Petræans were nothing if not adaptable to new ideas; whether they did or not it is almost certain that the work is the work of native stone-cutters. Not only were the Nabatæans famous for their masons' work, as can be seen from the remains of temples and buildings in the Hauran, but they were original in their manner of starting it, beginning from the top and working downwards.

The Jewish tombs have been mentioned by several writers, including Mr. Fergusson in his " History of Architecture in All Countries," as resembling the earlier Nabatæan tombs, though they are later in date than many of these. The so-called Tomb of the Kings was once that of a certain Queen Helena of Adiabene, who built it for herself and her son Izates, who left twenty-four sons and twenty-four daughters, which may account for the size of the Mausoleum. It is approached by a rock-hewn staircase which leads down to the catacombs. There is a façade of what the author just quoted calls " corrupt Doric," but the general effect is picturesque as can be seen in the illustration.

Josephus gives an interesting account of this Queen and her son embracing the Jewish faith and of Izates being instrumental in restoring the Parthian King to his dominions and receiving in return permission to wear his crown upright and to sleep in a golden bed. He was afterwards involved in a quarrel with the Arabians, which brings him into touch with Petra.

The other tomb of which we give an illustration has more resemblance to the Petra tombs, although it has a mixture of ornament that is never seen here. The pillars are Ionic, the architrave and frieze Doric and the cornice Egyptian; it is crowned with a structural spire. It is said now to date from the Herodian period and has certainly no claim to its old title, the Tomb of Absalom. Looking down on the Valley of Kidron from the road leading up to Jerusalem, this tomb presents a picturesque appearance and is interesting on account of the recent excavations.

The rock tombs of Petra have a great likeness to each other especially to the casual observer. They must have been completely rifled at a very early date, for nothing remains to suggest the use to which they were put except a niche for the Dusares emblem, or

ROCK-CUT ENTRANCE TO THE "TOMB OF THE KINGS," JERUSALEM

The Nabatæan City

evidence of funeral feasts having been held, or simply the niche that once held the remains of dead Nabatæans. Some have vestiges of water supplies and enclosures for gardens; in one, and I believe in one only, were skeletons found. The probability is that the idea of finding the treasure which is always supposed to have remained hidden here, inspired the Arabs to ransack the tombs in the hopes of discovering untold riches. Petra must have represented a sort of El Dorado to the older nomads as it does still to some of them to-day.

One of the decorations that strikes the eye at once is the often repeated urn—the urn in which treasure, according to the Arabs, is still stored. There are immense urns of which the biggest crowns the top of the Deir. These urns are placed at the summit of a pediment or at either end of a cornice; great fluted urns decorate the larger monuments, which have sometimes a little cord sculptured at the top and bottom of the body, while a groove, which is sometimes double, decorates the lip. On less important tombs small amphoræ of elongated form are surmounted by a long neck. Are these urns symbolic? There appears to be some symbolic meaning attached to the representation of the masks that are sculptured in relief on some of the façades and to the serpents twined together with the heads disappearing behind a human head. The serpent came from Egypt, as also later from Greece and Rome; the Arabs had a superstition about good spirits inhabiting the " serpent of the house " and the serpent may have served as a sort of mascot. An eagle is also represented on some tombs; it is, of course, a symbol of Jupiter and Ba'al, but was also that of Royal Petra. The Arabs have been accused of adoring the eagle, but it was evidently a national symbol as it was engraved on their coins.

The oldest monuments must have been far older than the dates given by Dr. Dalman; we do not know when Petra was first occupied by the Nabatæans, but if they came in after the captivity of the Jews in 596 B.C., when the Edomites moved away, they must have begun to carve in the rock very soon after. The type of Assyrian and Egyptian tombs that they copied or adapted to their own views, prove that the date was an early one. And then, we must remember that it was after Alexander's conquest of Syria in 332 B.C. that the great Grecian influence was felt and that, before then, it had reached Petra through Palmyra and other centres of trade. The Greeks were the first to inspire the Nabatæans to accomplish something more elaborate than they had yet achieved and they practically learned their art from Greece. The curious part of these remarkable people was that, with all their receptivity and their desire to copy works of art invented by other nations whose civilization was ahead of their own, they had a certain sturdy originality which showed itself in their choice of orders and decoration. They were also the inventors of a capital not quite like any other, and of some peculiarities in their architecture which showed their independence of thought without sacrificing the appearance of unity which the more rigid adherence to type would have ensured.

As architects the Nabatæans are famed for their management of masses and for their large conceptions of form; they excel as stonemasons, treating the hard, unyielding black basalt of the Hauran as well as the red sandstone of Petra and the softer inter-stratifications of limestone that are to be found there with equal success. They had the advantage, in both cases, of finding their material to hand.

Perhaps the mystery that surrounds the past of Petra—however disappointing from an archæological point of view, has something to do with its charm. To wander up and down the street of tombs leading from the Khazne Fur'un to the theatre is quite an interesting experience. The great, very dark, red buildings with open doorways yawning wide have an unearthly appearance; the whole place is absolutely silent, not a footfall is heard. On one afternoon I waited there thinking that the spirits of long-dead Petræans might well haunt this abode of silence, when the sound of footsteps came faintly from the interior of one of the largest of the tombs. What could it be? The footsteps grew louder and there appeared quite suddenly, framed in the doorless opening, a young and very handsome black bullock! The creature, that looked for all the world as if he were the genius of the place and had lost his worshippers, gazed at me with a large, contemptuous stare and then turned and walked slowly away in the direction of the Siq.

The theatre, which is, of course, labelled as being Roman, is a large one capable of seating about three thousand people. It is placed quite among the tombs; the lowest rows, which are just above the top of the amphitheatre, have been broken into when the work of excavating was accomplished. This, at least, is the usual view though there are some writers who think that the openings, that look like opera boxes, were really windows from rooms opening on to the theatre. It seems curious that the theatre should have been placed so near the tombs, but possibly they were of a much older date. I have read somewhere, but cannot at the moment remember where, that this theatre was excavated at a time when the Greek influence predominated, but it is usually said to have been made by the Romans after they took possession of Petra in the first century A.D.

From the theatre you have excellent views to right and to left, and it is good to sit in comparative comfort on the rock-hewn seats in order to take in the position of some of the tombs and the general aspect of the city. In the afternoon the sun shines down here on the smooth red stone where lizards crawl about contentedly and the great headlands and fantastic peaks of the rocks around and above stand out boldly against a sky of brass, while the mass of oleander fills up the course of the stream and wild flowers star the scanty green grass at your feet. At such moments it is good to rest and to take it all in subconsciously, for they do not come too often in this crowded and hectic affair that we call life.

CHAPTER IV
THE KHAZNE FUR'UN

CHAPTER IV

THE KHAZNE FUR'UN

ALTHOUGH the older Nabatæan structures are undeniably the most curious and interesting of all the tombs of Petra, the so-called Treasure House of Pharaoh is certainly the most beautiful. It owes much to its position, whether it be seen from the dark ravine of the Siq, or whether it be seen from the inside surrounded by overhanging cliffs. The soft flame colour of the sandstone which forms the greater part of the façade contrasts with the cream colour of the sculptured entablature; the mass of green bushes makes a foreground that must be even more effective when the pink flowers of the oleander are in bloom.

Some writers think that this graceful monument is due to the Romans and was executed after 105, some say even as late as the visit of Hadrian in 131, A.D.; but Dr. Gustav Dalman, who has written so much about this very subject, thinks that it is certainly anterior to the Roman conquest. He suggests that it was inspired by Greece and that it may very well have been the Mausoleum, or a memorial set up in honour of one of the later Nabatæan Kings, erected not long before the Romans "put an end to royal splendour in this Hellenistic outpost between two deserts." The architecture and decoration, he says, contain nothing that might not be derived from the first century of our era; the pomp of the later Roman period is wanting, the style is Hellenistic rather than Roman.

Let us look at it a little more in detail.

The Khazne consists of several large chambers excavated from the rock with the front of a prostyle temple, approached by a flight of steps. It seems to have had originally only four columns supporting the entablature and pediment ; in order to broaden the effect two more columns were added and the entablature extended. Over the lower order is a colonnade which recedes in the centre to admit a small cylindrical temple, that contains a statue of Isis ; on either side is a recess in which are sculptured winged Victories, over which a broken pediment connects the outer decoration with the central shrine. This combination of a tomb with a shrine in an upper story is said by most authorities to be peculiar to Petra, but I notice that the Duc de Lunyes says it has a striking analogy to the Choragic Monument of Lysicrates at Athens. " It appears," he writes, "that one must be an imitation of the other." Now this beautiful example of Greek art at a time of transition dates from 335 B.C., just at the time when the Greek influence was strongest in Syria, following on the conquests of Alexander. So that whether the design, which was twice copied in Petra itself, was copied from Greece originally, or whether the idea was due to the genius of the Nabatæan architect, it certainly did not come from Rome.

The lower order of columns has Corinthian capitals, with two rows of acanthus leaves and scroll work and flowers between the helices ; they are very original in design and typical of Petra. There is no cavetto between the shaft and the capital, therefore there is no difference between the upper diameter of the shaft and the lower diameter of the capital. The entrance doorway, which was meant to have been closed by double doors, has holes for the lower hinges and other holes of a different shape to support a beam with sockets for the upper hinges. There is also a curious cup hole with a channel leading to the right end of the highest step which was probably used to pour in libations for the dead.

The entrance doorway has an entablature consisting of three fasciæ of different width. The first ends with a cyma reversa, the third with the same and a fillet. The cornice has egg and tongue, and bead and reel decora-

THE KHAZNE FUR'UN, PETRA

The Khazne Fur'un

tions and dentils painted in red and white ; a very unusual detail consists of a projecting acroteria which gives a massive appearance to the upper part.

The pilasters of the upper order have a shaft without base or ornament, the shafts diminish very slightly and the capitals have acanthus leaves only towards the sides, but the rest of the decoration resembles that of the lower order. Over the main entrance is a frieze beautifully ornamented with an intricate design in which canthari appear between winged panthers ending in scroll work with heads of Medusæ at the corners. In the pediment is also scroll work and a Medusa head and an eagle which, as we have seen, was an emblem of Petra and also of royalty.

The figures represented on the façade besides the enshrined Isis, which, by the way, resembles with her sheaves of corn, the figure chosen to represent Petra on coins, are Dioscuri and Amazons and Victories, all symbolic of some triumph, making it all the more likely that it was executed to glorify a King.

No vestige of a grave has been found here and yet the ground plan is that of a tomb, which perhaps, as Dr. Dalman suggests, was never used owing to a political upheaval. Inside we find a large plain hall with doorways in the side walls leading into side chambers. These doorways have Corinthian pilasters surmounted by a frieze and a cornice supported by consoles. Fabulous birds stand on the cornice flanking a circular opening framed by an architrave. A back chamber, where the body should have rested, is approached by four steps and has a Medusa head over the entrance.

The peculiar feature of the upper story having a circular temple or shrine in the middle, is imitated in the fine tomb called the Corinthian and in the huge Deir. Ed-Deir, the Convent, is placed in a magnificent position and is colossal as to size. From the plateau where it stands magnificent views are obtained of the whole Wadi Musa with a distant glimpse of the summit of

Mount Hor. The surroundings are so beautiful that the temple itself appears all the more disappointing. The graceful centre shrine has become an excrescence like the bow window of some enormous seaside atrocity, and I confess that I fail to appreciate the æsthetic beauty of an erection that has been held up to admiration by many writers. It is probably my want of appreciation, but I am not alone in this view. As a feat, it certainly deserves all the praise possible, but as a work of art, and a work of art that is framed in such a setting, it fails to satisfy the eye. Perhaps also, the cold yellowish stone from which it is cut has something to do with its failure to please after the wonderful colour of other rock tombs.

The strongest appeal that it makes consists in the element of surprise. After the long climb up into what appears to be the most solitary and almost inaccessible spot, you suddenly catch sight, over the natural rock, of a huge sculptured urn. How did it get there? It seems unreal, fantastic. A turn in the stony track brings you on to a flat plateau covered with grass and tulip leaves and wild flowers, and there is the great temple, for it looks more like a temple than anything else. You enter with some difficulty, climbing up over some stone blocks, and find yourself in a huge hall that has no other outlet. In a niche there is something that may have served as an altar; all around is desolate.

One cannot deny that the sheer weight and the great mass of the Deir have their fascination, but, as a work of art, it is far below the Khazne. In speaking of it Mr. Fergusson says that it is of an order neither Greek nor Roman, but with something like a Doric frieze over a very plain Corinthian capital. Of the Khazne he writes that it " consists of a square basement, adorned with a portico of four very beautiful Corinthian pillars, surmounted by a pediment of low Grecian pitch. Above this are three very singular turrets, the use and application of which it is extremely difficult to understand. The central one is circular, and is of a well-understood sepulchral form, the use of which, had it been more important, or had it stood alone, would have been intelligible enough ; but what of the side turrets? After suggesting that these might have been derived from a five-turreted tomb, like that of Aruns, he ends by this note on the Khazne : " Though all the forms of the architecture are Roman, the details are so elegant and generally so well designed as almost to lead to the suspicion that there must have been some Grecian influence brought to bear upon the work. The masses of rock left above the wings show how early a specimen of its class it is, and how little practice its designers could have had in copying in the rock the forms of their regular buildings."

It will be seen that this is a different view from that formed by de Luynes or Dr. Dalman ; speaking of the Corinthian tomb, he says that the design is similar to the Khazne but inferior in execution and detail, " showing at least a century of degradation, though at the same time presenting an adaptation to rock-cut forms not found in the earlier examples."

The absorbing interest taken by the Arabs in the Khazne is due, not to the appreciation of its beauty, but to a mistaken idea that in the urn that crowns the summit is the last remains of the treasure that once made Petra famous. In order to get hold of this hoard they have repeatedly shot at the urn which they have injured without releasing floods of gold and without altogether destroying the receptacle of the supposed treasure.

It is not difficult to see how Greek influence came to Petra. From Damascus and Palmyra, an important caravan station long before it is heard of under the Greek name, from the Hauran, and from the Greek cities of the Decapolis, the Greek influence filtered down those trade routes that formed a connecting link with the outer world and the Arabian desert. Before those times it came to them through their contests with the Seleucid

Kings. They are said to have learned their first lessons in monumental art from the Greeks; in early inscriptions they used both Greek and Aramaic. This attempt at culture was favoured by the Kings who reigned over them from the apparent founder of the dynasty, Aretas I, to King Rabel, who was presumably deposed by the Romans when they annexed "Arabia belonging to Petra" in 106 B.C. Aretas I was reigning in 169 B.C., when Jason took refuge with him, the Nabatæans being friendly with the Maccabees at that time. He was succeeded by a vigorous King called Erotimus, who appears to have consolidated the monarchy. Aretas III, surnamed the Philhellene, who reigned about 85 to 60 B.C., was one of the greatest promoters of Greek culture; he also got possession of Damascus and greatly increased the Nabatæan domains. Aretas, which is written "Haretath" in Nabatæan inscriptions, but which is always given the former spelling in Josephus and other old writers, appears to have become a name that was assumed by a Nabatæan King. This leaves us uncertain whether all these Kings—we know of eleven in succession—were of one family or not. Aretas IV, who succeeded Obodas II, changed his name from Æneas on his assumption of the throne; on this occasion Cæsar was very angry with him because he did not apply to him before he "took the government," which looks as if the monarchy had been elective. Aretas sent a letter and presents to Rome, which were at first refused and only accepted later.

The destiny of this outpost of civilization was completely changed by a clever schemer whose ambition had a disastrous effect on the destiny of the Jews also. Antipater, the Idumæan, lived in Petra in his early days and was on intimate terms with the reigning King. When, for his own ends, he woke up the embers of the quarrel between the two sons of Alexander Jannæus, Aristobulus and Hyrcanus, he persuaded the latter to fly to Petra in order to get military help from the

ABSALOM'S TOMB, JERUSALEM

Nabatæans; Hyrcanus, who had no taste for public life and was quite happy in a subordinate position, was not keen for this move, but he allowed Antipater to go to Petra to see how the land lay. When Antipater returned, he fled from Jerusalem with him one night and went a " great journey " to Petra, where he was kindly received by the King in his palace.

His palace! Where was it, and what was it like? Perhaps it resembled the houses in the Hauran, vestiges of which still remain, only the material was so different; that hard, unyielding black basalt, that must have been so much harder to handle than the softer sandstone, was necessarily developed in a style of its own.

Aretas promised to lead an army against Aristobulus and, in return, was to have back the twelve cities that Alexander Jannæus had taken from him. Josephus says that Aretas led an army of fifty thousand horse and foot against Aristobulus, beat him in a hard-fought battle, and laid siege to Jerusalem, aided by many of the Jews who were on the side of Hyrcanus. What would have happened next who can say had not Rome intervened? What did happen was the inevitable. Rome appeared on the scene and got the better of both combatants.

Pompey happened to send a general to Syria named Scaurus, to whom both parties sent embassies as to the arbiter of their fate. Both parties offered a bribe of equal value, that of Aristobulus being accepted because he was the richer man; Aretas was ordered to retire on pain of being considered an enemy of Rome. After a last battle with Aristobulus, in which he was beaten, the Nabatæan King took the remains of his army back to Petra, and we can imagine them marching up the defile of the Siq in very different spirits to those with which they had marched out.

The Jews, on their part, because of internal quarrels which need never have occurred, had made the Romans masters of the situation. " Now the occasions of this misery," writes Josephus, "which came upon Jerusalem, were Hyrcanus and Aristobulus, by raising a sedition one against the other; for now we lost our liberty and became subject to the Romans." He might just as well have said that Antipater was the cause of this misfortune. In his dealings with the Nabatæans he was always out for his own interests, and more than once he used their King as his tool, though he appears to have lent Obodas money that he had some difficulty in getting back.

After the Nabatæans returned to Petra, they were punished for their audacity by Scaurus, the Roman general who was apparently sent to take possession of Petra, but who did not like the look of the place. Instead, he burned and destroyed everything that he could find in the neighbourhood, and was only induced to go by the usual payment of a sum of money. This was manifestly unjust, as the Romans had finally decided against Aristobulus and had reinstated Hyrcanus as High Priest and Ethnark.

Aretas III, the Philhellene, under whose influence Petra had been Hellenised, died and was succeeded by Obodas or Obodath, a man feeble in mind and body, who left the direction of his affairs to his Prime Minister Syllæus. Strabo relates that, in this reign, the Romans sent a force under Ælius Gallus with instructions to find out how the land lay in Arabia Felix. He was to make friends or to fight with the rich inhabitants of the land of spice, whichever seemed the most profitable course. The general decided to fight and made a compact with the Nabatæans, who were to guide his army through this unknown country and to fight in its ranks.

This Syllæus was young and good-looking and crafty; he was ambitious and as unscrupulous as Herod himself. He led the Romans by pathless wastes where no water was, and he directed their fleet to shores where there were no harbours. When the Roman found out that he had been deceived by the clever barbarian, who had hoped to kill off some enemies and to weary out the Romans by hunger and thirst and the long marches, his rage was great. Syllæus, however, managed to escape punishment for the time and no doubt chuckled to himself after he got back safely inside the walls of his native city, thinking that he had outwitted Rome.

Antipater's son Herod, surnamed the Great, had a sister called Salome, who was always intriguing against the other members of that amiable family. She had already got rid of two husbands when Syllæus came to supper with her brother and fell in love with her. She returned his passion and when he proposed for her to Herod she accepted with alacrity. Syllæus, however, was rejected by Herod for various reasons, one of them being that he refused to adopt the Jewish religion; Syllæus said that the Arabs would stone him if he did such a thing and the affair was off. Salome, who was forced, some months after, to marry a third husband not of her own choosing, never forgave Herod for his highhanded behaviour and Syllæus took every opportunity of annoying his former friend.

When Herod was trying to introduce law and order into a wild part of his tetrarchy, Syllæus gave a band of robbers a refuge in Nabatæan lands and encouraged them to lay waste Herod's property. He also refused to repay the money that Herod had lent to Obodas and which he appears to have appropriated himself. Herod took an armed force and went to collect what was due to him and Syllæus fled to Rome and accused the great man of waging war without the approval of Rome. Herod was, for the time, in disgrace and Syllæus triumphant, but it was not for long. When Obodas died and the government was taken on by Æneas, under the name Aretas IV, the ex-Prime Minister, who wanted the kingdom for himself, went to the Emperor dressed in black and told him, with tears in his eyes, that things were not as they should be in Nabatæa. Aretas had no right to the crown. The haughty Roman rejected the golden crown that Aretas sent with a letter announcing his succession, and for some time it appeared as if Syllæus was going to win his risky game. When, however, enquiries were made, and Syllæus was accused, whether rightly or wrongly, of having had a hand in the death of Obodas, the pendulum swung in the other direction. The old offence, too, of leading the Roman troops astray, was brought up against the schemer, who was beheaded in Rome while Aretas was received back into favour and Herod became more powerful than ever. So ends a story that is without political significance but not without interest as conveying a little picture of the times in which a King lived for whose sepulture, or to celebrate whose glory, the beautiful Khazne may perhaps have been hewn out of the living rock.

CHAPTER V
Pre-Roman Petra

CHAPTER V

Pre-Roman Petra

ANTIPATER, the founder of the Herodian fortunes, had been Procurator of all Judæa; he had made himself indispensable to Rome, and his son, Herod the Great, more than followed in his footsteps. The Roman emperors found it very convenient to have a man with apparently inexhaustible riches at their beck and call and, no doubt, they saw in him a man devoted to their interests and one who would go far.

Herod the Idumæan never forgot his kindred in far away Petra. He was friends with them and lent them money when it suited his game; he fought them quite indifferently when necessary. When Antigonus, the son of the murdered Aristobulus, got possession of Jerusalem, Herod fled for safety to Petra on his way to Egypt and Rome. He came back, of course, the titular King of the Jews, and eventually took Jerusalem with the help of Rome.

Cleopatra of Egypt was another celebrated personage who played a part in the chronicles of the Nabatæans. When she came to Syria she took a fancy to that land and asked Mark Antony to give it to her. Antony did not dare accede to this rather comprehensive request, and he could not refuse her altogether, so he gave her the Phœnician coast with the exception of the cities of Tyre and Sidon that were free—a very annoying exception and one that made the acquisitive Queen justly indignant. He also handed over to her part of the Nabatæan and Iturian domains and Jericho, which she subsequently leased to Herod.

Herod is said to have been the one man who resisted the charms of the Serpent of Old Nile; he thought her dangerous and tiresome; he even went so far as to advise Mark Antony to have her assassinated, and was grieved that the infatuation of the great soldier for that Queen prevented this simple, and for Herod, always available solution of a difficulty to be adopted. When Cleopatra came to Syria, Herod loaded her with costly gifts and conducted her back to the frontier of her dominions, which did not prevent him from being heartily glad to see the last of her. Cleopatra resented the fact that this wretched little Idumæan upstart had proved so difficult a fish to hook, and she tried to pay him back later on.

It happened in this way. Herod was preparing an army to fight for Mark Antony against Octavian when he received an order to direct his attack against the Nabatæans instead. This unexpected order was inspired by Cleopatra, who argued that she would reap the benefit whichever side lost. If Herod lost, she would score heavily and acquire all his lands; if the Nabatæans lost, she would take Petra and Arabia belonging to Petra. She sent a general to see that all went well, and awaited the result. The dice were loaded; whichever won, she would be no loser.

Now Herod was on the point of winning the battle when the general, who happed to dislike him, came up to the Nabatæans with reinforcements and turned fortune in their favour. In another battle Herod won a great victory, and went back to Judæa covered with glory and on to Rome to explain to Octavian that, however much he had loved Antony he was capable of loving him just as well. So Cleopatra did not win after all, and after her death her possessions went to Herod, who took on her guard of four hundred Gauls, and must have felt that he had got the better of her in the long run; as, indeed, he did of most people with whom he came in contact.

The Nabatæans, although they won some fine battles, were not very celebrated as warriors; probably their forces were more in the nature of police to protect the trade routes than of actual fighting men.

THE THEATRE, PETRA, AND THE ENTRANCE TO THE SIQ

Pre-Roman Petra

The story of Herod's political life and that of his blood-stained domestic tragedies have nothing to do with Petra, but the link is there and the connection comes to the fore again in the reign of Aretas IV. One of the tyrant's sons who was lucky enough to escape his father's murderous rage, Herod Antipas, married the daughter of the Nabatæan King; we can imagine the Princess leaving the familiar and friendly scene with some state, for the marriage was a great one politically, her prospective husband being the tetrarch of Peræa among other things. The two lived together for some time—how long we do not know—whether happily or unhappily, whether there were children or whether there were not. And then Antipas was called to Rome on business, as all princes were when Rome was the centre of the universe.

While Antipas was in Rome he lived with his brother Philip—not the tetrarch, but another Philip—and his brother's wife, Herodias, who was also his niece. The drama seems to have unfolded itself rapidly, and with the rapidity with which news travelled in those days it soon reached the ears of the wife who had been left at home. Antipas had fallen in love with his brother's wife, and he had proposed to her to leave her husband and to join him in Palestine. Herodias accepted, but made one condition, which was that the Nabatæan should be divorced before she herself went to live with Antipas as his wife. Antipas agreed to this suggestion and hurried home to make his arrangements. What the brother thought of the transaction does not appear, but when the Nabatæan Princess heard the news she resolved to fly to her father in order to escape the ignominy of being turned out. She asked leave to go to Machærus, which was situated just on the extreme border of Herod's land, where it marched with that of her father. She pretended that she was going for a short time, but directly she got there she collected her possessions and fled over the border, where she was received by her father's subjects and passed from one strategus to another, from one fortress to another, until she reached Petra. One would like to know what thoughts she had as she entered the long defile of the Siq; whether she was thankful to have escaped or sick at heart, whether she brought children with her or whether she had failed to add a soul to the race that began so prolifically and was wiped out before a hundred years ran. All we do know is that she told her story to her father and that Aretas declared war on his son-in-law.

Once more the Nabatæans marched out of Petra intent on war, and this time they must have felt that Herod had offered an insult to their nation. Herod Antipas came to meet them, perhaps a little disturbed at the turn affairs had taken. His new wife and her daughter by her first husband, Salome, had taken up their abode at Machærus, and the former had been annoyed by the insulting references made to the marriage by a wild preacher, one John, called the Baptist. He was a dangerous fellow who had a great following, and might easily have made mischief, the people being ready to follow him anywhere, so he had been put in prison for lese-majesty. And then Salome had danced and Herod had promised her anything she liked, and the girl, prompted by her mother, had asked for the Baptist's head. It had perhaps been rather a hectic time, one way and another. Herod lost the first battle, receiving such a beating that his followers were alarmed; the defeat was followed by an earthquake, and they cried that God was angry—it was a judgment!

The Nabatæans were triumphant, as well they might be, but it was not for long; helped, no doubt, by the devil and by his own astucity, Antipas made a great speech to his army and attacked his enemy again, this time completely routing them. If the discarded wife felt sad when she saw the avenging force return defeated, she had afterwards cause to realize that the guilty couple did not always escape scot-free. Herodias became so

Pre-Roman Petra

jealous of her brother, who had been made a King, that she persuaded Antipas to go to Rome to ask if he could not have a crown too. The couple set off, arranging their journey as economically as might be, times not being very flush, but not only was the crown not bestowed, but the tetrarchy was taken away with all their possessions, and given to the brother whose better fortune she had envied. It is recorded that Herodias preferred to follow her husband into exile rather than to return to Palestine in disgrace. What happened to the discarded first wife history does not say.

It is curious that so very few inscriptions should have remained on the walls of the tombs. The inscriptions that are found at Medain Salah and elsewhere are not interesting. They are merely intended to make clear the legal rights of the dead and their descendants to the tomb, with minatory tags as to the curses of Dusares and Allat that will confound anyone who ignores them. In some of the oases there are simple lines to commemorate unimportant people who might have lived there or who might have been passing through with a caravan when death overtook them. Of such are these : " Greeting ! Uwaisu, son of Fariyyu ; Good luck !" and "Remembered in welfare and peace be Sa'adu, son of j'arm-alba-ali for ever !"

An inscription was found in Petra *in situ* in a chamber that is reached up a flight of steps. It appears to have been put up to do honour to the memory of Obodas II, that weak and ineffectual King who allowed Syllæus to rule his kingdom for him. A cult for him arose at the end of the first century B.C. ; and it was a very usual thing to deify kings after their death. The room has the appearance of having been a sanctuary, and the inscription runs as follows :—

" This is the statue of the divine Obedath, which the sons of Hotaishu son of Patmon made . . . . Teluk, son of Withra, the god of Hotaishu, who is on the ridge of Patmon, their ancestor, for the life of Haretath King of the Nabatæans, lover of his people, and Shugailath his sister, Queen of the Nabatæans, and Maliku, and Obedath, and Rabel, and Pesæl, and Sha'udath, and Higru, his children, and Haretath, son of Higru, his grandson .... in the 29th year of Haretath, King of the Nabatæans, Peace be upon him!"

It is described in Irby and Mangles' "Travels in Egypt and Palestine" as being placed in a tomb that has a large front of pure Arabian design, with four attached columns. Only the top part is finished, proving once more that the native workmen began at the top of a monument and carved downwards. The inscription is placed in an oblong tablet, without frame or relief; it is distinguished from the rest of the surface by being more delicately wrought. Wings project from the ends, those wings in the form of the blade of an axe which are common both in Roman and Greek tablets. They seem to have been intended to receive screws or fastenings; although the whole tablet is cut in the solid rock, there are stains where metal studs have been driven in to give the appearance of a separate piece. The letters are well cut and in good preservation owing to the shelter obtained from the projecting cornices.

Pliny, Diodorus Siculus and others give accounts of the life in Petra when the shadow of Rome already fell across the threshold, but before the liberty of the city had been taken away. Strabo says: "The capital of the Nabatæans is called Petra. It is situated on a spot which is surrounded and fortified by a smooth and level rock, which externally is abrupt and precipitous, but within there are abundant springs of water both for domestic purposes and for watering gardens. Beyond the enclosure the country is, for the most part, a desert, particularly towards Judæa. Through this is the shortest road to Jericho, a journey of three or four days .... It is always governed by a King of royal race. The King has a Minister who is one of the Companions and is called a Brother. It has excellent

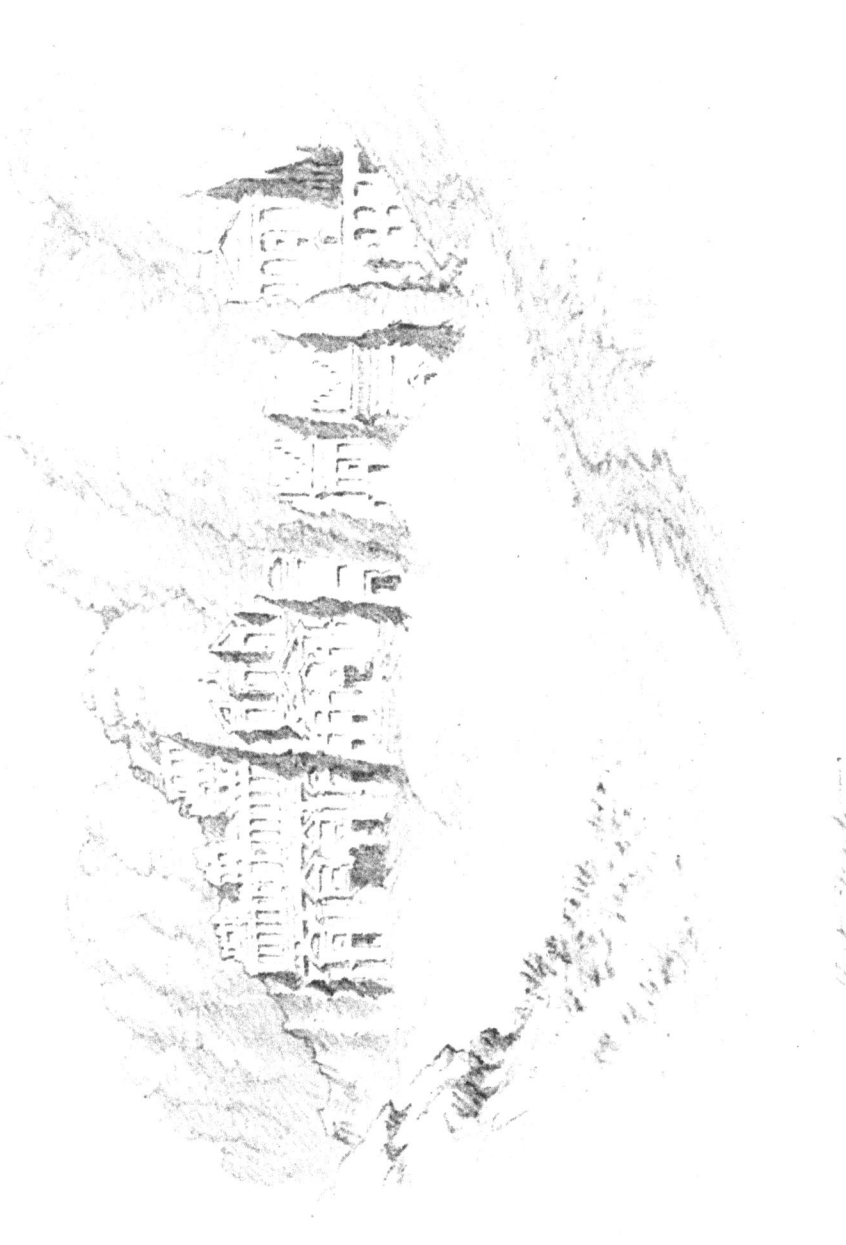

THE CORINTHIAN TOMB AND THE TOMB WITH THREE STORIES, PETRA

laws for the administration of public affairs.

" Athenodorus, a philosopher and my friend, used to relate with surprise that he found many Romans and others, strangers, residing there. He observed the strangers frequently engaged in litigation, both with one another and with the natives ; but the natives had never any dispute among themselves and lived together in perfect harmony."

Athenodorus was a Stoic philosopher, usually supposed to have been a native of Canana, near Tarsus ; he is now said to have been born in Petra about 80 B.C. In any case he knew the rock city well. He was high in the favour of Augustus Cæsar, with whom he used to speak quite freely. He once advised the Emperor to repeat the alphabet before replying to any remark that annoyed him.

It is evident that Rome had designs on Petra from an early period. The Romans who traded with the Nabatæans brought back wonderful stories of the wealth of the people and many, as we have seen, settled there. What did they talk about in royal Petra? Politics, of course, complicated by the eternal quarrels of Ptolemies and Seleucids ; the state of the stock exchange and the merchandise brought in by the latest caravan from the Levant. A scrap between Nabatæan guards and the Himyarites at some oasis like El-Ola, standing between the two dominions might furnish a few minutes' gossip. Perhaps Aretas might have had news from Damascus telling how his Ethnark had imprisoned an unruly preacher named Paul and how the man had escaped in the night, let down from the prison window in a basket.

When any question of importance had to be solved Aretas often went to consult the diviners. Once when Vitellius was marching on Petra, the King asked what would be the result of the attack and received the answer that Vitellius would not enter Petra and that either he or the Prince who sent him would shortly die. And, surely enough, Vitellius stopped half-way and turned back because he heard of the death of the Emperor Tiberius.

It was not alone in Petra and the surrounding districts that the Nabatæans made their mark. In the Hauran they built houses and temples, remains of which have been discovered by de Vogüé, especially in the temples of Si and Suweda. Although they copied the styles of other nations, although they took successively from Assyria, Egypt, Persia, Greece and Rome, they had a distinct individuality of their own. Their art had something oriental about it, their conceptions were large, their details often freely treated. Oddly enough for people who began as imitators, they were destined to influence the future styles of Roman and Christian art in Syria. They were original in construction and in ornamentation and, as everywhere in Syria, the classic forms were treated less rigidly than elsewhere, without losing that character which was the charm of the Greek and the good Greco-Roman architecture.

The capital that the architects of Petra evolved is used by them in the tombs of that city with hardly an exception. The Dominican Fathers, Jaussen and Savignac, say that these capitals constitute the most singular feature of the Nabatæan architecture. There are three special forms. The simplest have two horns at the angles and a rounded excrescence high up; another type has a claw under the horns divided from each other by a hollow and the third is that which is seen in most of the big tombs. It has a double capital, the first of which is formed of a moulding surmounted by the purely Nabatæan capital. M. Dieulafoy thinks that these forms are undoubtedly derived from the Persian; M. de Vogüé sees in them only an unfinished copy of the Corinthian capital.

Having once evolved a capital the Nabatæan architects kept to it, and we find it repeated over and over again in Petra. Even after the Roman occupation the double capital persists.

CHAPTER VI
ROMAN PETRA

CHAPTER VI
Roman Petra

IN 106 A.D. Petra was taken by the Romans, and we know little more of her story. The Nabatæans appear to have fought well to defend their liberties and kept part of the Hauran for some time longer. But the Petræans became quite Romanised and the city prospered; trade was kept up under Roman direction, the conquerors made one of their famous roads connecting Petra with the Red Sea, and others followed. They replaced the Nabatæan houses with others of a more important type, erected an arch at the entrance to the Siq, a Triple Gate and a Temple and the usual public buildings appeared in the basin of the Wadi Musa, where traces of the streets can still be seen. As usual with Rome, the religion of the conquered race was respected, and we find Epiphanius (A.D. 130-170) writing of a festival held in Petra in honour of Chaabon and Dusares.

Hadrian paid a visit to Petra, which was commemorated by a coin bearing the inscription " Adriane Petra "; the greatest period of prosperity was probably about the end of the first century A.D. But for centuries to come Petra was a commercial centre, which only began to decline in importance when the caravan routes changed, sea being preferred to land, and when the star of Palmyra was in the ascendant.

Most of the post-classical tombs belong to the Roman period. The tomb of the Urn is one of the most important, both on account of its simple but majestic style and of the prominent position that it occupies. Standing one hundred feet above the valley the temple, for it is undoubtedly a temple and not a tomb, dominates the scene with its four great pilasters supporting an architrave interrupted by small pilasters above which is a triangular pediment on which the urn rests. The temple façade is sculptured from the rock, which is here of a very beautiful rose or flame red colour, and it stands back on a square platform which rests on arched substructures of a very massive quality. The labour involved in this feat of engineering was great, and points to a date not earlier than the end of the first century A.D. The temple is approached by a great flight of steps, but both these and the substructures are in a ruinous condition, and it can only be gained by anyone who is prepared for a climb.

The architrave over the door is ornamented by shields between triglyphs; over it there is a window with three more in the attic; in the centre are two figures in basso-relievo. To right and left of the raised terrace are colonnades of pillars of the Ionic order, standing out from the wall of rock that forms the side of the enclosure. This feature is quite new to Petra, or rather to the remains of pre-Roman Petra that we know; no doubt there were many such in the town in the valley that has vanished from our ken.

Inside we find a large room with wonderful effects of colour in the ceiling and on the walls, which are finely grooved. The rainbow effect of the marbling is here very beautiful. An inscription tells us that the temple was consecrated as a church in the time of the " most holy Bishop Jason " in 477 A.D.

The tomb with three stories is in a very damaged condition, having suffered from time and weather more than most; it is also unfinished in the top story, which is built on, the rock not reaching high enough to complete the design. It is a copy of a Roman palace and not that of a temple as was more usual and is, indeed, the only example of its kind in Petra. The Persians used to erect palace façades as entrances to their tombs, but it was never a Roman custom. Fergusson says that it resembles the proscenium of some of the more recent Greek theatres and that, if it were a tomb, it is " one

THE TEMPLE OF THE URN, PETRA

of the most complete misapplications of Greek architecture ever made." The lower story has four portals, each flanked by two columns, which lead into four rooms; the centre columns are surmounted by triangular pediments, the outer by round arched pediments. A high architrave supports the middle story, on the face of which are eighteen smaller pilasters and some windows. The top story, that is composed of masonry, is supported by a quadruple architrave.

The Corinthian tomb is a Roman copy of the Khazne. The lower story has eight Corinthian pillars, the upper contains the centre shrine and two lesser projections; the whole is surmounted by the usual urn. Another very fine tomb is that of the Roman governor, Sextus Florentinus, with a Latin inscription. The façade shows a central portal flanked by columns; over the pediment is a Victory, a head of Medusa and an eagle with extended wings.

One of the most striking of the Roman monuments is well seen when climbing up to the Deir. Looking across the valley, seen through some steep and narrow defile, a vision of a temple strikes the eye; it stands upon a terrace, its lofty columns and simple façade give it a dignity which is enhanced by its position. As I did not go up to examine it I may borrow a description from Sir Alexander Kennedy :—

"The Lion Monument," he writes, "which is one of the few classical monuments, like the Deir, on the western side of Petra, is a triclinium and not a tomb. The lions are in low relief on each side of the doorway. The faces of the Nabatæan capitals between the horns have a little scrollwork decoration. The frieze carries two Medusa heads and four pateræ, and in general it is obvious that the monument must be a late one. But it is very noticeable that the feasts held in it must have been connected with the worship of Dusares, whose block symbol stands in a flat niche to the left of the doorway."

It is not certain whether the theatre dates from the Roman period or from the time of Aretas III, when there was a strong Hellenistic influence in Petra. It is well known that the Greeks looked on the theatre as a necessity, whereas the Romans preferred the amphitheatre in which contests of man and beast took place; so it is quite likely that it was excavated at the earlier date.

At first, apart from the change of government and the presence of Roman soldiers and the ever-increasing number of Roman colonists, there may not have appeared, on the surface, a very great difference in life in the old Nabatæan capital. Rome had always loomed large on the horizon, exacting tribute and sometimes men to fight in her armies; after Syria was annexed as a Roman province and Jerusalem became a Roman city, known as Ælius Capitolinus, the bonds tightened. For a long time Rome had coveted the trade of the East, and it seems that she carried it on energetically once she possessed the key to the position. It is often remarked that Rome was the first power that ever kept the desert hordes in order; the roads flung across the waste can still be traced by remains of milestones scribbled over, at times, by the Roman soldiers. The paved roads, with the borders marked by stones or blocks of black basalt, are still to be found here and there; no doubt the commerce profited by the general prosperity, for a time at all events. Whether, in the long run, the Romans understood the peculiar character of the business as well as the Arabs had done, who had grown into it rather than learned it as a trade, is another matter.

For many a long year the caravans plodded along the old routes, from the Persian Gulf and Saba to Petra, from whence the roads branched out to Egypt and Palestine and Syria, stopping at Arsinoe, Gaza, Tyre, Jerusalem, Damascus, and many other places of less note.

It is certain that Christianity penetrated into Petra

VIEW FROM THE COLONNADE OF THE TEMPLE OF THE URN, PETRA

and the surrounding country at an early date, and it seems probable that the Romans, who were usually large-minded as to the religion of other people, unless, as with the Jews, it was complicated by political struggles, allowed a certain amount of liberty to members of the new sect. It may even be possible that Saint Paul lived in Petra during the three years which he spent in the land beyond Jordan before beginning his ministry. In the fourth century it was the seat of a bishopric, but it does not appear when the first bishop was appointed.

But the Roman empire itself was changing, and with it the fortunes of Petra. When the empire was divided into two parts Syria was included in the Byzantine empire; under Constantine the Great Christianity became a great force, while, at the same time, the fire-worshipping Persians came to the fore once more. The Greek cities of the Decapolis, metamorphosed into Roman colonial centres, were now very prosperous; Palmyra was the chief centre of commerce. For long before the Roman débacle began, Petra gradually declined in importance, her nationality gone and with it her old traditions, her commerce diverted into other channels, she sinks away into the shadow. Then, quite suddenly at the end, she disappears. The coinage that began with Aretas III stopped dead; there is no more talk of the rock city after the beginning of the seventh century, and it may be that Chrosroes II of Persia took it by assault and looted the caves of their treasure.

Whether Persia began the destruction of Petra and the followers of Mohammed finished it, or how the complete ruin of the once prosperous capital of Arabia Petræa came about, is not known. Petra vanished from history as completely as if a curtain had been drawn across the stage; the players—those colonial Romans and Romanised Nabatæans—vanished also, and the curtain is only very partially lifted before the Crusaders came here in the early days of the twelfth century.

CHAPTER VII
THE CRUSADERS' CASTLE

CHAPTER VII

THE CRUSADERS' CASTLE

THE little "Château de la Vallée de Moyse," or "Selah," as the Crusaders called the fort that they built on the Obelisk Hill at Petra, was not such a tremendous affair as were some of the others that they erected about the same time. It must have been of considerable strength owing partly to its position and partly to the material out of which it was hewn, in addition to the engineering science of the builders. In times of war engineering progresses quickly; the Franks had their own military architects and they were not too proud to learn from their Roman and Byzantine predecessors.

The Crusaders arrived in Palestine at a propitious moment, when that unhappy country was, as usual, in the grip of civil war. The latest invaders were the Seljuk Turks, whose empire, founded by the Sultan Togrul Bey, was quite a recent affair, dating from 1038. These Turks had absorbed the territories of the Caliphs of Baghdad and part of the old empire of Greece; they overran Syria, subjecting it to a sort of guerrilla warfare. The Crusaders were at first very successful, though they never got hold of the whole country but only of isolated districts, which they bound together, much in the same way as the Greeks had united the cities of the Decapolis, by military roads. They formed at first four principalities, taking the names of the principal towns to distinguish them—Edessa, Antioch, Tripoli, and Jerusalem.

The new principalities were divided into fiefs; churches, monasteries, and castles rose up in the land as well as minor forts to protect the lines of communication. The principal cities had their dependencies and it was all arranged on the feudal system, which answered very well in the East. Christian and Moslem settled down quite peacefully when the fight was over; so much so that the Christians ended, after a generation, in adopting eastern dress and many of the eastern customs which had at first seemed so strange to them.

It was, therefore, not so much the inhabitants of western Palestine who were to be feared after the position of the Crusaders had become consolidated, as the Turks and the ever restless Arabs of the desert. The gentle and heroic Godfrey of Bouillon, who had refused to be crowned where Christ had suffered death, had died himself; his brother Baldwin, who had no such scruples, was crowned King of the Latin Kingdom of Jerusalem on Christmas Day, 1100, in Bethlehem itself. He was clever, brave and energetic; when he saw that danger threatened on the other side Jordan he set out in person to see about the defence of his western possessions and the possibility of acquiring land in the east. As Guillaume de Tyr, the first systematic historian of those times, says in the charming thirteenth-century French that has been reproduced in the present edition of his work: " Li rois desiroit mout a acroistre son roiaume et elargir en cele partie "—cele partie being, of course, Cœle-Syria, which the Franks called " la Syrie Sobale."

The Crusaders had arrived in Palestine in the summer of 1097; it was not till 1115 that Baldwin I collected an army, passed over the Dead Sea, and laid the foundations of the fortress of Shobek, which he called Mons Regalis because it was founded by a King.

The fortress that rose up on a terrace on the top of a steep sharp incline, was well placed because it commanded the Haj route, up and down which pilgrims and merchants passed. Besides the dues that could legitimately be collected from them, the Crusaders were

THE DEIR, PETRA

not at all above robbing the caravan of an infidel in a good cause; command of the trade routes was of the first importance now that the Christians were entering into the game with zest, and it was also by these roads that the Turks advanced to the attack.

Mons Regalis, or Montreal as it was more usually called, was also known as " le Crac de Montreal," a phrase that is supposed to be derived from the Greek word " charax," a pale or stake. In this sense it was used for the great fort that protected the route between Homs and Tripoli, " le Crac des Chevaliers "; Kerax is another derivation, but the other name, " The Stone of the Desert," by which it is so often mentioned, is of course given because of its rocky structure, just as Petra derived its name from the same reason. These various fortresses are all mentioned at different times as " crac," which is apt to be confusing if the derivation is not made clear.

Baldwin annexed much land around Shobek, where fruit trees and vines grew abundantly; the three great enclosed ramparts of the fort were so capacious that Lodolphe of Sudheim, who visited it between 1336 and 1341, saw in the outer a rock from which three springs gushed; in the middle enough corn was grown to keep the garrison for a year, and in the inner there were vines. Towards the end of the fourteenth century the Crusaders' fort was replaced by a Moslem fort that is much smaller than the original; it was dismantled by Ibrahim Pasha in the course of the last century.

Baldwin left a knight to command the fort, with others under him, and men-at-arms to supply the garrison; in feudal fashion, land was portioned out among the principal warriors. In 1116 the King went down to Elim on the Gulf of Akaba, where he seems to have established a maritime base. The monk Thelmar, who begins his tiny book of travels by stating that he took up the Cross, for the remission of his sins, in the year 1217, came here in the course of his wanderings over the Holy Land; he says that the island of Graye, which formerly belonged to the Crusaders, was then in the possession of the Moslems, who kept a great many Christian prisoners there of various nationalities. On his way to or from the Gulf of Akaba, Baldwin must have passed by Petra, where he intended to erect a fort to further protect the district.

One would like to know what impression Petra made on these men who had already seen so much that was strange to their western eyes, but surely nothing so strange as this weird chasm leading to a ruined city that might have been dropped from the moon. What remained of the Roman city? Had it completely disappeared under the inrush of the devastating Moslem hordes or, before them, of the Persians?

However much or little was left to astonish the new-comers, and whatever they thought as they marched up to inspect the place with a view to a convenient spot for a fort, this much is certain: historically their arrival is intensely interesting, for it fills in the gap between the collapse of Petra in the sixth century and the rediscovery of the city of tombs in the nineteenth. More than that, it stirs the imagination. Up the winding Siq had Esau walked or ridden, and perhaps Moses and the Children of Israel had followed in his footsteps during their exile in the wilderness. Up and down the tortuous ways of the ravine the Nabatæans had come and gone, Herod had hurried with his mind full of plots and counter plots; Greek architects, Egyptians, Babylonians, Persians, the motley crowds from the caravans, one generation after another, one civilization after another, had gone in endless procession up the now deserted Siq. The glittering helmets of the Roman legions had caught the rays of the sun when a chance shaft filtered down through the pass; and now came the Burgundian Prince with his followers from many lands, all bound together by the symbol of the Cross which they wore on their tunics and on their shields.

The Crusaders' Castle

There are the remains of two forts in Petra, but the one that was utilized by the crusaders stood to the north-east of El-Khubza. It stands high with deep gullies all around, one of which has been artificially widened to form a moat, making approach from the east impossible. The rocks on the further side have also been hewn so that they are almost perpendicular and quite impossible to scale. The fort stands on a platform that has been levelled on the eastern slope; on the west of the moat was a parapet of which there are some remains. It starts above the ravine Se'ib el We'jra, from a square building, running along the edge of the moat. Here, also, are to be seen the remains of a defensive wall, built along an artificially constructed platform. The walls are very thick and have loopholes in them, and sometimes steps leading down to a lower level. South of the wall the platform falls away and there is a stairway hewn in the rock leading to a lower platform, and again, lower still, the stairs run down to the moat. The moat, that runs from east to west, is divided by four cross-walls and is closed at its east end by a rock wall.

Bits of wall and the remains of stout square towers show where were the southern limits of the fort, and a little to the south-west is the entrance to a Gothic chapel, the apse of which is still standing; under the chapel is a cistern, which is approached by a vaulted passage. It has an incomplete cross moulding and a hole through which the water could be drawn up into the chapel.

A feature of this fort is a tower that is hewn from the rock; under it stands a round tower, and there are the remains of walls where once a drawbridge was let down; another could have been lowered over the entrance to the covered passage that led down to the Siq.

The Crusaders must have looked out over the wide prospect with dimly-felt awe; perhaps they stood by the two mysterious obelisks, which were part of age-old rites, beyond which the vague outline of the desert shut in the view, or gazed at the equally mysterious " Holy Place " with its great altar and all the arrangements for sacrifice. To leave the contemplation of nature in her most fantastic mood and human nature in its least comprehensible delight in shedding blood as an act of worship, in order to dash down and waylay a caravan, must have been quite refreshing to the average man.

The Crusaders were now in a position to exact dues from anyone passing along the trade routes; they also entered with enthusiasm into commercial projects. For the first time Europe became alive to the fascination of the East. Just as learning woke up afresh in Spain through the agency of the Moors, so delight in artistic and luxurious things came to Europe through the active co-operation of the Crusaders with the Moslems.

Trade was never more flourishing than it was at this time. The cities of the Mediterranean opened new business relations with the Latin colonists in Palestine; the extreme East and the West came into touch. Privileges were extended to the Mediterranean ports, and certain advantages were reaped by the Crusaders in return. Cotton and wool were sent to Europe, and linen and silk, raw or woven into tissue. The silks of Damascus became the rage, the spices of Arabia were in great demand; sugar, indigo, saffron, spices and drugs, to mention only a few of the products of Arabia and Persia, borne on the backs of camels along the immemorial routes, were shipped off to Europe. The Venetians, always to the fore in matters of art or commerce, were very active in this matter. Besides these more or less useful commodities, all sorts of oriental rugs, embroideries, objects of art, rare books, began to find their way into the European markets.

Every year there was a great fair by the lake of Phiala, near Banias and the sources of the Jordan; here the Arab tribes camped with their trains of camels

The Crusaders' Castle

and their merchandise which had been, perhaps, brought hundreds of miles across the desert from Arabia Felix and on beyond from the shores of the Red Sea; or which might have come from the shores of the Persian Gulf, past Petra and Shobek, and along by the Pilgrim route in a line with the Dead Sea until it passed by Rabboth Ammon and Gerasa and underground Der'aa, known then as Edrei. Besides the Arab merchants and the agents of the Crusaders, there would be the great mass of pilgrims going to Mecca, for the fair always corresponded with the date of the Pilgrimage.

It does not seem likely that the Crusaders built the whole of the fort of Wasaira; there must have been something in the way of fortifications before. But, in any case, even if they were able to use some rock-cut walls, and even though they were helped by the natural formation of the high ground surrounded by gullies, there must have been years of work before it was completed. And they had, after all, a comparatively short period during which they were able to profit by its strategic position and its strong walls.

There was, at one time, some hesitation in deciding whether or no the fort was actually in Petra or whether it was only in that neighbourhood. Guillaume de Tyr is certainly quite clear on the point.

"Cest chastiaux," he writes, "siet assez pres del leu ou Moyse fist issir les eues de la pierre par le cap de sa verge, quand le peuple Israel moroit de soif." He states that the Château de Moyse, which was in the command of "Petrocii Comitis," was taken by assault by the Franks in the year 1144, it having been in the possession of the Saracens. The Franks held it until the year marked by the taking of Jerusalem; that is, in 1189.

After this date Petra disappears until 1265, when Sultan Beybars, after receiving the submission of Kerak, came to Petra, climbed up the steep way, half stair, half path, and greatly admired the work of the gallant but unfortunate Crusaders. And then the veil falls in earnest. A city of tombs, with her dead past as securely buried under the soft red sand and the brushwood of the Wadi Musa as if that past had never been, Petra slept through the years until the beginning of the nineteenth century. Over a hundred years have passed since the brave Burckhardt offered up a sacrifice to Aaron as a pretext for getting inside the forbidden city; since then much has been done by those few that have interested themselves in the monuments of a vanished people, but Petra will never give up her secrets until excavations on a large scale are permitted. Let us hope that the time may soon come when the veil may be finally lifted which has hung over Petra so long.

CHAPTER VIII
KERAK

CHAPTER VIII
Kerak

HIGH up on the summit of the spur of a mountain lying between the Dead Sea and the desert, the ruins of a great fortress cut the sky line. It does not, at first, appear to be a ruin; the walls still stand, flanked by occasional towers of defence, outlining the whole vast enclosure where were once the fort and the castle of the Crusaders. Seen from a distance it presents very much the same appearance that it must have done in the days of its splendour. Now, as then, it dominates the scene, commanding the country that runs down for some thirty miles to the Dead Sea, as well as that which descends in the opposite direction, to the Pilgrims' road through the desert. Now, as then, it stands for aggression and defence, set up on high that all may see; proud in its strong position, superb in its own strength, with the added something that only age can give. In the midst of this mountain solitude it appears to be alive with the curious life of old buildings that outlasts the ephemeral existence of generations of men.

We are now in the heart of Moab, in the midst of that wedge of rock that stands sheer over the Dead Sea, making a great barrier with a long, level outline that is one of the most beautiful views to be seen from Jerusalem, when the setting sun turns the bare rock into a jewelled haze. Coming from Petra, where the landscape is so much wilder, the isolation of it makes less effect, but wild and grand it undoubtedly is. The whole scene is absolutely different, like something in another planet; the colouring is totally different, although, not so very far off, in the gorge of the Arnon, the same red sandstone rocks are to be found.

The rose and flame of Petra have gone, and with them the sensation of a dead world. Within those walls, still standing up on high, is the modern town of Kerak, and the road winding over the shoulder of a hill, plunging down into a valley where it crosses a river bed at right angles before ascending to that town, is not without life. A man is following a couple of camels; some boys are driving a flock of black goats; by the roadside, up by the arch that leads into the vaulted passage that was once the only entrance to the Castle, are some Arab women. The country, for all its grim mountains, cut through by innumerable twisting gullies, has verdant wadis and suggestions of cultivated land. The road, too, that crosses the ravine by means of a stone bridge is a good one; the impression, even before entering Kerak, is one of prosperity.

The first that we hear of Kerak is in the various references to Kir of Moab that are to be met with in the Old Testament. We learn from this source that Mesha, King of Moab, was a sheepmaster who paid tribute to the King of Israel of " an hundred thousand lambs and an hundred thousand rams with the wool "; after the death of Ahab he revolted and succeeded in making Israel serve Moab for eighteen years. All that Mesha did in the way of victories is engraved on the celebrated Moab Stone that was discovered at Dibon in the last century; his defeats he omitted. If we are to believe the accounts given in the Bible, the Kings of Israel and Judah, after nearly dying of thirst in the wilderness, where they were provided with water at last through the agency of Elisha, gave Mesha a severe beating, and Moab " was destroyed from being a people." It is characteristic of Mesha, who was as confident that his god Kemosh directed the battle as were ever the Israelites that God gave the victory, that he offered up his son as a sacrifice to his god when affairs seemed desperate. The Israelites destroyed the cities of Moab, leaving only one stone on another at Kir-

THE APPROACH TO KERAK

haraseth, another name for Kir of Moab, which suggests that it may have some connection with the name of the Nabatæan Kings, which became dynastic—Haretath. It must have been after this defeat that Isaiah sings :—

" The burden of Moab. Because in the night Ar of Moab is laid waste and brought to silence ; because in the night Kir of Moab is laid waste and brought to silence. . . . .

" In their streets they shall gird themselves with sackcloth ; on the tops of their houses and in their streets, everyone shall howl, weeping abundantly."

Jeremiah says that Moab and Kemosh are to be humiliated, hunted out and destroyed ; so that it was not only a war undertaken to subdue a proud enemy who had recovered the land that Israel had taken from him ; it was a war of religion intended to wipe out idolatry and to throw down false gods.

Kir of Moab must always have been fortified to a certain extent, whoever were the masters of the rocky tableland from which it stands up so boldly. The Moabites disappeared in the second century before Christ ; perhaps they became cave dwellers, following the scornful advice of the prophet Jeremiah :—

" O ye that dwell in Moab, leave the cities and dwell in the rock, and be like the dove that maketh her nest in the sides of the hole's mouth."

But it is not so much the fragmentary history of Moab that attracts us here ; it is rather the far more recent and less nebulous story of the Crusaders, who built the fortress and the Castle, the former being raised on existing foundations.

King Baldwin I died in 1118, two years after he founded the fort at Petra ; he was succeeded by his cousin, Baldwin II, whose reign was marked by great enterprises and by the consolidation of the feudal system that took root so naturally in the East. His daughter Melisande married Fulk, Count of Anjou, who was then sixty years old ; he was elected King after Baldwin died, leaving no male heir, and he reigned from 1131 to 1144. This was a glorious period in the history of the Latin Kingdom of Jerusalem. The great fortresses on the coast and in the north of western Palestine were erected at strategic points, protecting each other, and connected by military roads; in order to increase the protection afforded to eastern Palestine by Montreal and Petra and the castle of Ahamont, it was decided to fortify the already strong place known as the Stone of the Desert, le Crac du Desert, as it was also called, though la Pierre du Desert was the more usual name given by the Franks.

Kerak Castle was founded in the latter part of Fulk's reign, probably in 1140, by a great Neapolitan noble, who had been cup-bearer to King Baldwin II. He is called "Payen le Bouteiller" by Guillaume de Tyr, and by this name he signs various documents, such as the Diploma of Baldwin II as Seigneur of Montreal, and he witnessed an act of Guillaume de Buris, the Seigneur of Tiberias, in 1132, also signing his name as Payen; but in 1136 he signed an act of King Fulk as "Pincerna," which was probably his family name, as it sounds more Italian in character than Payen, which may well have been a Frankish corruption.

Payen le Bouteiller was given the Seigneurie of Kerak; he built the fine great Castle and he probably utilized the fortifications already made, erecting others on Roman foundations. The Romans called the place Kerak Ommanorun because it had belonged to the Ammonites, or rather the Moabites; the Greeks called it Charagmoba, the Pale or Stake of Moab. What the Nabataeans called it is not recorded unless it were Hir Hareseth, but it was one of their forts in the days of their power and may even have been their chief city before they took Petra.

There were originally only two entrances to Kerak, both being vaulted passages cut in the rock; the arch which stands at the opening of the tunnel that opens on to the present high road and leads up to the Beybars tower, is of Roman workmanship. The passage is very narrow, only admitting a few people abreast and could be closed altogether in case of a state of siege.

Kerak stands on a rocky plateau that is three thousand one hundred and fifteen feet above sea level; it is separated from the surrounding hills by deep ravines, one of which is spanned by a bridge—the Wadi Ain-es-Sitt, the Valley of the Spring of the Lady. In the valleys round about are many cornfields and good grazing land which also runs up the slope of some of the lower hills. Although the general character of the country is wild and grand, there are also fertile districts.

The road leads up a stiff hill into the modern town of Kerak, where the most conspicuous objects are a very large building, standing alone, that I think was a school, and the solid stone houses which contain the official residences of the Governor of Kerak and the Sheikh. Beyond these are the ruins of the Castle, the first impression of which is one of its great size; the second being the charm of the colour and the great extent of the view. The limestone of which the walls are made has taken on a warm creamy yellow with age and the beating down of sun and rain and wind; from many of the ruined walls creepers hang. Over the battlements a glimpse of the steep pinkish hills of Judæa are seen afar off, on the further side of a pool of glittering turquoise that is the Dead Sea. The deep blue sky, the warm sand and the sun-steeped rock, with this delicious distant view, are so admirably expressed in the sketch that any further words are unnecessary. From other points of vantage, great vistas of mountain and ravine and winding river beds were obtained; and everywhere the same feeling of spacious country and the picturesque contour of mountain tops was the dominant feature.

The remains of the great feudal Castle and its dependencies are really amazing from their sheer size. The storehouses where food was kept, the vaulted passages with loopholes through which to shoot at the encroaching enemy, the towers and the curtains that connected them, all give evidence of the care with which this important fortress was fortified and furnished. It is no light thing to feed a large garrison and a whole tribe of civilians for the space of two years, as was done once during the last and most severe siege that Kerak had to endure; the great extent of these storehouses is easily accounted for when it is remembered what emergencies had to be faced in a time of perpetual warfare. The fact that Kerak was in a commanding position with regard to the caravan routes made it eagerly desired by the Saracens, and many were the attempts made to wrest it from the Crusaders.

The Wadi Kerak is a steep and twisting gorge that leads to the Dead Sea just where the land projects into the translucent green waters a promontory that has earned for it the name of the Tongue. It is one of those semi-tropical ravines that contrast so amazingly with the bare desolation of the salt sea, like the grander and better-known gorges of the Arnon and the Zerka.

The most comprehensive views are, naturally, to be seen from a height, and the best place to see them is from the upper story of what remains of some of the magazines where provisions and material of war used to be stored. There is a ruined stairway that leads to a path running along between the wall, with its loopholes, and a green enclosure that was once part of the interior of the castle; in the masonry at the corner of this building is another turret stair, up which you climb to find yourself on a platform from which extensive views unfold themselves on all sides. Mountains and valleys, pasture lands and bare rock, the distant line of the desert, all have their charm; but that glimpse of the Dead Sea, with its green waters turned to the purest blue by the reflection of the sky, is the most fascinating of all. The

ANCIENT ROCK-CUT ENTRANCE TO KERAK

bare Judæan hills, pinkish in the afternoon light and the long stretch of distance right out to Jericho and the Jordan valley, make up a picture that is typical of the country, and one that remains in the memory.

Not only is this a good place in which to sit and admire the view, it is also one from which we can get a good idea of the disposition of the fortress and Castle as they were in the days of the Crusaders.

Kerak stands on the summit, as we have seen, of a steep hill; from this point of vantage it is easy to see how completely it is isolated from the other hills that surround it, some of them being as high as the one on which the citadel stands. Deep ravines divide the citadel hill from the others, while, on the south side, is a wide, artificial moat; there is another moat to the north, which, however, cannot be seen from this point. The Castle stands to the extreme south on a tongue of land; huge as it was with all its dependencies, it only occupies a relatively small space of the whole enclosure.

In order to get any idea of what life was like when Payen le Bouteiller reigned here as Lord of Kerak, and later as Lord of the important fief of Oultre Jourdain, which stretched from the Gulf of Akaba to the Zerka, we must remember what a multum in parvo a fortress like Kerak really was. The Seigneur in command of the fortress, who was sometimes the titular Lord of the place, had his suite, including esquires, pages, secretaries, doctors; he would have knights who were recruited from the stream of men who continued to arrive in the Holy Land, anxious to take up the Cross or to make a fortune. He would have a head engineer, probably a Syrian, with a crowd of workmen under him—a clever native artificer, who sold his skill to Moslem or Christian indifferently, blacksmiths, wheelwrights, and so on. The men at arms were of various nationalities, Franks predominating, but a certain number of Syrians were mixed with them as time went on.

The town, or rather the upper town, was also

included inside the fortifications, and in it would be little shops like those in the modern Arab markets, and, to the crowd of military men might be added those of the merchant and small shopkeeping class. Visitors to these forts, even to the more remote ones, were not uncommon. An occasional Moslem Prince, for friendship between the heads of both parties was not uncommon, a travelling merchant or a party of pilgrims, might come to ask hospitality for a time. The ladies who came over with the Crusaders appear to have adopted oriental dress with enthusiasm; they are described as wearing long draperies, using much paint and powder, over which they veiled their faces whenever they went out. The middle class, who intermarried most with the Syrians, shut up their women, who were obliged to adopt the harem life, and were never allowed to go out without a veil. The ladies were served by slaves, Armenians, Syrians, any prisoner of war, or those coal-black Nubians who were much sought after and who fetched a long price in the slave market.

All this population was divided up into the usual classes, which had the usual amusements in times of peace. The great Hall was used for a Court of Law, at which the Seigneur presided, but it was also used as a theatre in which jugglers, singers, dancers and musicians performed to amuse the society of the place. Perhaps, sometimes, when the gaiety was at its gayest, the towers that were placed at intervals on the lines of communication flashed out a signal that meant " The Saracens are coming! " and then all the frolic would cease, the women would go to their abodes in the towers and the men to defend the fort. These signals of fire, shown from a tower, were much used by the Crusaders, and it is said that they were even able to exchange them with Jerusalem, and did so during the many sieges that they had to endure.

From the top of the Castle the Mount of Olives is visible with the tower of the Government House faintly silhouetted against the sky; it is easy to see that, although that building did not exist, the so-called Tower of David, which was one built by Herod to adorn and fortify his palace, could have a fire lit on its summit which would have been seen at Kerak. And, equally, a fire burned on the top of the towers of Kerak would have been visible from Jerusalem, as the Castle can be seen from any high ground there on a clear day. Roman candles were not unknown to the Crusaders, and pigeons were often used as messengers.

There was not often much time between the skirmishes and the sieges; even when there was peace farther west and north, this fortress, that held the key to the caravan routes, was always in the eye of the enemy and continued to be a bone of contention long after the Crusaders had been swept away out of the land that they had fought for so valiantly.

CHAPTER IX
A Feudal Castle

CHAPTER IX

A Feudal Castle

THE ruins of Kerak are interesting from several points of view, not the least important being the insight gained into the manner in which the Franks adopted the ideas of the Moslem architects while retaining the chief features of their own system of defence. Several writers have taken up this subject, one of the most thorough being M. E. Rey, whose "Étude sur les Monuments de l'architecture militaire des Croisés en Syrie" gives many interesting details.

When the Franks started to build the fine series of forts that were placed at strategic points on their lines of communication, they adopted many features from the Byzantine plan, which included some taken from the Romans, such as the vallum, agger and Mænium. From the Greeks they took the double enceinte, two lines of defence one over the other, the first line being always lower than the ramparts to allow the machines full play. The outer walls were often as much as thirty feet thick at the base, reaching up to a certain height with a view to protection from the enemy's attacks and to safeguard against the danger of earthquakes. At the top of this immensely thick wall a passage was hollowed out, decreasing the weight, and forming a battlemented terrace which gave the wall a double crown.

In Byzantine military architecture the towers were generally comparatively small and were placed as near to each other as the nature of the ground would admit; there was, however, one large tower in which the Captain of the Guard had his quarters. The towers were generally round and had battlemented parapets at their summit. The towers on the "agger" were placed in the intervals of those that stood on the ramparts; they were often put to strengthen weak places and were the origin of the Bastilles that appeared some centuries later in Europe.

These fortresses were placed so as to command the country round, to cut the enemy's communications, to divide his forces and to provide a defence for the neighbourhood. In the case of Kerak and Shobek and also of Petra, the positions chosen were largely taken because these forts then held the key to the caravan routes.

The fortresses erected by the Knights Templars differed, in some particulars, from those built by the other Crusaders. They resembled more closely, than did these others, the Arab fortresses of that day. A fine specimen of the Hospitallers' art is seen in the ruins of the enormous fortress known as the Kalaat-el-Hosn or, as the Franks called it, le Crac des Chevaliers, which guards the defile leading from Homs to Hameh and Tripolis.

The Templars' forts were built, like those of the Moslems, on the top of a steep slope, which acted as a defence and did not need such thick walls. They had deep moats, laboriously hewn out of the rock and filled with water; their stone was always dressed. The towers were sometimes square and did not project much from the walls.

A third group of fortresses, of which Kerak is an important example, consists of the feudal Castle, generally owned by one who takes the title of Lord of the Fortress. Here, again, are certain differences, although the general features are preserved. Kerak was never owned by either of the two great Orders, and retained its character of a castle belonging to a great noble to the end.

The city of Kerak occupies the summit of a hill which is separated on three sides from the surrounding hills by deep ravines; it is only connected at two points with these other summits by ridges of rock. On one of these, at the extreme south of the enclosure, is the

KERAK CASTLE, OVERLOOKING THE DEAD SEA

A Feudal Castle

Castle, protected by an artificially-cut moat, and having here the large reservoir that was fed by water brought by an aqueduct from a spring that is still called the " 'Ain-Frenguy." On the other ridge of rock, to the north-west, is the tower called after Sultan Beybars, and the great building erected there also protected by a moat.

Feudal castles such as Kerak were intended to take in a great quantity of people, as we have seen, for an indefinite time, a fact that accounts for their enormous size. One of the chief necessities of life at such a time was an adequate provision of water, and we find that the Crusaders made four large reservoirs and any amount of cisterns to that end.

The map of Kerak that is in M. Rey's book, already referred to, shows the peculiar shape of the ground that was enclosed by the fortifications; it is rather like a leg of mutton with the Castle forming the bone. Within this space was the town, the Castle dependencies and the fortified towers of the inner line of defence. The keep stands to the south of the Castle, which ends here with a vast building forming a redoubt.

The remains of this fortress give an impression of great strength. The towers are connected with a curtain; down the slope of the hill to south and east masses of masonry show where the old walls stood. Wherever you look, it is the same story.

In order to enter the Castle, two gates had to be passed, each with a portcullis; it was only after passing through what M. Rey calls " complicated defences " that the courtyard was gained, which was on a lower level than the principal rooms, which were all in the upper part of the building.

The interior of the Castle is in such a state of ruin that very little of the original plan can be made out; there are great storerooms under buildings that once rose to four or five stories; many cisterns, long passages under arcades with loopholes through which a glimpse of the outer world can be seen. In the middle of the

Courtyard is the Gothic chapel, built on the same lines as those at Kalaat-el-Hosn, Margat and Safed. The aisle terminates in a semicircular apse, lit by four windows; in the thickness of the wall a staircase is concealed that leads up to the roof of the church. There are still faint remains of fresco on the walls.

The fief of Oultre Jourdain became one of the most important in the Latin Kingdom; not only did the territory extend from the river Zerka to the Red Sea, including all the land of Moab and Idumæa and those fortresses which had been placed there for the protection of the country, but it was increased by the addition of land west of the Dead Sea. Payen died, and was succeeded by his nephew Maurice; King Fulk died, and was succeeded by Baldwin III, in whose reign Hebron was added to the possessions of the Lord of Kerak, making him master of both sides of the Dead Sea; he had also a naval base at Aila, on the Gulf of Akaba, and he included in his dominions the vast deserts of the peninsula of Sinai.

These great possessions brought great riches to Kerak, because the Seigneur had the right of levying a tax on the merchants who passed up any of the roads in his dominion and on any ships that sailed on the Dead Sea. It was the seat of an archbishop and was like the capital city of all that region. The Lords of Shobek evidently preferred the liveliness of Kerak to the much more restricted amusement to be enjoyed in that solitary outpost of civilization, for they took up their residence there, leaving the care of the fortress to their seconds in command.

It is not difficult to realize that these Seigneurs, endowed with such vast possessions and with a position of so much importance, to which many of them were unaccustomed, should have become like little Kings, making war or peace as they liked, without reference to the King of Jerusalem, who was the nominal head of these scattered communities. The great Orders of the

A Feudal Castle

Templars and the Knights of Saint John of Jerusalem set a bad example ; they were always jealous one of another, and the ultimate expulsion of the Crusaders from the Holy Land was partly caused by the dissensions of the various parties. Had they been more united and had they been properly supported from the countries that sent them out to fight for the Cross, the history of Palestine might have been very different to what it actually was.

Modern historians tell us that the arbitrary division of the various expeditions sent out to reinforce the Crusaders into so many crusades is not right historically. Men and arms dribbled in all the time, but, little by little, the spirit and the fighting genius of the first Crusaders grew dim and their first enthusiasm died down. Intermarriages with Syrians and Christianised Saracens were not calculated to keep up the spirit of the race ; eastern costumes and eastern customs, more suited to the climate, seemed to have had an enervating effect on the Franks. In 1127, a cloud had appeared on the horizon, and by the time that Kerak, in all its splendour, was completed and frowned down over the mountains to the Dead Sea, the sky was already overcast.

In 1127 the star of a remarkable man rose, the star of the Prince-Governor or Atabek of Mosul, Imad ud-din Zengi ; he was the first of the Moslems to stand up against the Franks. His more famous son Nur ud-din Mahmud was to carry his father's conquests still higher and the Kurdish general Salah ud-din Yusuf was destined to sweep the Christians out of Syria.

The first great blow to the Crusaders was the loss of Edessa ; although it was recovered for a time it was definitely taken by the Moslems in 1146. This was a great triumph for the enemy and was of real use to him in his operations ; the troops in Syria were no longer divided from those farther east and the Crusaders' greatest fief was broken up.

In 1164 Saladin was sent with his uncle, a distinguished general, to Egypt; he was very unwilling to go, being apparently, at that time, not at all anxious to do deeds of valour. Although in a subordinate position he soon proved his talent for warfare and also for diplomacy and was rewarded by becoming the master of Egypt after the death of the weak Fatimid Sultan. It was then that his jealousy of Nur ud-din showed itself; in spite of the kindness that he had received from the family of Zengi he seems always to have feared that he would stand in the way of his ambition and he was never willing to share any part of his glory with another. After the death of the Prince in 1173, he rose to be the master of Syria and Egypt in name as well as in fact.

Saladin came back from Egypt determined to destroy, one by one, the isolated forts of the Franks. It was not only a question of religion, it was vitally important that the military roads connecting the far-lying parts of the Saracen empire should be free. And then the old question of commerce was still to be considered. The Franks owned so many of these routes, some of them made by the Romans, all of them paved with great slabs of stone and with upstanding posts to mark the limit. At convenient distances there were towers built in which the doles of merchants and others were collected, and the revenue arising out of this customs office by the wayside was not to be despised. The Trans-Jordan routes were particularly convenient because they branched out in so many directions; there was one road, for instance, that led from Petra to Hebron, a four days' journey by camel. So that both sides of the Dead Sea would be open to the caravans if once the Franks were dislodged from their key positions.

In spite of constant warfare, Syria still kept her place as a centre of commerce; besides acting as middleman to half the nations of the earth, passing on the products of one to another, she had many and beautiful

A Feudal Castle

things to dispose of that were either grown or manufactured in the country. In an earlier day the prophet Elijah, that inspired poet whose words were like the facets of clear-cut jewels, said of her in that beautiful lamentation over the lost glories of Tyre:—

" Syria was thy merchant by reason of the multitude of the wares of thy making; they occupied in thy fairs with emeralds, purple, and broidered work, and fine linen, and coral, and agate."

And again: " Arabia and all the Princes of Kedar they occupied with thee in lambs, and rams, and goats; in these were they thy merchants.

" The merchants of Sheba and Ramah, they were thy merchants; they occupied in thy fairs with chief of all spices, and with all precious stones and with gold."

Besides the merchants and their caravans, there were the pilgrims going to Mecca and Medina; it must have been a regular thorn in the side to the Moslems to see Shobek throned over the Haj route, exacting a dole from the pilgrims and even, sometimes, threatening to descend upon them.

Rénaud of Chatillon, proud and passionate, a man who was too much given to following his own impulses without thinking where they would lead him, came over in 1147, in the train of King Louis VII; he married the widowed Princess Regent of Antioch, was taken prisoner and remained in captivity at Aleppo for fifteen years. When he was released he went to Antioch, where he found his wife and his stepson, who was then reigning Prince. After the death of his wife he married again, another heiress. This time his wife was the widow of Humphrey of Toron in Upper Galilee, who was also Lord of Montreal and Kerak; in this way he was Lord of the fief of Oultre Jourdain and he took up his abode in Kerak. In spite of certain good points in his character, his coming to the Holy Land was disastrous not only to Kerak but to the cause of the Crusaders.

CHAPTER X
Kerak Besieged

CHAPTER X
Kerak Besieged

"LE Crach qui mout estoit forz de siege et bien fermez de mur," had many a siege to endure before the final capitulation; they were all quite unsuccessful, and nearly all were connected with the duel that went on continuously between Rénaud de Chatillon and Saladin.

That hero of romance, Saladin, whom most of us associate with our earliest recollections of the stories of chivalry, had his defects as well as his qualities. It is true that he did some gallant deeds, such as sending a couple of horses to Richard the Lion Heart when he saw him fighting on foot, and being merciful, when it suited him, to prisoners, but there is the reverse side of the picture. He could be cruel and cold-blooded, and he was certainly both ambitious and apt to be jealous. That this jealousy should have been intensified when the object of it stood in the way of his ambition was but natural. It is an ill wind that does no one any good, and the garrison of Kerak profited by it when he withdrew from the first siege, in 1173, for no other reason than that of being unwilling to meet his liege lord Nureddin.

It came about in this way. Saladin's father and uncle had done the old Atabek of Mosul a good turn in days gone by, and when they had to flee from justice they naturally went to his Court. They were well received and were eventually given high office, one as Governor of Damascus and the other as a general. The young Yussuf grew up in this Court and owed everything to Zengi and his family; when he was twenty-five he went to Egypt to serve under his uncle, and was fighting there when the Franks and the Moslems were each trying to annex Egypt. The Franks got the better at first, for they forced Saladin to leave Alexandria, but the arrangement made was little more than a compact between both parties to leave Egypt to its Fatimid owners. Saladin was, according to Mr. Stanley Lane-Poole, a hostage or guest in King Amalric's camp for several days, and he suggests that it may have been here that the young Moslem leader received the honour of knighthood from the hands of Humphrey of Toron. Many chroniclers have touched on this story, but none with such detail as we find in the pages of the " Chronique d'Ernoul et de Bernard le Trésorier." The chapter is headed: " Comment Saladins fu rechatez de prison."

The story told here is circumstantial. Saladin, after the Egyptian expedition, was a prisoner of war in Montreal; his uncle, a very rich Provost of Damascus, offered to ransom him, being induced to try this course because the Lord of Montreal was courteous and friendly to the Moslems. Now the Lord of Montreal was the same Humphrey of Toron; he consented to the ransom and was induced by the captive to bestow the order of knighthood on him before he rejoined his uncle in Damascus. However that may be, most historians agree that he did receive it and that, on many occasions, he proved himself worthy of that honour.

Affairs might have turned out very differently for the Franks had they not been ill-advised enough to be influenced by some of their number who insisted on an invasion of Egypt, in spite of their treaty with the Fatimid Caliph; the result was that the Saracens rushed in, allied themselves with the Egyptians, and soon became the ruling power. Saladin succeeded his uncle as Vizier of Egypt when he died, and he replaced the last feeble Fatimid Sultan after his early death. Although still Commander of the Army in Egypt and owing allegiance to Nureddin, Saladin was supreme at Cairo. It was an anomalous position.

And so it turned out that a siege of Kerak and

THE GATE OF KERAK

Kerak Besieged

one of Shobek were raised because Nureddin was approaching with his forces, and the haughty Saladin preferred to retreat on Egypt, with an excuse that did not deceive anyone, rather than meet the man who stood between him and the realization of his ambitious dreams. Nureddin was really angry at last, and was on the eve of invading Egypt to bring his general to book when Saladin's father advised him to make his submission in order to avert such a disaster. And then, at the right moment for Saladin, Nureddin died. The story of his offer to rule Syria through the little son of the late King and of his taking the crown for himself when the Zengi faction opposed him, has nothing to do with Kerak. But the fact that Saladin became King of Syria and of Egypt and that he spent his life between the two Courts of Damascus and Cairo, and was consequently always passing and repassing the roads guarded by the fortresses of Oultre Jourdain, explains his anxiety to possess them independently of his hatred of Rénaud.

There is no doubt that Rénaud did his best to make himself disliked. He more than once swooped down from his "Crow's Castle," as the Saracens called Kerak, and kidnapped a caravan, twice certainly, in a time of peace; once Saladin retaliated by seizing a pilgrim ship. Soon after that he hovered round Shobek, perhaps thinking occasionally of the time he had spent there as prisoner; but he did not attack either fortress then because the Franks were posted in the hills about Kerak waiting for him.

The Franks had a great loss in 1179 in the death of Humphrey of Toron, who was killed when trying to defend his young King. He spoke Arabic, and was on terms of real friendship with many of the Saracens although he fought them as fiercely as any of the other knights when it was a question of war.

"No words can describe Hainfrey," writes an Arab historian, "his name was a proverb for bravery and skill in war. He was indeed a plague let loose by God for the chastising of the Moslem."

In spite of this ferocious character, Humphrey had a lovable nature, and the various truces that were made between the contending parties were largely his work.

The fourth Humphrey of Toron was a young man in 1184; he was the son of the second wife of Rénaud de Chatillon, and was engaged to be married to Isabeau, the daughter of King Amalric, or Amoury, and half-sister to Baldwin IV. The wedding was planned to take place with great ceremony and rejoicing at Kerak, where the bridegroom was living with his mother and step-father. The preparations were all made, the wedding day dawned, and then a bombshell arrived in the notice of the near approach of the Saracens under Saladin. Whether the news was blazed out the night before by means of those fires that were lit as warnings on the top of the towers, or whether some breathless messenger, thankful to be within the gates of the strong city, brought the bad news, we do not know. All that appears is that the wedding took place on the very day that Saladin invested the fortress.

The bride must have been magnificently dressed, as can be judged by reading an account of a wedding that took place at Tyre in the same year; it was written by an Arab historian, who describes the bride :—

"She was splendidly dressed, and wore a robe of silk magnificently interwoven with gold; the trailing dress swept the ground behind her. According to their usual manner of dress, she wore on her forehead a gold diadem covered by a fillet of gold tissue, and round her throat the same. So dressed she advanced with little rhythmic steps, like those of a turtle-dove."

The historian adds that the bride was preceded by music and followed by splendidly dressed knights and ladies as she made her way between the Moslem and Christian spectators.

Kerak Besieged

While the wedding feast was going on at Kerak, Saladin, an uninvited guest, was at the gates of the town; he thundered through the lower fortifications, and got to the very gates of the Castle. An entrance was even effected through one of the gates leading to the Castle, but the attack was repulsed and the breach closed. It was then that Rénaud had one of those brilliant flashes that came to him sometimes; he sent a present to the enemy outside his gates in the shape of bread and wine (perhaps the celebrated wine of Engadi, made from grapes grown on the other side of the Dead Sea); with these were driven out cattle and sheep to provide a wedding feast. Rénaud sent a message by those who brought this unexpected gift, to the effect that he wished to salute Saladin, whom he had often carried in his arms when he was a captive at the fort; alluding, apparently, to the period of his captivity at Aleppo, when he might well have played with the little son of the Atabek's right-hand man.

Saladin was delighted—" si en fu mout lies, si le fist recoive, et si l'en merchia mout hautement "; he then asked which tower the young couple were to occupy, and when he heard he gave orders that no one was to dare to attack that point. These civilities over, he proceeded to bombard the Castle with all his biggest siege engines, always avoiding the tower in question.

A deep moat divided the Castle from the town where Saladin was, but it must have been an anxious time for the garrison. The food supply was not enough for the demand made on it by the mass of people crowded into the Castle and its dependencies. A messenger was accordingly sent down the precipitous side of the mountain, in the hope that he would be able to get to Jerusalem, which he evidently did; and the fire was lit as a signal that something was wrong at Kerak. The night before the King started from Jerusalem to relieve the fortress he lit the fire on the top of David's Tower, and then the beleaguered garrison knew that help was at hand. Perhaps Saladin understood the reason of that beacon flaming up in the dark night; when he heard that Baldwin had crossed the Jordan, and had encamped near the " Mer del Dyable," he raised the siege and left the proud fortress still unconquered.

Of all the rash deeds of Rénaud de Chatillon, the one that had the worst consequences was one that he accomplished after long deliberation and careful preparation. It sounded the tocsin that awoke the Moslem world to a religious war, and it gave Saladin a pretext, if one had been wanted, to wake up the smouldering animosity of the Saracens, and to force them to carry on a war of extermination.

Rénaud was lucky, at a time when disaster was overtaking the Crusaders in so many ways, to be able to preserve his dominions with the five strong places intact. Added to his position on land, he had the advantage of possessing both banks of the Dead Sea and of having a harbour on the Gulf of Akaba. He became rich with the dues of caravans and of ships, though he sometimes remitted these in favour of some such great power as the Knights of Saint John of Jerusalem; he used his base at Akaba as a harbour for his ships. In 1182, the workshops in Kerak were busy; there was a perpetual sound of hammering and of men coming and going. Great trees were cut down in the neighbourhood, and brought up to the shops where they were fashioned into boats. These boats were taken in sections, on the backs of camels, to the port on the Gulf of Akaba, where they were put together, and launched from the harbour in the Isle of Graye. When all was ready, Rénaud in person led an attack on the shore of Arabia, landed and took his troops to within a day's march of Medina, his avowed object being to destroy the holy places venerated by the Moslems. He did not accomplish his design; he only escaped with his life, leaving many of his unfortunate followers to be taken to Mecca, tied on to camels with their faces to the tail, there to be

Kerak Besieged

sacrificed in place of goats, amid the howls and yells of an excited mob.

This foolhardy attempt had taken place as far back as 1182; it had not led to any real disaster, and might not have brought one had not Rénaud again swooped down on a rich caravan and stolen everything belonging to the merchants. This was again done during a time of truce, and it exasperated Saladin, who swore to kill Rénaud with his own hand. He made the former exploit the spark that was to light the fire of Mohammedan enthusiasm, but it was, apparently, the last ill deed that led to the defeat of the Franks by driving the Saracens to immediate revenge at a time of weakness in their own ranks and irresolution in their counsels. Baldwin the Leper was dead, and the little boy who succeeded him was dead also. Sibylla, the elder daughter of King Amalric, had been made Queen, and her husband, Guy de Lusignan, King; Rénaud supported them, although his own stepson and the younger daughter, Isabeau, were put forward as rivals.

Things went on from bad to worse; one party wanted war, and the other saw that the time was unpropitious, but when at last the terrible day of reckoning came, differences were forgotten, and the Franks stood together in a last effort to save their cause. It was too late. Saladin had collected an immense force, all inspired by the idea of a Holy War; the Crusaders fought desperately, but the great heat and the total want of water made the battle of the Horn of Hittin one of the most ghastly on record. When it was finished, when the sad remains of the flower of chivalry that had gone out to fight for the Cross was counted, little enough remained. Guy of Lusignan, Raymond of Tripolis, Rénaud of Chatillon, Humphrey of Toron were among those who survived.

Saladin encamped on the field of battle; when he had refreshed himself he sent for Guy and Rénaud to come to his tent. The King was still parched with thirst, and

Saladin gave him a cup of iced sherbet to drink. Guy drank, and handed on the cup to Rénaud.

"Tell the King," Saladin said to the interpreter, "that it was he, not I, who gave that man to drink."

Rénaud must have known what was coming, when the Conqueror refused him hospitality; and he had not long to wait. Saladin, crying out that he would avenge Mohammed, fell upon him and killed him with his own hand.

Jerusalem fell that year and Kerak must have been invested soon after as it is generally supposed that the last siege extended over a period of two years. We know little of that siege, except that, at the end, the garrison capitulated on account of starvation. The women and children had been sent out to live how they could; the men had no leader and were mostly natives. It is stated that Rénaud de Chatillon's widow gave up Kerak to ransom her son who had been a prisoner since the battle of Hittin; was she in the fortress herself? Probably not, as there is no mention of that in the old chronicles. Bernard le Trésorier says that Saladin sent her son back to her: "Quant li rois si compaignon furent delivré, si envoia Salehadins a le feme le prince Renaut del Crac sen fil Hainfroi, tout delivré." The same chronicler says that Saladin restored the women and children to the garrison of Kerak and sent them all into Christian territory. Perhaps he felt that with that one blow, when he had killed his enemy with his own hand, he had exhausted his longing for vengeance.

When the tide of war went badly with Saladin after Richard the Lion Heart delivered those tremendous blows that did something towards wiping out the disgrace of Hittin, he dismantled many fortresses, but Kerak and Jerusalem were kept in a state of defence. He even strengthened the fortifications of the former, which continued to be a bone of contention between rival factions long after the Crusaders had left the scene of their short-lived triumphs and their long misfortunes.

Kerak Besieged

The last person of interest of whom we hear in connection with the Stone of the Desert, is the Mameluk Sultan of Egypt, who came here, unexpectedly, dressed as an Arab and riding on a camel. Beybars did a good deal to the fortifications; he restored and partially rebuilt the tower that bears his name. Since then, the history of the fine old Crusaders' Castle is unwritten.

Looking back at it from the valley below, it still has an air of strength and grandeur; up there, on the summit of an almost precipitous hillside, it has all the appearance of a mediæval fortress that is still inhabited. The Arabs, clothed in their picturesque garments, astride on camels or walking after their sheep and goats, do not belong to any age; they are quite in the picture. Looking up at the Beybars Tower and the huge construction near it, or looking down on the group of peasants on the bridge, the illusion is preserved. The whole scene is so romantic that one would not be surprised to see Rénaud de Chatillon and his knights riding down bent on a foray, or Saladin himself at the head of his forces coming to invest the place once more.

A last vision of Kerak, enthroned among mountain tops, overlooking the desert and the Dead Sea, leaves one with a vision of something remote and made desolate yet not really lonely because of the ghosts of the past that still inhabit its ruined shell.

CHAPTER XI
THE CITIES OF THE PLAIN

CHAPTER XI

The Cities of the Plain

BLUE sky, green sea—not an ordinary green, but the clearest translucent green imaginable—bare rocks on either side; a silent sea with no cry of wild bird, though they abound in some parts of the shore, with never a sail to be seen from one end to the other—such is the Dead Sea. Lovely in colour, striking in the outline of the cliffs that come down so sheer to the waters, the chief impression that it leaves is one of desolation. That, at least, is the impression left after navigating its waters one Sunday during last Spring. It is true that salt is still collected at the south end of the lake, and also, I believe, commandeered by the Bedu, and the bitumen still forms a part of local industry, but there was nothing to be seen that day. The solitude was untroubled by any modern innovations; it was strangely impregnated with the tragedies of the past. No place has ever given me the sensation of past tragedy more strongly than did the oily waters and the desolate shores of the lake of Asphalt.

The water, that looks turquoise blue from a distance with the sky reflected in it, appears quite green when looking down into its depths from a boat; it is so clear that you almost expect to see Sabrina braiding her hair with pearls down there beneath a curious long streak of white foam with crystallized balls that glisten in the sun like brilliants. But it is not even peopled with shadowy nymphs; its history is too far back and too tragic for such pleasant visions.

To the right are the steep hills of Judæa, rising some three thousand feet odd over the level of the water; to the left are the picturesque crags and the level plateau of

Moab, rising to almost the same height. The gorge of the Zerka-Main is visible where some wild palms come down to the brink of the sea—farther along the great red cliffs, reminiscent of Petra, guard the entrance to the Arnon ; stretching across the waters, and looking from a distance almost as if it were the further shore, is the long promontory called the Tongue-el-Lisan. At the southern extremity is the mountain of salt, the Jebel Ousdom, a name that may have some connection with that of Sodom.

Geologists tell us that the subsidence of the Jordan depression dates from the end of the tertiary period ; in prehistoric times it was a great inland lake that had collected the immense rainfall of the Ice Age ; the level of the water was then fourteen hundred feet higher than it is at present. This fact is proved by the lacustrine deposits and traces of fresh water fauna at that height. It once filled the valley of the Jordan as far as Lake of Galilee, but was never connected with the Red Sea, as has been suggested. When the rainfall grew less and the temperature increased the lake shrunk, and along the fertile southern valleys were apparently erected the three famous cities that perished because of their sins and the small town or village that was saved at the prayer of Lot.

The Sea of Lot ! The Arabs cherish any story that appeals to their imagination, especially if it has, as in this case, been introduced into the Qoran. But their favourite story is quite different to the Bible narrative, being concerned with a breach of hospitality as well as with the fatal curiosity of the lady who was turned into a pillar of salt. There was a real pillar of salt, in days of old, that was always pointed out as being Lot's wife, and the statue was supposed to be endowed with life and to wax and wane with the moon in some mysterious way. Another effigy of the Curious One is in rock, and just below it is a rock resembling the dog that was roasted for the traveller's dinner, called back to life by the

THE GATE OF THE ARNON

The Cities of the Plain

naturally angry prophet, only to be turned to stone with his foolish but well-meaning mistress.

The Bible story is quite clear. Lot was no saint; he liked the good things of life and he was too fond of the wine of the country. He chose the fertile Jordan valley when Abram gave him his choice and he pitched his tent near Sodom, a town that, even then, had a bad reputation. The Cities of the Plain, which were very rich, were attacked by the four Kings who were, in their turn, defeated by Abram, who came to the help of his nephew Lot. But the wickedness of the people had to be punished somehow, and the only way seemed to be that of absolute annihilation. Lot, as we know, was warned to fly, and the angels told him to be quick about it as they were only waiting to get him out of the way before starting work. They told him to go to the mountain, but Lot, characteristically, and thinking no doubt of his little comforts, suggested that he might be allowed to go to Zoar, because it was such a little place—evidently not worth while blowing up. This permission was accorded him and he went there, though, after the awful catastrophe, he moved up to a cave in the mountain.

What happened when the wicked Cities of the Plain were engulfed? Many suggestions have been made. The Bible says that it rained brimstone and fire from Heaven, that the cities and all their inhabitants and " all the plain " were overthrown. The next morning when Lot looks out over the scene of desolation, " the smoke of the country went up as the smoke of a furnace."

One suggestion concerning this event is that it was a natural convulsion of nature which took the form of an earthquake and thunderstorm, and the lightning set in a blaze the inflammable products of the Dead Sea. Even so, where are the remains of those cities? The probabilities are that they lie under water at the southern and shallow end of the Sea; an idea that has often been ridiculed but that seems now about to be proved by the archæologists' labours. It is curious how often the light of modern research proves, instead of disproves, the old traditions.

The American School of Archæology has been lately studying all this neighbourhood, with the result that several interesting discoveries have been made. One of these was that of a quantity of Iron Age pottery dating as early as 1400 B.C.; near to this find an altar was discovered, and the inference is that there was a shrine and pilgrims' station here. The extraordinary thing is that the relics cease at the period when the cities are supposed to have fallen and do not begin again for a thousand years. As to the sites, it is certain that each of these cities must have been built in a wadi, as water was a necessity; Zoar was probably on the same wadi as the mediæval town, but lower down; Sodom and Gomorrah were evidently placed on the only other wadis at the southern end of the lake. It remains to be seen whether any effort will be made to excavate in the shallow waters which now cover the soil.

Strabo, who was living and writing in the Augustan Age, says that near Masada "are to be seen rugged rocks bearing the marks of fire; fissures in many places; a soil like ashes; pitch falling in drops from the rocks; rivers boiling up, and emitting a fetid odour to a great distance; dwellings in every direction overthrown; whence we are inclined to believe the common tradition of the natives, that thirteen cities once existed there, the capital of which was Sodom, but that a circuit of about sixty stadia around it escaped uninjured; shocks of earthquakes, however, eruptions of flames and hot springs, containing asphaltum and sulphur, caused the lake to burst its bounds, and the rocks took fire; some of the cities were swallowed up, others were abandoned by such of the inhabitants as were able to make their escape."

Strabo and Diodorus Siculus give us various details concerning the Dead Sea industries. According to them the natives knew when the asphalt was going to rise to the surface, because all metal was immediately tarnished, even gold not being exempt. Thus warned they went out on rafts made of reeds or bulrushes and hacked the great lumps of bitumen or asphalt, for both floated on the surface, into smaller lumps and placed them on the raft. The bigger lumps were called bullocks and the smaller sheep, because they often had the appearance of a headless animal. Those who collected were armed, and frequent fights took place between rival claimants.

The Nabatæans had, at one time, the monopoly of collecting the bitumen, which they sold in great quantities to the Egyptians, who used it to mix with other ingredients when they embalmed the bodies of their dead. It was even said that they could not make sure of preserving the body from decay without this bitumen which they do not seem to have been able to procure anywhere else.

The Dead Sea, which is so unique in its scenery, must also surely be uncommon in its composition. Although writers differ as to the exact quantity of each detail, the general accounts agree that six million tons of water are poured into it daily which cannot be carried off in any other way than by evaporation. In the water are chloride of sodium, chloride of magnesium, which gives the water its bitter taste, and chloride of calcium, which makes the waters oily. The asphalt is said to form in the crevasses of rock at the bottom of the sea, whence it is loosened by any disturbance of nature; the bitumen rises up and floats on the surface in lumps, as we have just seen. A famous Arabic chemist of the thirteenth century gave a list of the uses that bitumen could be put to for medicine and other purposes. " The stinking sea," he remarks, " throws up bitumen from the bottom, smelling of naphtha, that is formed in the fissures of rock, as amber comes out of the sea." There is another sort, he says, that is used medicinally for ulcers, inflammations and stomach troubles, as well as for killing vermin off the vines.

One would like to know if anything remained of the Cities of the Plain in the days when the Nabatæans collected bitumen to sell to the Egyptians : the tradition has subsisted through the centuries, whether or no any trace was left. Colonel Conder, whose researches in eastern Palestine have made all this region so interesting, apparently thinks that it is impossible that they should have been sunk in the sea. He says :—

"The cities were destroyed, blotted out so that their names never appeared again in the Bible topography, and Josephus believed—as some still do in England—in spite of geological evidence, that they lay beneath the salt waters of the Dead Sea."

The latest archæological opinion seems to point to the old idea agreeing with tradition, which has so often proved right in the end ; we can only hope that as the oldest history unfolds, bit by bit, as fresh light is thrown on it, something may be yet found out concerning these cities that have vanished more completely than any of the others that we have so far considered.

In the days of the Romans, there were several landing stages ; the Lord of Kerak had his harbour just at the mouth of the Wadi Kerak. It has been suggested that Herod went to the baths at Callirrhoe by boat in order to avoid the long land journey. There must have been a good deal of life all about the lake Asphaltitís in old days, but the Moslems do not seem to have used it much. Probably the sons of the desert, who were trekking about in the neighbourhood, kept traders off, while preferring their quick horses to the boats to which they were not accustomed.

The Dead Sea remained unnavigated until quite recent times. The first to sail there was an Irishman named Costigan, who died from the effect of the climate, combined with want of water ; the second was an Englishman named Molyneux, who had the same fate. The two capes of the white marl "Lisan," which is reflected in the green waters so picturesquely, are called after these pioneers, both of them having been taken from its inhospitable shores in a dying condition. Costigan went to make his unfortunate attempt in 1835; Molyneux in 1847; the third adventurer was an American, Lynch, who was luckier than his predecessors, being far better equipped by his Government.

Since then various people have taken advantage of a couple of motor boats that are sometimes available; one of these, Père Abel, has written a very interesting account of the voyage undertaken by him, during which he explored the shores very thoroughly. Before penetrating into the gorges by which the cities near the Dead Sea are approached, we must take one brief glance at those that are on the western shore, and so have no claim to be considered here at any length.

Masada, near which Strabo said that he saw the ruins of other vanished cities, was a fortress rather than a city. It stands seventeen hundred feet above the Dead Sea, on a plateau at the top of a bare rock. Nearly every city overlooking the Dead Sea has a tragic story; that of Masada is a horror that was redeemed by heroism.

Jonathan Maccabeus climbed up to this eagle's nest, and built a fortress here; Herod the Great refortified it, encircled the whole of the plateau with a great white wall, which had thirty-eight towers, and then erected a palace for himself. It was a wonderful affair, that palace—very strong outside and luxuriously furnished inside. He had baths, no doubt arranged on the Roman plan, and his floors were covered with coloured mosaic; he had gardens and roads, and a marvellous view, which perhaps did not appeal to him, of the Dead Sea, lying, like a jewel, at his feet. The description which Josephus gives of the approach to the earthly Paradise is so typical of the country that it must find a place here.

" Now of the ways that lead to it," he is speaking of the way up to the Castle, " one is that from the lake Asphaltitis, towards the sun-rising, and another on the west, where the ascent is easier : the one of these ways is called the Serpent, as resembling that animal in its narrowness, and its perpetual windings ; for it is broken off at the prominent precipices of the rock, and returns frequently into itself, and lengthening again by little and little, hath much ado to proceed forward ; and he that would walk along it must first go on one leg and then on the other ; there is also nothing but destruction, in case your feet slip ; for on each side there is a vastly deep chasm and precipice, sufficient to quell the courage of everybody by the terror it infuses into the mind."

Herod fortified this place, also according to Josephus and others, to protect himself against two dangers : one that of the Jews, who might return to their former Kings, and the other that ever-present danger that arose from Cleopatra's ambitions and Antony's weakness. He provisioned the place so thoroughly that when the Romans took the fortress nearly a hundred years later, grain was still found in the storerooms ; wonderful to relate, it was still eatable.

The Roman general, Flavius Silva, who came there after the Romans under Titus had taken Jerusalem, had no easy task to accomplish. He got possession of the country round, and then climbed up the hill and made his camp there, where still remains are to be seen. And then he built a great wall all round Herod's fortifications, and put his siege engines on it. The garrison consisted of those extremists the Zealots, under Eleazar, the fanatic ; they were brave men, and women too, as the sequel shows. They built another wall inside the outer fortifications to keep out the enemy, but all in vain. And then, when it came to a certain capitulation, Eleazar made a speech in which he set forth the horrors of the fate that awaited them as prisoners to the Romans, and begged them to kill themselves rather than submit. The garrison consented, and the massacre began ; men killed their wives and children, and then each other ; in silence, so that the enemy should suspect nothing, the dreadful scene took place, only two women and five children hid themselves rather than give up their lives.

The next day, when the Romans at last got into the fortress that they had besieged so long, they found a mass of dead bodies, and an awful silence took the place of the clamour that they had expected. The last of the Dead Sea tragedies has, at any rate, an element of greatness about it.

CHAPTER XII
Aroer and Machærus

CHAPTER XII

Aroer and Machærus

ABOUT thirteen miles east of the Dead Sea two streams unite to form a river that, in spite of its short length and its sometimes scanty flow of water, is one of the three great rivers of the Trans-Jordan district. Like other rivers in Palestine it depends more on the extraordinary beauty of the gorge through which it runs than on the actual extent of its waters.

Somewhere about the Haj route, a quantity of small streams arise mingling their waters until they meet those of a southern brook; after the junction the river thus formed runs down through a tremendous cleft in the rocky plateau of the Moab mountains, pouring its torrent down and down until it empties itself into the salt waters of the Dead Sea at a point that is very little north of the middle of that inland sea and just opposite the site of Engadi. This gorge is formed chiefly of red sandstone cliffs that rise up in bold headlands and lofty crags; the width is two miles across at the top, narrowing down to something about a hundred feet at the outlet. The river is overhung with willow and oleander, with tamarisk, castor bean and cane; it is the haunt of wild birds, and there were, until quite lately, a number of wild animals lurking about in the neighbourhood. Jackals and hyenas are still common, wolves used to abound; gazelles and roebuck and ibis have all been seen here by travellers. As to the birds, there is a peculiar bird only known to these regions which has been named, not very poetically, the " grackle "; there are also sand grouse, bee-eaters, Greek partridges, wild duck, kingfishers, storks, as well as eagles and vultures.

The human beings who frequent these valleys used to be as wild as the four-footed animals, lurking in the shadow of some mighty boulder to pounce on any unprotected wayfarer. Burckhardt, writing in 1812, states that he found heaps of stones at regular intervals in the gorge of the Arnon, and noticed that his Arab guard always added a few stones to the pile. When he asked the reason, he was told that the stones were there to provide weapons for any unarmed traveller who might be attacked by robbers. We have left those uncivilized customs behind us in the course of more than a hundred years, but the Bedawin tribes are still liable to relapse into banditti if an occasion arises.

Seen from the Dead Sea, the entrance to the Arnon is scarcely perceptible; the cliffs seem almost to meet, the great pylon that guards the Bab-el-Mojib—the Gate of the Mojib, as the Arabs have rechristened the old river—bars the way. In front of the cleft in the rock a sort of promontory of sand, on which the oleander grows with its usual lavish abundance, stretches out, half hiding a great pool of water in which the vivid red rocks are reflected with dazzling effect. It is only after climbing over rocks and splashing through pools of water that the entrance to the gorge can be approached. The conditions, however, vary; it is sometimes possible to wade up the Arnon for some way, while at others the water is comparatively deep from the beginning. The theory that the water of the Dead Sea is rising seems to be corroborated by the change in the conditions of the shore, much of which is being gradually submerged.

The view up the gorge is very striking. The cliffs have all the fantastic pinnacles and the Gothic tracery that are such a marked feature of those at Petra; some of the rocks might be taken for the work of the architect, others present a flat surface. The ravine twists and turns, the walls rise up sheer and steep to a height of four hundred feet, and below the clear water reflects the gaunt red rock and the feathery green tamarisk in its blue depths, as well as the cloudless blue sky above. The refreshing shade, dappled with intense splashes of sun-

THE DEAD SEA

Aroer and Machærus

light, make the entrance to this strange ravine both restful after the glare of the Dead Sea and exquisite as a picture to remember long after many others, less weirdly beautiful, have faded from the memory.

Climbing up by the rocky bed of the Arnon is no easy task, but it can be accomplished by the active and enterprising. Having, unluckily, only a short time to spend here, I was unable to go farther, and must rely on accounts given by others so far as Aroer is concerned.

"I built Aroer, and I made the highway by the Arnon"; so Mesha wrote on the Moabite Stone that was found at Dibon, only a few miles north of the site of the old fortress and city that stood on the border of Moab. It was no vain boast, especially as regards the road that was a feat of engineering, considering the difficulties to be overcome. Traces of the old Roman road that probably followed the Moabite track still remain: "Par maints zigzags," writes Père Abel, in his "Croisière autour de la Mer Morte," "la voie romaine en facilitait autrefois le passage, succédant peutêtre au sentier que, huit siècles avant notre ère, Mesa se vantait d'avoir établi." The modern road crosses the ravine at a depth of two thousand five hundred feet, which makes the journey through the old northern boundary of Moab one not to be attempted in a hurry.

The ruins that mark the site of Aroer are on the northern bank of the Arnon, just where the Roman road dipped down from the heights and ascended again. In the Bible it is often mentioned as "Aroer and the city that is in the midst of the river," which has given rise to the suggestion that the town may have been astride the stream, but the more likely proposition is that there was a fort actually in mid-stream which helped to protect the town. The town itself was originally, as far back as we can at present get, built by the Moabites; it was rebuilt, probably on the same site, by the tribe of Gad, but was finally handed over to Reuben, who owned the land immediately to the north of the bank on which Aroer stood. The Israelites took the city from Sihon, King of the Amorites, who had taken it from Moab, an act which embittered the Moabites for ages to come; they seem to have resented this later affair more than they had done the earlier. They never lost the hope of getting back all this country, and went to war with the Jews three hundred years afterwards because they refused to restore it to their kinsmen.

Very little remains to tell us what sort of a city Aroer was; it stood down by the river among high limestone cliffs, surrounded by scenery that suggests a volcanic eruption. Near by is the Roman road and some milestones, one of which bears the name of Severus; higher up there is the remains of a Roman bridge. The allusions to the Arnon and its city that are to be found in the Bible are all minatory.

The inhabitants of all the southern part of eastern Palestine were idolaters, and steeped in wickedness of every sort. Whether their fate would have been different had they given leave to the Israelites to pass through their countries is not told. Perhaps they would have been spared the worst of their troubles; perhaps contact with those who worshipped the true God would have taken them from that of Ba'al. The fact remains that they resisted the Israelites, although they had some communion with them when they inveigled them into the worship of their tribal god, which does not look as if they were easy people to convert.

And they were clearly terrified at the idea of this invasion. Balak, King of Moab, sent for the prophet Balaam to do what he could in the matter, meeting him on the banks of Arnon. He asked him to curse the multitude that had come out of Egypt, and was swarming over all the land, and he took him to three high places to accomplish the deed. The sequel is too well remembered to need repeating, but it is interesting to hear that seven great stones have been found at the edge of a ridge south of Bamoth Ba'al, which may have been

Peor, where Balaam caused seven altars to be raised to the seven planetary gods. The stones are very ancient, the Arabs know nothing of their history ; the ridge commands an extensive view.

Besides their extreme wickedness, the children of Moab and Ammon were also children of nature. They did not hide their joy when anything evil happened to Israel ; they rejoiced exceedingly and boasted of their own victories. The Ammonites said " Aha " when the Sanctuary was defiled, and " Aha " when Israel was desolate and Judah went into captivity. No doubt they said " Aha " with a double zest when the conquering Israelites were stopped at the Ammonite border, because it was " very strong."

Many interesting events are connected with the Arnon. When David sent Joab to number the tribes, he encamped " in Aroer, on the right side of the city that lieth in the midst of the river of Gad " ; and Jeptha came here when he fought the heathen and vowed a vow that he would sacrifice whatever met him coming out of his house, on his return from war, if God gave him the victory. Whom had he in his mind's eye when he made that singular vow ? Surely not his only daughter who came to meet him with timbrels and dancing, and whose immolation has provided artists with a pathetic subject and poets with a theme !

In Roman times the gorge of the Arnon was considered so dangerous that it was always guarded by soldiers ; the " Cohors III Alpinorum " occupied a fort near the top of the pass.

Another even more celebrated gorge is that of the Wadi ez-Zerka Main, between the Arnon and the northern end of the Dead Sea. The river runs in a deep ravine of sandstone and limestone rock ; all along its course is a semi-tropical vegetation, including palms and cane and gnarled trunks of wild fig. Hot springs, with the water at 145 Fahrenheit, issue out of the rocks at the Hammam ez-Zerka, which have been identified with the springs of Callirrhoe. There are opinions for and against this theory, but it is now usually supposed that the springs of ez-Zara, about three miles south of the Zerka Main, were the baths used by Herod.

Of the intense majesty of the gorge that leads up to another vanished city, Machærus, there are no two opinions. Colonel Conder, who believes that the hot springs of the Zerka are those frequented by Herod, gives a fine description of the scene. It does not seem obvious why the baths and the gorge were called after Callirrhoe, the heroine of a tragedy concerning a stolen necklace and peplus, but the explanation is probably only a simple one. During the days of Rome's greatness, the Greek myths and the Greek culture became the fashion, and any Greek name may have been taken without much thought as to the meaning.

Concerning the gorge, Colonel Conder writes :

" It took a full hour to reach the bottom of the gorge, and the scene beneath was wonderful beyond description. On the south, black basalt, brown limestone, gleaming marl. On the north, sandstone cliffs of all colours, from pale yellow to pinkish purple. In the valley itself the brilliant green of palm clumps, rejoicing in the heat and in the sandy soil. The streams, bursting from the cliffs, poured down in rivulets between banks of crusted orange sulphur deposits. The black grackle soared above, with gold-tipped wings, his mellow note being the one sound re-echoed by the great red cliffs in this utter solitude. The brooks (which run from ten springs in all) vary from 110 to 140 F. in temperature, and fall in little cascades amid luxuriant foliage, to join the main course of the stream, which is far colder and fresher, flowing from the shingly springs higher up the valley, and forming pools beneath white rocks of chalk, which we found full of fish, and hidden in a luxuriant brake of tamarisk and cane.

" And of all scenes of Syria, even after standing on Hermon, or among the groves of Banias, or at Engadi, or among the crags of the Anti-Lebanon, there is none that so dwells on my memory as does this awful gorge, ' the Valley of God ' by Beth Peor, where, perhaps, the body of Moses was hid—the fair flowing stream which Herod sought below the gloomy prison of John the Baptist at Machærus—the dread chasm where the Bedawin still offer sacrifices to the desert spirits, and still bathe with full faith in the healing powers of the spring."

Père Abel, on the other hand, is convinced that the springs of Zara are those which provided Herod with the healing baths which were unable to cure his malady. He says that the Hamman ez-Zara is in a vast amphitheatre shut in to westward by the side of the mountain. Towards the sea the ground is covered by a thick layer of tufa. The natural and artificial beds of the currents of hot water are so covered by deposits and incrustations that they form promontories of travertine that descend to the shore. At the edge of the ridge of chalky tufa there are buildings that may have served for baths, and a canal for bringing the water to the baths is still to be seen. Following the shore to the north you come, in about five minutes, to some rising ground crowned with a little ruined fort; five minutes more brings you to a mass of rubble of hydrothermal origin, and to a shapeless rock inside which a room has been excavated, with an entrance towards the sea and a canal to bring the water. The Wadi ez-Zerka is at the northern boundary of this vast amphitheatre, and here are hot and cold springs among reeds. In the bed of the hot springs there are hollows for the bathers.

Père Abel is convinced that this is Callirrhoe, and he brings the Madeba mosaic in as evidence. In this remarkable mosaic map there is a group of three sources placed between two unnamed wadis in the eastern shore of the Dead Sea. The first of these founts escapes from a circular basin and shoots down into the lake, the second, which is larger, is placed in an apse, and the third comes down from the mountain, is caught in a basin, and is lost in the sea in a long yellow trail. On the shore are two palms. Furthermore, he notes that the Herodian paved road that is seen in the Zara gorge disappears under a mass of black basalt on the platform that dominates the hot springs.

Herod did not seem to trust in the medicinal qualities of the water, for Josephus says that he was put into a bath of hot oil in which he turned up his eyes and very nearly died and soon after he did die at Jericho, keeping up his character for villainy to the end. Here was no death-bed repentance; he died as he had lived. In the last year of his life he had ordered the massacre of all the male babies at Bethlehem, for fear that a rival King had been born there; among his last acts were the murder of his eldest son and the imprisonment of a number of Jewish notables who were to be executed when he himself died, so that there should be mourning in every family in Jerusalem. But we must get on to Machærus, the city up above the ravine of the Zerka Main, to which we are slowly gravitating, " par maints zigzags " like the Roman road in the gorge of the Arnon.

Machærus, the ancient fortress, castle and prison of the Herods, was built by Alexander Jannæus, destroyed by the Roman general Gabinius and rebuilt by Herod the Great. Like everything that he touched, the Castle was magnificent, rivalling that other palace in a desert at Masada. But the interest centres now in his son Herod Antipas, who became the ruler of Peræa and succeeded to the tetrarchy of his father. Antipas was educated in Rome, married the daughter of King Aretas of Petra, as we have seen, and was about to divorce her for his sister-in-law Herodias, when she came to Machærus and from there escaped to her father's dominions. It was here that Salome danced her dance of death and here, somewhere in the dungeons, that the Baptist died, not for the cause for which he stood and for which he was prepared to die, but because he had

Aroer and Machærus

protested against the unnatural union of Herod Antipas with the wife of a brother who was still alive.

The last siege of Machærus was something in the nature of a farce. The Romans looked on this fortress as a most dangerous place and one that ought to be dismantled. They invested it, but without much hope of success owing to the inaccessible position that it occupied. The valleys were so deep that it was useless to think of filling them up as had been done in other cases.

The Jews were all in the citadel, which was really almost impregnable ; they put a large number of aliens in the lower town. The siege had been going on for some time when a young and foolhardy man walked outside the gate to show his contempt for the assailing force. As he stood there, a Roman soldier came up and carried him off armour and all. The horrified garrison saw the youth first beaten and then a cross was erected, on which apparently the victim was to suffer ; this was too much for his friends, and the garrison actually capitulated in order to save one man. The hero of the comedy, unlike some who had found themselves in the same position, strongly recommended the capitulation. A breath of farce is, perhaps, not to be despised after the recital of so many tragedies.

CHAPTER XIII
The Desert

CHAPTER XIII

THE DESERT

IT is impossible to speak of the cities of Arabia without turning aside, for a brief moment, to consider those strange nomads, the true Arabs of the desert, who made of its wilderness their transitory home. The country that they inhabit is, for the most part, lacking in actual beauty; it has not often that wide prospect, stretching out to a far horizon, that one associates with the idea of the waste places of the earth. The strip of desert that runs through the eastern border of Palestine and that is merged in that of Arabia proper is monotonous, but often shut in rather than open as to the view. The sand is pale in colour, it abounds in stones, sometimes it is covered with slabs of black basalt; very often scanty grass and abundant brushwood grow somehow without moisture. When the ground is undulating, as it often is, the nearer hillocks shut in the prospect, but when it opens out, as of course it often does, there is much of the charm that comes from a wide view over an extensive plain, fringed, perhaps, with distant hills. Among the scrub that grows freely in the sand are many wild flowers; I remember chiefly pale flowers such as mauve orchids and anemones. In the middle of the day, when there was a hot haze abroad, there were mirages seen, the distance took on the appearance of lakes fringed with palm trees or a strip of sea coast with a lighthouse.

Of the great desert stretching out to the south and the east I have no personal experience; of course the Bedawin tribes came from much farther afield than this narrow strip belonging to Palestine; they trek from the interior of Arabia to Palestine and northern Syria, not only to change their pasture but also to raid the settled inhabitants, from whom they often exact tribute in one kind or another.

There are few sights that take one back more completely to the state of what life must have been in the primitive world than that of a Bedawy camp on the move. The horsemen have perhaps gone on before or are following after; an old man leads the long procession consisting of several women " camel borne," sitting up on their high seats nursing a baby or carrying their pet possessions, while their less favoured sisters carry household properties on a sort of litter which they support on long poles. There will be men too, walking occasionally but more often riding on camel or donkey, bringing up the rear of the long procession with the inevitable collection of Pi dogs snuffing round. Very slowly they move, as if time did not exist, and with a total absence of that nerve-racking fuss that so often accompanies a move when a good many people are involved.

The women do most of the hard work; they strike the tents, pile up the baggage, unpack when they get to their destination, pitch the tents, and set to work to perform their household duties while the men smoke their narghillies in peace. If you come on a Bedawin tent you may find the women sitting there doing nothing, but it is far more likely that each one will be fulfilling some special task. One will grind the corn in a little prehistoric hand mill, another will be making coffee, while others will be weaving the black goats' hair that they have collected in order to make it into cloth to cover their " house of hair." In Arabic poetry a great deal is written of the love felt for the beautiful damsel whose almond eyes have inspired the poet, and love matches are not uncommon, but the lot of the married woman is a hard one. She is not veiled or secluded like other Moslem women, but the hard work of the family devolves on her, the man considering that he has done his part when he has tended the cattle or shot something

IN THE DESERT—ON THE PILGRIMS' WAY TO MECCA

for the larder or perhaps raided the felaheen for forage for the camels.

The Bedawy has been described as being proud, serious, shy, and reserved; he is naturally inclined to mistrust strangers, but once his confidence won, he is true as steel. His ideal is courage, he is a good lover and a good hater; he keeps the desert laws of hospitality and revenge. A brief experience leaves the impression of people who are always smiling, always anxious to offer you what they have, whether coffee or the excellent partly soured milk they call Lebban; the women seem moved by a gentle and quite inoffensive curiosity, the men are courteous to strangers who treat them decently.

There are two sorts of Bedawin, the regular nomads who are camel breeders and who have been called the "nobles of the desert," and the semi-nomads who breed sheep and goats and often cultivate a patch of ground and even sometimes pay taxes. The camel breeders have the advantage because their beasts travel fast and can go for days without water, while the flocks of sheep and goats have to be watered every day. The camel breeder is the terror of the felaheen, for he exacts his share of the harvest or sometimes lets his camels pasture in the cornfields. He introduces an element of uncertainty into life in the Trans-Jordan district which is still an evil to be reckoned with, as it has been from time immemorial.

It is said that the desert Arab, with all his cunning, keeps an element of childlike simplicity; certain it is that not so very long ago they still kept up some of their old superstitions. Perhaps they do so now, for they seem to be more inclined to Paganism than to the self-denying precepts of Mohammed, although they are nominally Moslems. One of these superstitions took the form of a rather curious prayer for rain. It consisted in tying two sorts of bushes to the tails and hind legs of some cattle, setting fire to them and driving the unfortunate beasts up into the mountains. Whether the local

Ba'al would have his attention attracted by the unusual sight, or whether there were any occult meaning in the burning bush, one cannot say. Another idea was that if a hyena stepped on your shadow, you became deaf and dumb—quite natural in the circumstances!

The Arabs have their poetry, handed down orally, as all literature was before Islam; very typical and characteristic, even when it is presented through the veil of a translation. They had their time of civilization and literary output, as we may remember, during the darkest days of European ignorance. As geographers and philosophers, and as the first to study and translate the classics, they prepared the way for the Renaissance. Here, in Arabia, there were various centres of culture, two of them being the seat of courts held by kinglets who owed their position entirely to the Bedawin terror.

"About the middle of the third century of our era" writes Mr. R. A. Nicholson in "The Literary History of the Arabs," Arabia was enclosed on the north and north-east by the rival empires of Rome and Persia, to which the Syrian desert, stretching right across the peninsula, formed a natural termination. In order to protect themselves against the Bedouin raiders, who poured over the frontier provinces, and after laying hands on all the booty within reach vanished as suddenly as they came, both powers found it necessary to plant a line of garrisons along the edge of the wilderness. Thus the tribesmen were partially held in check, but as force alone seemed an expensive remedy it was decided, in accordance with the well-proved maxim, *divide et impera,* to enlist a number of the offending tribes in the Imperial service. Regular pay and the prospect of unlimited plunder—for in those days Rome and Persia were almost perpetually at war, were inducements that no true Bedouin could resist. They fought, however, as free allies under their own chiefs or phylarchs. In this way two Arabian dynasties sprang up—the Ghassanids in Syria and the Lakhmites in Hira, west

The Desert

of the Euphrates—military buffer states, always ready to collide even when they were not urged on by the suzerain powers behind them. The Arabs soon showed what they were capable of when trained and disciplined in arms."

Ghassan served Rome and Hira Persia, which brings in an interesting point, that of Persian influence on the Moslem world. Hira, by its position, was peculiarly liable to receive Persian influence, which, as far as poetry and literature went, was spread all over Arabia. The rival Courts of Ghassan and Hira attracted all the talent of the day, and their princes were great patrons of the poets who wrote flowery poems in their honour. Religious liberty seems to have been enjoyed at Hira, where there was a Christian Bishop as early as 410 A.D.; and where the people were on equally good terms with the Persian Zoroastrians.

The Ghassanids ruled the country round Palmyra and Damascus. Although they had no fixed abode and remained nomads their Court was luxurious, or so it appears from the well-known account of it from an Arabic writer of the time. He writes that he had seen the King sitting on a couch of myrtle and jasmine, surrounded by gold and silver vessels of ambergris and musk. During winter he had fires of aloe-wood in his apartments and in summer he cooled himself with snow. He was being entertained by Greek singing girls singing Greek songs, girls from Hira chanting Babylonian airs, and Arab singers from Mecca. He was handsome, agreeable and generous.

If such was the state of an Arab prince, how much grander was that of the Persian monarch, the "King of Kings." The Sasanid monarchs were those who had most influence on the art and the architecture of the Arabs, and they certainly set an example of luxury and magnificence. In the old Parthian capital of Ctesiphon Noshirwan the Just held his state. He sat enthroned behind a curtain and only those who were invited might venture behind and prostrate themselves before the great King. Noshirwan was the son of the founder of the dynasty, but his mother had been a peasant girl; when his succession was disputed by other members of the family he had all his brothers and all their male children killed, which makes his surname of the Just appear rather a misnomer. But, once this act of fratricide committed, he turned out the most just and enlightened ruler, caring for the development of his country as well as for those conquests abroad which made him famous. Noshirwan, or Chosroes as he is usually called, when not fighting or playing polo with the Court ladies, or chess with his Courtiers, received the gay world of Persia in an immense audience hall which held, literally, thousands of people, he himself being hidden by the curtain.

Chosroes entered this inner hall closely veiled; he then took his place on a great golden throne with ruby feet, and carefully inserted his head into a huge crown that hung suspended from an arch, it being too heavy to wear. Under his feet was the famous carpet on which Paradise was represented as a garden, with the ground wrought in gold and the walks in silver, the rivers in pearls and the meadows in emeralds; trees, fruit and flowers were each worked in jewels of appropriate colours.

When he was quite comfortably settled his draperies were removed, and he was ready to receive the favoured ones, who fell flat on their faces, as anyone would who saw a sight so gorgeous.

The grandson of this King was Chosroes II, whose reign began and ended in flight. But he had a time of greatness, during which the arts and literature reached their highest development. His Court was also one of great magnificence, and he, too, had a period of success in arms, although it did not last his lifetime, and he was finally put to death by his own subjects when his star began to set. Chosroes had some great victories over the declining power of Rome; he sacked Antioch and Jerusalem. He fought with the Jews against the Christians, and stole the True Cross, after which he took Alexandria. He evidently meant to keep Syria, because he built the palace of M'Shita in the desert; he laid wonderful plans, and then was defeated by Heraclius, deposed and imprisoned in " The House of Darkness." His children were killed before his eyes, and he died a lingering death, a sad end for the man who was called in Persia, Khusru Parviz, the Conqueror.

The Palace of M'Shita was built by Chrosroes II early in the seventh century. It was never finished, but the decorative stone work is wonderfully finely executed. It stands about seven miles east of el-Kalat Ziza, a station on the Haj railway, and was called by a name that means either the Mother of Rain or the Mother of Winter, which may have been intended to suggest that it was to be a winter abode of the Persian King.

The palace seems to have been on the plan usual in Persia. The entrance arch was of the very lofty type characteristic of Sasanid architecture; it contained a huge audience chamber like the one in which the Great King received his Court in his own country. It is totally unlike any other building to be seen in Palestine, and does not even resemble the Sasanid structure at Amman. The massive walls that surrounded the square enclosure measured five hundred feet each side; they were made of limestone and had twenty-five towers, which were circular at the corners and semi-circular to right and left of the entrance. The marvellous and intricate carving of the great façade, the octagonal towers and the frieze that ran along the finished part of the building, has excited the admiration of all those who have had the privilege of seeing it before the final vandalism of native and foreign despoilers laid it low. It must have presented an astonishing appearance standing, as it did, in the heart of the desert, a monument of greatness, showing the talent and the magnificence of another vanished civilization.

The Palace itself stood within the open court, and was approached by a triple gate. It has been suggested that it was intended to serve as a hunting-box for Chosroes, and that the vast enclosure, with its fortifications was an afterthought. The palace was built of brick, and had the audience hall with a dome on pendentives and vaulted halls and courts leading out. But it is not the palace that remains as a thing of beauty and a joy for ever, it is the sculptured stonework that ornamented the outer walls. The great façade was decorated with a zigzag pattern in which were hexagonal rosettes surrounded by the most intricate lacework, showing wild animals and birds, arabesques, flowers and leaves. The great fragment, that was *in situ* until quite recently, was taken by the ex-Emperor William for the Berlin Museum, and the Arabs followed it up by using the stone lying about to build the railway station at Ziza on the Haj line, defacing the carving to hide their evil deed.

The wall was never finished: it was evidently left in a hurry when Chosroes' defeats began to show that his day was over. Although the design is purely Persian, of the Sasanian order, the workmen are said by the late J. Fergusson to have been Arabs, brought from Antioch or some Syrian city, an assertion that is proved by the introduction of such a feature as the vine introduced into the decoration, which was a typical motive used in Syria from the time of Herod onwards.

" Its greatest interest "—I am quoting from the " History of the Architecture of All Countries "—" lies in the fact that all the Persian and Indian mosques were derived from buildings of this class. The African mosques were enlargements of the atria of Christian basilicas, and this form is never found there, but it is the key to all that was afterwards erected to the eastward."

This Persian palace was unique in its day, planted out there in the desert, and the remains of the sculpture are considered extraordinarily fine. Historically it is a symbol of the power and the downfall of the last great Sasanian King, and also of the fall of Persia before the might of Islam.

It was, perhaps, the answer to the contemptuous action of the great King who tore up Mohammed's haughty letter : " In the Name of God, the Merciful, the Compassionate. O Khusraw ! Submit, and thou shalt be safe, or else prepare to wage with God and with His Apostle a war that shall not find them helpless. Farewell ! "

The King tore up the letter before the envoy of Mohammed, who is reported to have said :—

" Thus, O impious King, shall God rend asunder thine empire and scatter thy hosts ! "

Although it is quite beside the subject we have set out to study, it is hard to leave the desert without a thought of those great ones who have left a spiritual mark on the shifting sands that have engulfed empires.

Job, that monument of patience, lived not far from Petra, near to the desert land where people " remove landmarks " and " steal and pasture flocks." Somewhere in the neighbourhood of the Dead Sea Elijah the Tishbite lay down to rest under the juniper—the feathery white broom that is so often seen here. John the Baptist preached here, and met his death in the Machærus dungeon ; Christ himself came over Jordan, and was met by people who wanted to be taught, and who brought the little children to be blessed, by the man with great possessions who went sadly away. He went back deliberately to Jerusalem, after foretelling His death. Saint Paul persecuted the Church in Arabia as a young man, and spent three years in the desert before taking up his ministry. Whether from a psychical or an historical point of view, the desert is surely a theatre on which some of the great dramas of life have been played.

CHAPTER XIV
Madeba

CHAPTER XIV

MADEBA

THE Roman road runs up to Madeba through a smiling plain which appears doubly verdant and fertile after journeying through the desert. The young corn was standing six or seven inches high, poppies and other wild flowers made splashes of colour, the sky was clear and the air delicious on the April morning when I made acquaintance with the old episcopal city. Walking slowly along the road were two Church dignitaries, the younger holding an umbrella over the head of the elder and more important; they were followed, at a respectable distance, by a one-horse carriage. The key-note was struck at once, for Madeba, in spite of its ancient history in the days of the Jewish wars, has come down to us as a Christian city, a reputation that is kept up to-day.

Madeba stands on rising ground in the middle of a plain where many battles have been fought; the town does not show any remarkable feature with its flat roofs like those of any Eastern village. To north of the hill on which the modern town has been built on the old foundations is another on which are some ruins, the outstanding object being a pair of pillars surmounted by an architrave. These pillars are popularly known as " el Masnaqah Abu Rok—the gallows of Father Rok, who was a Sheikh reputed to have administered justice there. Although Madeba does not present any special feature of interest from the outside, and is more remarkable for the charm of the sylvan scene than for anything impressive about its architecture, it is extremely interesting when you penetrate inside.

It is not that there is any great building to attract the attention, any group of columns or the remains of a temple or theatre well enough preserved to delight the eye, it is rather that, poking about among the little houses and outhouses of the people, you come on the foundations of Byzantine churches, and everywhere are the Greek mosaic pavements for which Madeba is famous.

Madeba or Medeba, as it is called in times past, lies on the Roman road between Dibon and Heshbon; to north is the long ridge of Mount Nebo where Moses may have gone to survey the Promised Land, though there are some who think that the more beautiful and extensive view seen from Mount Osha was the one on which he looked. In any case Nebo is a mysterious place, where there are dolmens and menhirs, and where, as we know from the Moabite Stone, there was once a shrine sacred to Jehovah.

The Moabite Stone was discovered at Dibon in 1868; it relates the victories of that King Mesha, whom the Bible calls a sheep-master, obliged to pay tribute to Israel. The tables were, however, turned during his reign, and he was able to recover a good deal of lost land, including "Mehedeba," which King Omri had held for forty years. Mesha also, following the orders of his god Kemosh, sacked the Sanctuary of Jehovah on Mount Nebo and dragged the holy objects before his idol. This is how he relates the event:—

"And Kemosh said to me: 'Go, take Nebo against Israel.' And I went by night and fought against it from the break of dawn till noontide, and I took it and slew all . . . seven thousand men and women and damsels, for I had devoted it to Ashtar-Kemosh. And I took thence the . . . of Yahweh and I dragged them before Kemosh."

It is a song of triumph and one can almost hear Mesha saying " Aha ! " and showing an indecent joy at the success of his arms, such as brought an immediate punishment on his nation. For God was not to be mocked by the gods of the heathen.

THE LITTLE RUIN OF THE MARKET

Madeba

Madeba belonged to Reuben, who owned the land from " Aroer, that is upon the bank of the river Arnon, and the city that is in the midst of the river, and all the plain of Medeba unto Dibon " ; but, in the time of Herod it was known as " the city of the Nabatæans." It was always a prosperous place, and never more so than under the rule of the Kings of Nabatæa, who seem to have wished to make another centre of their dominions farther north, yet not so far as Damascus. It was governed by a Strategos, whose office was sometimes hereditary ; in an inscription that was found sixteen miles south-east of Madeba and which is now in the Vatican Museum, it is stated that it was erected to one Abd-Obodath and his son " in the seat of their jurisdiction, which they exercised for a period of thirty-six years, in the time of Haretath, King of the Nabatæans, lover of his people ; and the above work was executed in the forty and sixth year of his reign (A.D. 37).

Alexander Jannæus took Madeba after a severe siege ; his son Hyrcanus promised to restore it to the Nabatæans, and apparently did so, with other cities in return for the support given to his cause by King Aretas. Rome took it over with the rest of Arabia Petræa, and it became a prominent city of the Eastern empire, its time of greatest splendour being in the fourth and sixth centuries. The ruins that we now see date from those periods, the town having been of Byzantine architecture built upon Roman foundations.

Owing to the exposed situation, standing on a gentle slope instead of being perched on an inaccessible hill-top, Madeba suffered a great deal from the battles that raged round and the sieges that invested her walls. Once a band of robbers had their headquarters there, and they murdered the son of Matathias Maccabeus ; in return for which crime the city was besieged and taken by that party. The result of so many upheavals is that very little of the old city remains, though the foundations and some fragments of twelve churches are still to be seen with the few pillars that mark the site of the street of columns. The modern town is built on the Acropolis hill; between this hill and the other to the north, the street of columns ran. To the north-west is the remains of one of the city gates and bits of the walls; the northern hill is crowned with ruins. There was once a fine basilica, over which the modern Greek church is built that contains the mosaic map; at the other end of the town is the Latin church and hospice, near which was another basilica. The two columns that the Arabs have nicknamed " the Gallows " were once in the porch of a temple. They are not monoliths, but are composed of three separate pieces. The drum is in two pieces; it is older than the capitals that are too small and that do not even agree with each other, one being Ionic and the other a Byzantine copy of Corinthian. The shafts are older than the capitals and are said to date from the fourth or fifth century A.D. Tribal marks of the Bedawin have been cut on them at some time.

The chief interest centres in the remarkable mosaic map that was only discovered quite recently; what remains of it is on the floor of the Greek church, but unfortunately most of it has been destroyed owing to the ignorance and carelessness of those who should have treasured it as a unique possession.

Very little is known about the history of mosaic and tesselated pavements, but it is probable that the Greeks took the art from the East after the conquests of Alexander the Great. There is no term for this branch of art, we are told, until a comparatively late time, which proves that it had not been in common use at an earlier date. Greece may have taken the idea from Egypt or Mesopotamia, or from the glazed tiles, arranged in symmetrical patterns, of the Persians; the earliest known example is in the pronaos of the Temple of Zeus at Olympia, dating from the first half of the fourth century B.C. In the third century B.C., it was used in Greece and then Rome took it and certainly made a great deal

Madeba

of use of it, as it suited the great rooms with flooring over central heating, to perfection. Whether Syria got it from further east or from Greece does not appear, but almost certainly it was from the latter source; the Madeba mosaics are all Greek or Byzantine.

The great map was only found by an accident. The new Greek church was built in 1896-1897, on the site of a basilica ending with an apse; the new church was smaller than the old one, but also ended with an apse. During the building of the church and dependencies, the mosaic pavement was irreparably injured.

The first to take any notice of the map was a monk who wrote in the year 1894, to the Greek Patriarch of Jerusalem, Monsignor Nicodemus, to the effect that he had seen a most curious mosaic map at Madeba. He asked for instructions, but received no answer. The Patriarch was removed to Constantinople and Monsignor Gerasimus came in his place. The new Patriarch found the monk's letter in 1896, saw that he had made an important discovery and sent a master-mason to look into the matter, and to include the mosaic in the church that was about to be built.

The master-mason, as M. Clermont-Ganneau relates in his "Recueil d'Archéologie Orientale" was certainly no architect. He reported that the map was not so important as had been said, and he allowed it to be mutilated quite unpardonably during the building operations. According to the testimony of four monks, the great map was practically whole before the new church was built; after its erection part of it was outside the church, and that part which was preserved inside had been cut ruthlessly to admit a pilaster.

Monsignor Gerasimus did not visit Madeba, but he never lost his interest in the map and he persuaded Father Cleopas, the librarian of the Greek Patriarchate, to visit the church with a view to seeing what its value really was. Father Cleopas made drawings and reported that the discovery was one of great archæological and historical importance, and after his visit the map was seen by experts who pronounced it quite unique.

When you enter the Greek church you see portions of the floor covered by boards, which are removed if you wish to inspect the precious fragment. You see before you part of a map of Palestine, of which the most interesting portion is the now well-known map of Jerusalem. It shows the Holy City as it was in the days of Justinian, early in the sixth century. It is Ælia Capitolina, with its walls and gates and a street of columns cutting right through from west to east. The principal buildings are here shown, the most interesting being the Church of the Holy Sepulchre, quite recognizable with its triple doors and its dome.

The stones are not artificially coloured, they are evidently taken from the neighbouring mountains; the walls and buildings are light in colour, the thick outline is black, brown or violet. The names are written in Greek.

The street of columns in Madeba led from the north gate in the east wall, where there is still the remains of a watch tower; outside is the reservoir with a flight of steps leading down into what was, for long, an empty pit, owing to the Bedawin watering their flocks there. Inside the gate, on the south side, was the old church of St. Elias, dating from the seventh century, which was completed in the year 607-8, under Bishop Leontius. All that remains of it is a bit of wall and a mosaic pavement; an old, partly demolished stairway leads down to the crypt, which also ended in an apse and has a mosaic pavement, with four inscriptions, according to which the crypt was completed in 595-6 A.D. by Bishop Sergius. A little to the east of this church is the site of another with three aisles. The mosaic pavement represents rhombuses in which are gazelles, birds, plants and fruit. An interesting description of all these churches, besides five others, is given in Professor Musil's " Arabia Petræa."

The curious part of these pavements is that they all appear to be *in situ,* but built over with cottages, or left on the floor of outhouses, where they are covered by hay and chaff and dust. The owner will produce water and a brush and clean his pavement, or part of it, so that it can be inspected ; he will probably stand there surrounded by the females of the family, each armed with a brush or pail of water, intensely amused at the curiosity of the stranger within his gates. One pavement that made a great impression on me was on the floor of a barn ; flowers and fruit and animals were represented in a most decorative manner, and in each corner was a human head.

Madeba calls for more than a flying visit ; among the hovels and the waste places all sorts of interesting things may be found by those who have the time and the understanding to appreciate them. Ruined vaults with round barrel roofs, fragments of lintel stones, of pillars and sculptured capitals, old tanks to hold water, relics of a vanished people. The country round is very pleasant, and there are very many places of interest near by. Dibon, Heshbon, Arak-el-Emir—to name only a few— are all worth a visit. The latter is, of course, one of the most interesting ruins in all the country, and one of the few that show the Greek influence in the architecture and decoration.

Arak-el-Emir—the Cliff of the Prince—was built in 176 B.C. by a priest named Hyrcanus, of the family of the High Priest, who was a ruler in Jerusalem. Hyrcanus quarrelled with his brothers, as people blessed with this name always did ; he fled from them and came across Jordan, where he built a wonderful white castle by a rock, and in the rock he excavated another palace, the whole place being elaborately protected by strong walls. He called his palace Tyre, and he lived in it for seven years, retiring into his rock when danger threatened. Among other curiosities to be seen here is a sloping ramp, cut in the rock and leading from one floor to another ; up and down this passage the horses were led to their stable, in which there are still more than a hundred mangers, each separated by a stone partition and each with a stone ring for a halter.

Hyrcanus decorated his palace with enormous carved lions, fragments of which still remain ; he had a courtyard in which fountains played, and there were gardens surrounded by a deep moat full of water. It is sad to think that the poor man, who appears, by the way, to have been very cruel and to have treated the Arabs badly, had a tragic end. He was quite safe as long as Seleucus was King of Syria, but when he died and Antiochus replaced him, he was afraid of his brothers' vengeance under the new regime, and he killed himself in his beautiful pleasure house. Antiochus took the castle and all the riches of the sybarite, who does not seem to have been regretted by anyone.

Another site of a vanished city, of which, however, little remains, lies just off the road between Madeba and Amman. The remains of a mausoleum and some Ionic pillars standing up in a field, which is a blaze of wild flowers, catch the eye as you pass along the road. This is the so-called " Khareibet es-Suk "—the little ruin of the Market.

Owing to the kindness of the Latin priest, the Abbé Zacharie Chomali, it is possible to get a room in the hospice in Madeba if due notice is given.

Madeba was always a great centre of Christianity and the seat of a bishopric ; like all the other cities it fell into ruins after Rome fell, and it was only re-inhabited in 1881, when two thousand Christians from Kerak were allowed to settle here. It is probable that there were a certain number of squatters, as the population is not entirely, though it is principally, Christian. The newcomers settled at first in the caves that abound in the neighbourhood, but gradually a new town was built and churches were endowed.

Christians were, at one time, favourably treated in

Kerak; it does not appear why they left. In 1845, the Christians were ordered to wear a distinguishing blue turban—except at Kerak and Shobek, where they could apparently wear what they pleased. The Kerakians were connected with the fanatical Wahibis at one time, though they never paid them tribute; whether that fact contributed to make the position of the Christians difficult I do not know. The refugees from Kerak were converted from the Greek Church to the Latin, and came under the charge of some Jesuit priests. There are now a good number of orthodox Greeks for whose use the Greek church was erected over the pavement decorated by the mosaic map.

CHAPTER XV
RABBOTH AMMON

CHAPTER XV

RABBOTH AMMON

AMMAN, the Circassian village that has become the capital of the modern state of Trans-Jordan, stands on the site of the ancient capital of the Children of Ammon and of the more recent Greek and Roman city of the Decapolis. It is a curious, rambling place, following, for some distance, the river Amman, an upper reach of the Zerka, the biblical Jabbock. The stream was full of water when I saw it in the early spring, and the banks were green with willow and flushed with the pink of apple blossom, making, as is so often the case in this country, a sharp contrast with the towering hills that enfold the winding valley.

There is a good deal of vegetation on the lower flanks of the hills, but they are riddled with caves, and the upper part is pure rock. The exceedingly steep hillsides and the narrow gorges between them make the first impression of Amman one of strength and seclusion rather than beauty. The fine Roman remains are quite in harmony with this rather severe setting, but the modern street, with its noise and its vivid colour, strikes another note.

Rabboth Ammon, the stronghold of the Ammonites, consisted of a lower town, spoken of as the " City of Waters," and an upper town and citadel on the Acropolis hill. All round about are traces of the Megalithic people, who were the first to inhabit this region—or, at any rate, the first people of whom we have any shadow of knowledge. Round about in the country are also many tombs and cave-dwellings.

In Colonel Conder's " Survey of Eastern Palestine," published by the Palestine Exploration Fund Committee, fifteen examples of rude stone monuments are mentioned as being in the immediate neighbourhood; ten dolmens and six menhirs. Sarcophagi, rock tombs, Jewish kokim tombs are also found hereabouts.

After the prehistoric race came the giants, some of whom were still to be met with when the Israelites began to fight their way towards the Promised Land. The first reference to Rabboth Ammon in the Bible concerns the great iron bedstead of Og, King of Bashan, who cannot have been the " only remnant of the giants," as others are mentioned, and the Children of Israel were very much frightened at their bulk and fighting qualities. It has been suggested that this bedstead was really a throne, and an idea has been started that one of these great dolmens may have been called the throne of Og; I confess that I am loth to part with the original statement and the picture that it conjures up of a huge iron four-poster, measuring nine cubits by four !

The drama with which one chiefly connects Rabboth Ammon is one that has been told so often that it seems superfluous to try to fit it into the setting in which it took place, but these old stories are all that we have to help us to call up a vision of the past. It is a sordid drama, too, as sordid as any that we can boast of in these latter days.

The land beyond Jordan has always been a land of refuge for those in trouble. When David was warned by Jonathan that Saul was going to kill him he crossed over and took refuge with the King of Moab, who received him kindly. His grandmother Ruth was a Moabitess, and perhaps for that reason he was inclined to ask for help from a people to whom he was related; he also asked the King to receive his parents and to keep them until the storm was over, which was done. After David succeeded Saul he heard of the death of Nahash, King of the Ammonites, who had also been kind to him in his time of trouble; he therefore sent messengers to the son, Hanun, to condole with him on his loss. It is easy enough to blame the Ammonites for

PORTRAIT OF KING HUSSEIN OF THE HIJAZ

insulting David's messengers, but we must remember that it had always been a case of war between the two countries. Nahash had always had the right eyes of Jewish prisoners taken out, so that they were no use afterwards as archers; David might have wanted revenge, and it was quite on the cards that his message of condolence might have been a device for spying out the secrets of the citadel. It is not said that the messengers went alone, but they cannot have had many men with them; they were apparently unarmed, bent simply on their peaceful mission.

How did they come? Did they ride up the defile between the high hills, gazing up at whatever fortifications crowned the summit of the northern scarp? They may have felt nervous, or more likely proud of being the messengers sent by a great King to someone infinitely inferior. With what different feelings they must have hurried away, thankful to have escaped with their lives, yet full of wrath at the indignity put upon them.

The Ammonites knew what they had done, and they prepared for a fight. They hired mercenary troops from Syria and placed them near Madeba, while they themselves protected their citadel and lower town. When David's general came he was caught between the two armies, but he beat the Syrians with half his force and attacked the Ammonites with the other. They retired into their fortress, and Joab went back to Jerusalem.

The following spring Joab returned to Ammon and besieged it while David remained in Jerusalem, where he fell in love with Bathsheba, whose husband Uriah the Hittite was at the siege. The story is, of course, one of those "human documents" that is told in the Bible narrative, with cold-blooded realism. We seem to see the soldier called back from the siege of Rabboth and interviewed by the King, who asks him the news from the front and sends him a mess of meat from his own table, and even drinks with him and makes him drunk before sending him back to the seat of war, the bearer of a letter to Joab which concerned him nearly if he had had the curiosity to open it. " Set ye Uriah," he wrote, " in the forefront of the hottest battle and retire ye from him, that he may be smitten and die."

Nothing could be more explicit. The instructions were carried out to the letter, somewhere at the foot of the citadel hill, and there was a brave man less in the world. David's comment is given : " The sword devoureth one as well as another." And he sent for Bathsheba and made her his wife before the birth of her child.

Joab managed at last to get possession of the lower town, the " City of Waters "; he thought that the citadel would soon fall and so he sent a message to David asking for reinforcements and for the King to come in person in order to have the glory of taking the Ammonites' stronghold. David came and the city fell ; he met the conquered King who had despised his embassy of condolence and took off his great crown that weighed a talent of gold and put it on his own head. After which he treated the garrison with unexampled severity. He took a great deal of spoil, both gold and silver, which he afterwards offered up in the Temple at Jerusalem and he went back over Jordan feeling, no doubt, that vengeance was sweet.

The Ammonites continued to pay tribute to David and we find them bringing all sorts of provisions to him when he once more came over Jordan to fight his own beloved son Absalom. They brought " beds and basons and earthen vessels and wheat and barley and flour and parched corn and beans and lentils and parched pulse, And honey and butter and sheep and cheese of kine for David and for the people that were with him to eat ; for they said, The people is hungry and weary and thirsty in the wilderness."

Absalom the Beautiful was killed in a forest in Gilead, apparently caught up by his long hair as he rode through, and David's lament for him is one of his most pathetic utterances : " O my son Absalom, my son, my son

ROMAN RUINS AT AMMAN

Absalom! Would to God I had died for thee, O Absalom, my son, my son!"

The Ammonites, though often beaten, were always coming up to the surface again. They were always fighting and always hostile to the Jews. They were beaten by Jotham and made to pay tribute, they were tributary at one time to Babylon. They were always trying to hinder any development on the other side Jordan and always eager to assist the enemies of Israel or Judah. "Cœle Syria took it heinously that the building of the Temple in Jerusalem went on apace," Josephus says. The Ammonites joined the Syrians against the Maccabees and were defeated by them.

One of the most unfortunate battles, as far as the Nabatæans were concerned, took place here. They had beaten Herod the Great, helped by Cleopatra's general, somewhere near Kanawat; Herod returned to the charge at Amman or Philadelphia, as it was then called, and gained a decisive victory, after which he was able to get himself nominated as ruler of Cœle Syria. The Arabians, as Josephus calls them here, appear to have taken refuge in the citadel, from which they were forced to come out when exhausted and suffering from hunger. Without space to deploy, they were killed miserably, courting death rather than trying to escape from it, too far gone to attempt to cut their way out.

The Ammonites died hard. They recovered their possessions when the tribes went into captivity, and we find Jeremiah turning the thunder of his eloquence against them after he delivered the judgment against Moab.

"Concerning the Ammonites, thus saith the Lord: Hath Israel no sons? hath he no heir? why then doth their King inherit Gad, and his people dwell in his cities?"

It does not seem certain at what date they finally ceased to be a nation and their remnant dispersed and became part of the mixed population of eastern Palestine. Rabboth Ammon was one of the stations on the Petra caravan route, and seems to have enjoyed a certain amount of prosperity; the lower town must then have contained some fine buildings, as " palaces " are spoken of as existing there, and we know that David got a vast amount of booty from people that, in their barbaric way, had luxury and magnificence.

" Wherefore gloriest thou in the valleys, thy flowing valley, O backsliding daughter? that trusted in her treasure saying : Who shall come unto me? "

Probably the wars of Alexander the Great put the finishing touch to the desolation of Rabboth Ammon; the great old days were over, but the " flowing valley " still attracted the builder in search of a site, and those who were instructed by Ptolemy Philadelphus of Egypt to look for one on which to build a city, chose it for that purpose. It had a great many advantages. The river running through the twisting wadi was of course a real asset in a country where water is precious; the beetling crags on which the remains of the Ammonite fortress must still have stood presented an ideal situation for an acropolis. On the ruins of whatever remained in the lower town the new Greco-Roman city arose, white and gleaming, a thing of beauty and symmetry, built with a view to convenience as well as splendour, as all these classic cities were. And up on high tremendous engineering works were in progress for a long time before the place was transformed and modernized and brought up to the standard of the day. The new City of Waters was named after the founder, and was henceforth known as Philadelphia of Herakles of Cœle Syria. The Greek god, the good fortune of the Philadelphians, with Pallas Athene as his companion goddess, was the patron deity instead of a manifestation of the cruel old god Ba'al. The change must have been complete, even if a remnant of the Ammonites formed part of the population of a city that added one more to the increasing number of those ten towns known as the cities of the Decapolis.

CHAPTER XVI
PHILADELPHIA

CHAPTER XVI

PHILADELPHIA

ALEXANDER the Great, dying in Babylon, left his ring to his favourite general Perdiccus, with the inscription that it was for " he who is worthiest." Perdiccus, therefore, became Regent, and there was a conference of generals held in order to decide how the empire was to be divided up among the most powerful of them. Philip, the brother of Alexander, was nominally King, but was not present; the generals argued the question of the dismemberment of the empire while the body of the great conqueror lay unburied and forgotten. It was only nine years since he had crossed the Hellespont and into those nine years he had compressed all the colour and the tumult and the great deeds that has made his name live through the ages.

The empire was to be governed by Satraps; Ptolemy got Egypt and meant to hold it as a sovereign; an ambition in which he succeeded. He attracted the anger of Perdiccus, who marched into Egpyt to punish him and was himself assassinated there. The man who gave the first blow was one whom the murdered man had always advanced in his career and favoured—Seleucus, the founder of the Seleucid dynasty. Curiously enough, these two men—Ptolemy and Seleucus, and their descendants—were both to profit by the death of the tyrant Perdiccus, yet were to be the cause of ceaseless war for generations to come. The wars of the successors devasted Syria as well as other countries; ceaseless, insane wars made up of jealousy and a desire to snatch the territory of a neighbour for fear he should grow more powerful than yourself.

Seleucus was the son of one of Philip of Macedon's generals; he was a soldier of fortune himself and was about the same age as Alexander. At the famous marriage of Susa, where Alexander presented his generals with wives from the conquered race, Seleucus received Apama as his lot. Unlike most of the others, who treated the whole affair as the fortune of war, Seleucus made Apama his lawful wife, and she became the mother of his heir. He was a fine fellow, good-looking and well set up, a good soldier and a prudent man. If his descendants had been like him the history of the Seleucid dynasty would have been quite different to the disastrous affair it became eventually. Even the one great man, Antiochus III, the Great, lost almost all that he gained with the sword.

The great rivals of the Seleucids were, of course, the Ptolemies of Egypt. The Seleucids founded Antioch, and made there a most beautiful city, superb in architecture and luxurious in accordance with the ideas of that day. The Ptolemies lived in state among the immemorial glories of Egypt and in the new city of Alexandria, founded by the leader that they had lost in the prime of his life.

Ptolemy Soter I took Palestine and lost it, fought over Cœle Syria with Seleucus, disinherited his eldest son and associated his second with himself in the kingdom, leaving it to him when he died. This son, Ptolemy II, Philadelphus, was the founder of Philadelphia, as well as various other cities, such as Berenice, Arsinoe, Ptolemais, in Pamphilia, and Arsinoe in Lycia.

Philadelphus repudiated his first wife in order to marry his sister Arsinoe, one of those women who leave a trail behind them. Her career was singular, even for those times. She married Lysimacus, was obliged to flee after his death, married first one brother and then the other; her last husband, Philadelphus, adored her, and deified her after her death as the divine Philadelphia.

Ptolemy Philadelphus visited his city many times during his flying visits to Cœle Syria; whether

THE GREAT THEATRE, AMMAN

Philadelphia

Arsinoe II accompanied him we know not. He must have meant to inhabit it sometimes himself, for it was built on a scale that made it quite suitable for a royal residence. But the first intention was evidently to furnish a protection for the lines of communication with Egypt and a fort to oppose the attacks of the enemy.

The citadel was placed on the northern hill, which is completely isolated from the other hills that surround it except at one point. At that vulnerable spot an artificial depression has been made, either by the older defenders of the place or by the Macedonian conquerors. The whole space was covered with buildings enclosed in great walls flanked with towers; buildings which included an L-shaped fortress, and a mighty temple among many others of less importance. These structures stood along three immense terraces, each one at a rather lower level than the one preceding it, and the columns of the temples and of a palace gave an air of classic beauty to the whole scene.

The lower town—for there were two towns, just as there were in the days of the Ammonites—was built on both sides of the stream, though most of the important buildings seem to have been placed on the western bank. There were all the usual features of a Greco-Roman town ; the street of columns lay beside the river, which was vaulted over for a considerable way ; the temples and civic buildings, the baths and the private houses were disposed on the usual symmetrical plan. The theatre, a fine one for a colonial city, was excavated out of the side of the hill on the pattern of all the early Greek theatres ; Greek culture had come in the wake of the wars that had not brought unmitigated evil to the conquered people.

The cities of the Decapolis, of which Philadelphia ultimately formed one, are said to have been populated by Alexander's veterans, left behind after the war. But the whole of the population can hardly have been composed of foreigners. The soldiers probably married the natives, and the great new city, placed in a desolate district as it must have been after the earlier dwellings had been swept away by successive wars, would have attracted many. Those who wanted to sell their camels or sheep, or the corn from the threshing floor, would have found a ready market in the new metropolis. One can picture their wondering glances resting on the magnificence of Philadelphia. Perhaps the merchants, still travelling with their caravans up westwards and northwards, compared it to Petra in the desert, or to the newly-built Gerasa, or even to proud Antioch astride on the Orontes. And perhaps they saw a show in the theatre, occupying the strangers' gallery, and carrying away with them material for a dozen talks over their camp fires at night time.

The various countries resembled the piece of elastic even more in these times than in any other. At one time Seleucus added to the Satrapy of Babylon, with which he had begun his rule, the whole of Syria from the Gulf of Issus to the frontiers of Egypt; at another time the Macedonian ruler of Egypt wrenched Syria from him. It was never more than a partial rule, whichever was preponderant, certain cities standing out and having their own privileges.

Seleucus I, founder of the dynasty, was murdered at the age of seventy-five by Ptolemy Keraunus, the elder brother of Philadelphus. The old King had disregarded the omens which were all against his expedition to Macedonia, but he was anxious to see his native country again and was suspected of wishing to end his days as King of Macedonia, having left his eldest son, Antiochus, in charge of his eastern empire. Ptolemy Keraunus was a common murderer, preferring to strike himself; he had already killed several people and the children that were born of his sister Arsinoe. Having slain Seleucus he took possession of the Macedonian kingdom himself and made friends with Philadelphus, to whom he left the undisturbed possession of Egypt.

Keraunus was assassinated by the Gauls before he actually got the supreme power for which he had dared so much.

"It is not easy," writes M. A. Bouché-Leclercq in his interesting "Histoire des Seleucides," "to disentangle the situation in Asia when Antiochus I came to the throne. One must, first of all, put aside those countries that, neglected by Alexander, threatened rather than conquered by Perdiccus, by Eumenius and by Antigonus, are only connected to the Seleucid empire by a sort of theoretic vassalage. Such are the Satrapies or future kingdoms of Atropatenia in Media, Pontus, Cappadocia and Bithynia. The dynasties that were planted there had, later on, their Court historians and genealogists, who put their origin farther back and credited the ancestors with the independence which their descendants acquired little by little. All these towns, including the Hellenic cities on the shores of the Euxine Sea and the Propontus, were under the yoke of the Persians, and after a period of unrest during the Median wars, they took every opportunity to relax the bonds that united them to the Persians as well as resisting, as well as they could, absorption into the Macedonian empire."

Antiochus I, Soter, came to the throne in the year 281 B.C., and he reigned for twenty years. His first duty was to avenge the death of his father, which it was impossible to do in Macedon because Antigonus was now King, who had before been a pretender to the throne, following in the footsteps of his father who had usurped that title. There remained the Ptolemies, although the principal offender was dead, and so began the first great war between the Seleucids and the Ptolemies in the year 279 B.C.; it lasted for three years.

Philadelphus must have found Philadelphia very useful about this time. He was master of the sea, having a fleet, while Antiochus had practically none; this strong fortress protected quite a stretch of country besides the roads up which he sent reinforcements and supplies from Egypt. Ptolemy was very active in this war. He was not only to be found at the seat of war, wherever the contest was hottest, he found time to send an embassy to Rome, and he never allowed Antiochus time to concentrate his forces on Egypt. Pausanius says that Ptolemy sent pillagers to all the unprotected regions belonging to Antiochus and soldiers to all those that were protected. Wherever his fleet could act, along the coasts of Syria or Asia Minor, Ptolemy was victorious; on land Antiochus had some advantage. The long war ended in a compromise and Antiochus died, maybe a natural death, aged sixty-four years. He was succeeded by his younger son, Antiochus II, having put to death his elder, who was accused of conspiring against him.

The reign of Antiochus II, Theos, saw the second Syrian war, which has been called the war of Laodicea, and which was inspired by one of those domestic tragedies that stain the annals of all this time.

Antiochus, who appears to have gained his title of the God, and consequent divination, because he had rid the Milesian cities from a tyrant, made a peace with Ptolemy that was very much to his advantage. It included, however, a clause that was to undo any good won by battle or political cleverness. This was the alliance between the warring dynasties, to be consummated between Antiochus and Berenice, daughter of Philadelphus. The Syrian King had married his sister Laodicea and had had children by her, but he agreed to this political measure and even divorced the sister-consort or, at best, made her Queen-Dowager and also divinized her, giving her a special worship of her own.

These trifles did not appease Laodicea, who went to live in Ephesus with her two sons, Seleucus and Antiochus. She bided her time, and it appears that Antiochus returned to his allegiance and used to visit her at Ephesus, especially after the death of Philadelphus,

SPRINGTIME IN THE VALLEY OF THE UPPER ZERKA

who kept watch over his daughter and her little son. It was after his death that Laodicea struck; if she had waited patiently for about three years before doing anything, she was swift to act when opportunity came. She made Antiochus sign a paper in which she and her sons were recognized as his legitimate wife and children and then she had him poisoned; after which she caused the death of Berenice's child and then of herself.

Ptolemy III, Evergetus, set about to avenge the death of his sister and her child and so began the third Syrian war. The Egyptians were triumphant by sea and land and affairs went badly for the Seleucid; but, in the end, nothing very drastic happened and the usual truce ended the years of useless fighting. The Seleucid King and his brother occupied the interval between wars by getting up a civil war among themselves.

After the short and inglorious reign of Seleucus III, came the long and glorious one of his younger brother, Antiochus III, the Great. He reigned from 223 to 187 B.C. In 221, Ptolemy IV, Philopater, succeeded Ptolemy III in Egypt. He was a curious creature, half artist, half decadent, but he conducted the war against Antiochus with vigour.

Antiochus was busy with his campaigns in Syria and Asia Minor from 221 to 218 B.C., in the spring of which year he crossed the Jordan after receiving the submission of Scythopolis, the only city of the Decapolis west of the river. One after another the cities submitted to him and the Arabs began to join the ranks of his army as all his efforts were crowned with success. To protect these new allies against the garrison in Philadelphia, and to gain an important fortress, Antiochus resolved to invest the town and citadel.

The most detailed account that we have of this event is in the History of Polybius. The Arabs told Antiochus that there was a great multitude of men in " urbem Arabiæ Rabath-ben-Ammon (which others called Rabatamana) "; I quote from the Latin translation of the Greek original, showing that the older name was not quite sunk in the new. Antiochus examined the place carefully; going all round the hills he perceived that there were only two entrances to the citadel, or rather two approaches which might yield to his attack. He therefore divided the attacking force in two parts, giving the command of one to Nicharchus and of the other to Theodotus, two of his most trusted generals. He posted one at each of these places, and managed to instil into each commander a spirit of rivalry with the other which caused them to prosecute the siege with great vigour.

Day and night, without intermission, the siege engines that the generals had placed in what seemed to them the most vulnerable spots assailed the citadel, without doing more harm than infuriating the garrison and doing some damage to the walls. The siege might have lasted for a very long time had not a captive betrayed the secret passage along which water was conveyed to the fortress; after that it was only a matter of time. Antiochus caused the passage to be blocked up with rubbish and stones and the garrison was forced to capitulate; so ended the last great siege of Rabboth Ammon.

Antiochus left a strong garrison to guard his new possession under the command of Nicharchus and went into winter quarters at Ptolemais.

Philadelphia probably reverted to the Egyptians after the great defeat of Antiochus at Raphia, beyond Gaza, on the modern frontier between Syria and Egypt, which took place the following year. It was a tremendous battle. Antiochus had collected recruits of all nations, including ten thousand Arabs; he had a great force of infantry and cavalry and one hundred and two elephants. Ptolemy had an even larger force and seventy-three elephants, but these were smaller than the Indian elephants of Antiochus.

For five days these giant forces stood and looked at each other; Ptolemy began the battle because he had the desert behind him which made the provisioning of his men difficult. The shock, according to Polybius, was terrific, the battle raged with varying fortune. The two Kings were facing each other, one on the right wing, the other on the left; Ptolemy had his sister-wife with him, Arsinoe III. Antiochus had the best of it at the first, but Ptolemy scored a decisive victory and recovered Cœle Syria.

Having made a great effort on this occasion, probably realizing that his crown was at stake, Ptolemy returned to Alexandria, where he resumed his life of a mystic voluptuary.

He and Arsinoe died mysteriously in 204-203, B.C., the date was not really known. Sosibius and Agothocles, who were governing the country in the name of the King, suddenly produced two silver urns in which they said were the remains of Ptolemy and Arsinoe; they also produced a will giving the supreme power to themselves, and proclaimed the child King of five years old. It was the signal for Antiochus and others to think of dividing the spoil; but Antiochus the Conqueror had shot his bolt; as time went on he had one disaster after another until he lost nearly all the rich empire that he had inherited. And through it all the shadow of Rome was thrown before; he defied Rome, fought Rome and, failing, made ready the place that Rome was to occupy in Syria. He died ignominiously, being caught robbing a temple to fill his depleted money-bags.

CHAPTER XVII
The Decapolis

CHAPTER XVII

THE DECAPOLIS

THE League of the Ten Cities took shape soon after Pompey's campaigns in 64-63 B.C.; at least that is the most reasonable hypothesis, no exact date being known. Confederacies of Greek cities planted down in foreign lands were well known before that date, and we find the Greek cities of western Palestine crying out about their rights during the wars of those times. The Seleucids and Ptolemies frequently promised freedom to these cities as a reward for taking their side in the contest, but it does not appear that their promises were ever fulfilled.

The Greeks, living in their groups of islands, were naturally sea-going people; they swept the shores of Palestine, and took the Phœnician and Philistine maritime cities. When they came over Jordan, in the wake of Alexander's conquests, they found the countryside in a much wilder and more dangerous state than it was in the west, and no doubt they felt that some more stringent rules were necessary, some more definite means of defending their commerce and their very existence from the inroads of the Bedawin.

The Greeks already settled in western Palestine, as well as the more recent comers in the eastern region, welcomed a multitude of colonists who came out to join them; they probably intermarried with the natives, and some of these must have lived in the Greek cities, but the general character was carefully kept up, the religion, the manners and customs were all Greek. Their constitution was democratic; they aimed at an independence that they were not able fully to realize; they had a strong civic life, they encouraged Greek literature and culture generally; they had athletic games, entertainments in the theatres; they worshipped the Greek gods in their temples. The cities of the Decapolis had commercial freedom, their own Councils, the right of coinage and asylum, the right of holding property in the neighbourhood and of administering justice there; they were allowed to make an alliance among themselves as to offence and defence. On the other hand, they were put by the Romans under the Province of Syria, the Governor had power to revise their laws, they were liable to military service, and were taxed for Governmental purposes. No Roman garrison was given them, but they were liable to have a Legion quartered in their cities. Although they had their own civic arms on their coins, they had also the image of Cæsar.

This civic life dates from the Roman era. The Romans were always anxious to encourage Hellenism, and, even after Syria became a Roman province, they kept up the Greek character of these cities. It is evident that the Romans lived in these Greek cities, and that they imposed some of their own customs without disturbing the Hellenic religion.

Ten cities were included in this League when it was started, but others were added later on. Eleven original ones are mentioned: Scythopolis, Pella, Gadara, Abila, Hippos, Philadelphia, Gerasa, Dion, Kanatha, Damascus and Raphana, but Damascus was merely an honorary member as far as can be ascertained, leaving ten active members. Pella and Dion were the oldest, Philadelphia came next; then Gadara and Abila were added.

The plain of Esdraelon and the valley of Jezreel run down into the Jordan valley just by Scythopolis, the modern Beisan, the only city of the Decapolis that was situated west of Jordan. The position was excellent, both for keeping in touch with the Greek cities on the coast through the plain of Esdraelon, and for connecting these with the other cities of the League over Jordan. At Pella, on the eastern side, the modern Tubukat Fahil, three roads opened out and spread up to Damascus and

ROMAN VAULTING OVER THE RIVER, AMMAN

down to Philadelphia with a central road leading past Gadara and the unknown site of Raphana to Kanawat, or Kanatha, as it was then called, at the foot of Jebel Hauran. It was evident that the Decapolis, without having a district that could be called its own, had a good solid block of land in eastern Palestine, some of the properties even joining and all connected by these military roads.

Some of the towns composing the League are well known to us; some, as for instance Raphana, suggest nothing. Damascus is, of course, the greatest, the most ancient of them all, but very little is known as to the connection with the League. Abila was about twelve miles from Gadara on a branch of the Yarmuk; Hippos, which had a Pegasus on the coins led by a female form, gave a name to the country round which became Hippene, as that round Gadara became Gadarene, and round Philadelphia, Philadelphine. The finest remains, leaving Gerasa and Philadelphia out of the question, are those of Kanawat and Mukeis.

El Kanawat is mentioned in the Bible as Kenath; the Greco-Roman remains, built over older foundations, are still very picturesque. The streets are paved, there are ruins of temples and houses and two fine theatres, enclosed in great walls of an earlier date. Mukeis, once Gadara, and possibly the capital of Peræa, though Ajlun is also suggested, was taken and partly destroyed by Alexander Jannæus and rebuilt by Pompey to please, so the story goes, one of his freedmen who was born there. Like the other cities it became the seat of a bishopric in the Christian period and, like all of them, it became a ruin owing to the Moslem rising and the devastating incursion of the Mongols.

Kanawat or Kenath was one of the cities taken by Nobah of the tribe of Manasseh: " And Nobah went and took Kenath and the villages thereof and called it Nobah after his own name." The country round is extremely attractive, with forests of evergreen oak.

The Greeks preferred a site through which a river ran and round about which there were gentle hills; they chose far wilder situations in a country where you had to be always on the defensive and where, water being scarce, there had usually been cities built before. Very often these would be built, like the citadel of Rabboth Ammon, on a steep hill, but it seems certain that their ideal was rather in the character of the lower town by the river or of Jerash, set in the midst of pastoral country. Scythopolis was situated four hundred and thirty feet below the level of the Mediterranean Sea; Pella stood a thousand feet above the Jordan valley.

The histories of these cities differ very little; Pella, which was called after the capital of Macedon, and was almost certainly founded by some of Alexander's generals and populated by his veterans, was taken by Antiochus the Great just before he took Philadelphia in 218 B.C.; it was destroyed by the Jews under Alexander Jannæus because the Greeks refused to conform to Jewish rites. It was restored by Pompey, who did so much to revive the past glories of Syria, became an episcopal city and afforded a refuge for Christians during the siege of Jerusalem by the Romans. It was destroyed by the Saracens.

In these cities, bound together by so many ties of nationality, of culture and of common interests, there arose a special type of civilization, which has been described as " a curious, unique civilization, talking Greek, imitating Rome, at heart Semitic."

How far the inhabitants of these cities were at heart Semitic seems open to doubt. The Decapolis was an anti-Semitic League; the Semites, whether of the governing class who took away their privileges or of the class of the desert Arabs against whose depredations they had to protect themselves, were unfriendly. However well protected, the Greek colonists were aliens in a foreign land.

The Decapolis is mentioned several times in the

The Decapolis

New Testament. Christ was followed by "great multitudes of people from Galilee, and from Decapolis, and from Jerusalem, and from Judæa, and from beyond Jordan."

This may refer to Scythopolis, just west of Jordan, or to Gadara and the other cities to west of the Sea of Galilee; it was in the country " of the Gadarenes " that He cured the man who was possessed by devils and told him to return to his friends and to tell them what great things God had done for him. " And he departed and began to publish in Decapolis how great things Jesus had done for him; and all men did marvel." Jesus also went through " the midst of the coasts of Decapolis," after crossing the Sea of Galilee, that is on that part of the land of Gadara bordering on the sea, and there he cured a man of deafness.

In all the linked lands belonging to the Decapolis, they must have been talking of Christ and the miracles that he did; for there, before their eyes, were the men who had been freed from physical and mental evils and perhaps they heard also of the girl of their nation from whom He had cast out a devil on the sea coast.

When the Romans finally beat Antiochus the Great, the Greek cities began to ask for their rights and privileges to be guaranteed by the conquering party; the Romans gave the freedom of the city to those who had supported their cause, and they made the others tributary to the King of Pergamos. We do not know how this affected Philadelphia, which had stood out against Antiochus, because the eastern cities are not mentioned, but, in any case, they must have enjoyed their rights after Pompey annexed Syria as a Roman province.

The lower city of Philadelphia lay along the banks of a brook, for it is hardly more, part of which was vaulted over according to Roman practice. One bold arch is all that now remains of this vaulting; near to it are the remains of a building that may have been the baths. An aqueduct runs to it which looks as if that were the case, but it has apparently been used as a fort in later times. It contains a wall in which are three alcoves, richly decorated, and holes that suggest that metal ornaments may have been inserted here. A few columns without capitals are still standing. By the river there are remains of Roman masonry, besides various ruined walls in among those of the modern Circassian village. There is also a Roman bridge at the southern end of the present town.

Passing along modern Amman, the capital of Trans-Jordan, the impression is one of movement and noise, and, above all, of colour. The many coloured draperies of the modern Arab, his flowing head-dress and his dignified appearance would fit him for playing a part in any age; his garments are ageless. He might have ridden in on camel or horse, or walked in after his sheep and goats at almost any period of the world's history. We can imagine him coming in to the market at Philadelphia intent on getting as much for his flocks as he could, bargaining, possibly, in Aramaic, though that was the written language of the desert folk rather than the spoken, the language of the inscriptions and that of the educated, who used it for business.

Leaving the street of columns and the river gurgling over the stones, we cross a modern bridge and come to the theatre that is the glory of Amman. It is excavated out of the hillside and is in very good preservation. It is calculated to hold about four thousand people, not a great size when you remember that some Greek theatres held twenty-five thousand spectators, but sufficiently large for the audience of a provincial town. Up at the top is the seat for the Emperor with a scallop shell canopy; the tiers of seats are there and the stairs intersecting the rows mount up to the broad passages that run round the theatre. Between the theatre and the river are some fine columns, the beginning of the street of columns that cut through the town by the river.

It is a great pity that so little remains of the colonnaded street that must have given character to the riverside part of the town. Very few traces of it are to be found now; an occasional pillar embedded in masonry, part of the shaft of a column serving as a doorstep to a shanty, bits of old wall and old masonry, these are all that remind the passer-by of the departed glories of a city of the Decapolis. When the extent of the town is considered and the beauty of the temples and the public buildings and private houses that once stood here, one can but regret once more the vandalism of past ages.

There is one interesting building left which may have been the wall of a part of the forum; the group of ruins of a mosque and a Byzantine basilica, which are described at length in some books, I did not see, and I fear that part of the ruins may have disappeared beneath the new white mosque that is in process of being built. There are two aqueducts and many old walls and some particularly fine tombs outside the town. The ruins are interesting as coming from different periods; starting with the Ammonite foundations of the walls of the citadel, they include Byzantine, Greco-Roman, Jewish, Sasanian, Moslem, as well as the prehistoric cave dwellings and dolmens that have been noticed.

With so much that is interesting it seems ungracious to grumble, but one cannot help regretting that so much has, even quite recently, disappeared. Judging by the pictures of the Odeum, for instance, only about half is now standing compared to what was there only a comparatively short time ago. Until quite recently two columns stood up on the citadel hill, but they have fallen and lie prone among the enormous quantity of fragments of stone that literally cover the ground up there.

The theatre alone seems to have resisted the hand of time and the even more destructive hand of man; it is very imposing, and the group of columns add immensely to the effect. Whether seen at midday, with the old stone glowing against a deep blue sky, or at sunset, when all the colours latent in the stone shine out and a shadow cuts across the seats which were once filled by eager spectators, the effect is most beautiful, and suggestive of a whole civilization that has vanished.

Perhaps it would have been better for Philadelphia if the city had been suddenly deserted and left to decay, as was the case with Gerasa; more of the original buildings might then have been left standing. But in Christian times it was a town of note with a great Byzantine cathedral and other churches; the Moslems built mosques and certainly destroyed the cathedral, which, with its five aisles, must have been a fine specimen of architecture. The remains of the mosque and the cathedral are more interesting to archæologists than to ordinary mortals, and a great new mosque is being built over part of the remains of the former.

It is evident that Philadelphia fell on evil days after the Romans went in the seventh century. It was not entirely demolished as so many of the Decapolis cities were, first by the Moslems and then by the Mongols; but it must have appeared very different to the fine city with paved streets and great civic buildings of former days. Muqaddasi, the Arab geographer, describes it as being on the border of the desert; he writes: " In the city near the market place stands a fine mosque, the court of which is ornamented with mosaic. We have heard said that it resembles that of Makkah. The Castle of Goliath is on the hill overhanging the city, and therein is the tomb of Uriah, over which is built a mosque. Here, likewise, is the circus of Solomon (the theatre). Living here is cheap, and fruit is plentiful. On the other hand, the people of the place are illiterate, and the roads thither wretched. But the city is even as a harbour of the desert, and a place of refuge for the Bedawin Arab."*

---

* Translated by Guy Le Strange.

This was written towards the end of the tenth century by a man who journeyed all over the country in order to write his book of geography. And a very entertaining book it is!

Why he calls the citadel the Castle of Goliath or the theatre the Circus of Solomon; why, still more, he speaks of the tomb of Uriah is more than we can guess at this time of the day. It seems very unlikely that anyone should have put up a monument to an unfortunate and not very important soldier, unless David ordered it in a moment of repentance when he received the submission of the Ammonites just above the place where his " servant Uriah the Hittite " had been left to his fate.

The question of the building over the tomb having ever been a mosque seems doubtful; it is the most interesting ruin left standing on the citadel hill.

CHAPTER XVIII
THE CITADEL

CHAPTER XVIII

The Citadel

THE citadel hill is strewn with a mass of fallen stone. It is true that a good part of the walls remain, but of the temples and the Castle and the buildings of the upper town, nothing remains standing, except the Moslem building about which there is a certain amount of controversy.

The hill lies to north of the theatre and the river, to the west of it is another hill on which are many old walls and some cromlechs; the valley winds between the hills and is met by another valley in the middle of the town. One road runs to Salt, another goes east passing by the Haj railway about three miles away and pushing on either up the old Pilgrims' route to the north or straight across the desert to Bosra. Still another, the old Roman road, leads south to Heshbon.

The view from the hilltop is comprehensive; just below are the ruins, with the river winding away between its green banks, the town is spread out over the widening valley and runs up the lower slope of the opposite hill. The distant prospect is suggestive of wide space and gives an impression of indulating downs on the top of a high plateau.

It is no easy task to put back the clock some fifteen hundred years, and to reconstitute the Greco-Roman town and fortress as it must have appeared then. Wandering about among the heaps of fallen stone, noting where the great Temple to Herakles once stood because the bases of the pillars of the Pro-Naos are still in situ, is a melancholy amusement. Near by is part of the structure, just a bit of wall up which you can climb to gain a better view of the fallen glories of that Temple—great broken shafts of columns, the mighty fragment of a pediment, a Corinthian capital half-buried in the ground. And it is everywhere the same. Wanton destruction, possibly earthquakes, which are not uncommon in this part of the world, neglect, natural decay, all these elements of disintegration have combined to make of the once proud citadel a heap of ruins.

Towards the nothern edge of the curiously shaped plateau on which the fortress was built, stands the one building that gives any impression of its former beauty. It is approached through a great ruined archway and, as you pick your way over the heaps of stones, you see before you a great hall which is still protected from the weather by a domed roof. In this hall are four alcoves, which gives it the appearance of being cruciform—an appearance only, as the four chambers at the corners make up the square.

When you have had time to take in these preliminaries, you see that the walls inside these alcoves are most beautifully sculptured and that the decorative scheme consists of round-headed panels, standing on a string course, supported by small arches springing from dwarf coupled pillars; the designs used in the sculptured stonework are very beautiful and often intricate. As there are various opinions concerning this palace, it will be best to consider them, as the subject is one of some importance.

After describing the building in detail, Colonel Conder writes in the "Survey of Eastern Palestine" :—

" The arrangement of panels in different tiers, flanking large arches with recesses, resembles that of the walls of the Tak Kesra, at Ctesiphon, which is ascribed by Mr. Fergusson to the Sasanian period about 550 A.D. The Tak Kesra arches appear to be horseshoes, while the panels have segmental and pointed arches, with coupled columns as at Amman."

The late James Fergusson, who had no hesitation in ascribing the palace at M'shita to Chosroes II, speaks of Amman as of a similar building of the Sasanian period.

THE SASANIAN BUILDING, AMMAN

" The palace of Rabboth Ammon," he writes, " also in Moab, consists of a central court open to the sky, and four recesses or transepts, one on each face ; two of these are covered with elliptical barrel vaults, and two with semidomes carried on pendentives. The decoration of this palace is similar to that found at M'shita, but not so rich in design or so good in its execution."

The description hardly leads one to suppose that the writer himself visited the place that he speaks of with less than his usual care.

M. H. Saladin gives a more detailed description in his fascinating study the " Manuel d'art Musulman." Before quoting from the page that he devotes to this monument of Moslem art, we may as well remind ourselves of the manner in which the transition from classic art to Moslem was made in Syria.

If Syria had been Hellenised from early days, another artistic influence had come from still earlier times from Persia. And we must remember, as M. Saladin points out, that Moslem civilization is not purely Arabic ; it has been influenced by the peoples amongst which it has developed—Greek, Persian, Syrian, Egyptian, Spanish, Indian. In each country it has received a different impress ; and in each country one must study the former development of art when considering the great school of architecture that followed on the rise of Islam.

We know nothing of the earliest Arabic civilizations, except that of the Nabatæans, as seen in the remains of their work in the Hauran, which I do not think that M. Saladin mentions. The architecture of the dwellers in Yemen, or in the two kingdoms of Ghassan and Hira, have vanished completely. Hira, however, was in Mesopotamia, and it is from thence that the Sasanian art was inspired ; that was, of course, just a school of Persian art that developed under the Sasanid sovereigns of Persia. It is suggested that the annual pilgrimage to Mecca may have been instrumental in introducing new ideas to the people from so many different parts of the world, all brought together by the faith that united them. Many of these pilgrims were poor artisans who had to make a little money by the way ; they may easily have introduced new methods of work or new designs to those they met among the pilgrims or in the halting-places set apart for them at different points of the long route.

The earliest decorative work seems to have been inspired by the embroiderers and goldsmiths and the masters of the ceramic craft ; their intricate designs were reproduced in brick, or perhaps in the tiles for which Persia is famous. In Syria these decorative designs were reproduced in stone, because stone, rather than brick, was the medium to which they were accustomed. The carved and moulded plaister work of the Persians was copied from embroidery, the painted cottons of Ispahan were copied in ceramics, so one art gave to another.

The Moslem style in architecture superseded the Byzantine, without losing it altogether, just as the Byzantine had superseded the classic Greco-Roman. It is the fashion to say that Byzantine is debased Greek, but it is rather the Syrian development of the severer style with its own characteristics, the result being at once typical of the countries in which it chiefly flourished and exceedingly beautiful in itself.

The Assyrian and Chaldean influence is evident in Mesopotamia, for so many centuries under the dominion of one or the other of the great empires by which it was surrounded. The cupolas came from this source and passed over to Persia to reappear in Sasanian art ; from Chaldea and Assyria we have the fashion of covering a wall with enamelled terra-cotta tiles or metal, so often seen in Persia and Mesopotamia. The finest monument left by the Sasanids is the palace of Ctesiphon, Takhti-Kesra, to which the Amman building has been likened in some particulars.

The Sasanids gave the Arabs the models for their

The Citadel

hydraulic works which were accomplished with the help of the Roman prisoners as workmen. The influence of Sasanian art, the successor of the Mesopotamian, extended all over the East before the rise of Islam. Its principal characteristics were the vaulted or domed roof, the wide arch, decorative plaister work, either cut or moulded, walls covered with enamelled tiles and exterior coverings in metal.

It is interesting to find that there were several fine Moslem buildings in Amman. One of them was the Mosque mentioned by Muqaddasi, the remains of which are described in some detail by Colonel Conder.

This is what M. Saladin says about the Amman building :—

" The palace at Amman, rather than that at Machita, may be considered one of the most interesting examples of Moslem art. One ought perhaps, to date it from the beginning of the Hejira, as the arches have a curve that resembles that of the Mosque of Ibn Tonoun at Cairo. But if the springing of the arches, the engaged columns that support them, and the arcades of the base remind one in any way of Takh-i-Kesra, the outline of the semi-circular arch on the left of the section is certainly Greco-Syrian.

" It has been classed as a building of the twelfth century, but there is nothing in the decoration of the twelfth and thirteenth centuries that resembles it; neither the little recesses in the wooden cupola of the Kubbet-es-Sakra, or those of the Mihrab of the Mosque of El-Aksa, or those of the Mihrab of the tomb of Kalaoun (1279-1290), with its three recesses, where we find little double columns. The columns without capitals of Amman appear rather to be inspired by those at Ctesiphon. The decoration does not resemble the sculpture in form of a candelabra of Takht-i-Bostan. It is rather Arabic in style. Taking into consideration the dog-tooth moulding on the archivolts, the columns without capitals, and the decayed aspect of the stone, I think it compares with the Mosque of Toulouna and is consequently constructed by a Mesopotamian architect."

As the flight of Mohammed took place in July, 662, this interesting building must belong to the seventh century. The likeness to the outer walls of the Kubbet-es-Sakra, mentioned by Colonel Conder, can hardly amount to anything, as those walls were originally built in the reign of the Caliph Abdul-Malek ibn Marwan, in 691, A.D., but collapsed in an earthquake shock in 1016 and were re-erected in 1022 by the Caliph Hakem. The present walls seem to be the work of Sulaiman the Magnificent, who restored the Dome of the Rock in the sixteenth century.

Leaving this relic of Moslem art, we can make one more effort to reconstruct the fortress of Ptolemy Philadelphus.

It was built on three great terraces, running, more or less, east and west. The highest and most western was one thousand two hundred feet long by six hundred feet wide; then there was a drop in level of about thirty feet to the second terrace, which was one thousand feet long by three hundred feet wide. A triple gate led from one of these terraces to the other, apparently on the level of the lower, which itself sloped down to the third terrace of one thousand feet long and from two to three hundred feet wide. There was a moat at the foot of the lowest terrace.

The whole enclosure measured about twenty-nine acres and in it were two temples, the fortress itself, the buildings of the upper town and the fortifications. The principal buildings stood on the terraces. The south wall of the Qalah, or Castle, is still standing, composed of great blocks of drafted stone. A doorway has a winged tablet in low relief on the lintel, probably Byzantine, fourth to fifth century.

The best preserved monuments of Greco-Roman or Byzantine period, next to the theatre, are the sarcophagi which are to be found in the country round about. One

INTERIOR OF THE SASANIAN BUILDING, AMMAN

of these is the Sultan's tomb, built against the cliff at the entrance to the valley. It is described as having place for seven sarcophagi, only two of which were found. It has a wall adorned with a simple string course from which a round arched tunnel vault springs. There is a recess over this, evidently to hold a statue and a "round-headed or half-dome roof." Another tomb of importance is the Western Tomb, a square structure of masonry with walls five feet thick. It was once roofed with a dome. In the "Survey of Eastern Palastine" this tomb is described in detail; I quote a few lines because they help to explain the only one of these tombs that I had the advantage of inspecting :—

" The masonry resembles all the other masonry of this date at Amman, the stones being well set and dressed, of square proportions and not drafted. The soffit of the arch in the south wall has a ' rose and coffer ' pattern, like that in the roofs of some Roman basilicas.

" The most curious feature of the building is, however, the arrangement of the dome. About three quarters of the circle is visible, the two lowest courses being left. These do not spring from pendentives, but directly from the angles—large voussoirs projecting inwards, their faces being cut to the required arc."

The Kasr-en-Nueijis, the Palace of the Princes, which we went to see quite accidentally, being told that a small building called locally " The Little Temple of the Bell " was worth a visit, is another of these Greek mausoleums, dating from the second century after Christ.

About six miles away from Amman, in the middle of a cornfield, a small square building attracts attention. It stands quite alone, with waving corn all around, just a little off the track that was once a Roman road. The square building is rich in the colour of the stone and it has a domed roof on which a short column carries what remains of a vase. It is this broken vase, standing on its little plinth, that has given the name of the Little Temple of the Bell to the tomb. The dome rises from spherical pendentives, there are recesses for sarcophagi, but I think that none were found there. The outer wall has corner pilasters with Ionic capitals, the entablature has a fluted frieze and, at one place, a frieze showing sculptured animals and foliage. Mr. Ernest Richmond is of opinion that the Kasr-en-Nueijis may have been a Roman guardroom and not a tomb; it is, at any rate, a most picturesque feature in a desolate landscape.

CHAPTER XIX
Ptolemy Philadelphus II and the Greek Theatre

CHAPTER XIX

Ptolemy Philadelphus II and the Greek Theatre

PTOLEMY II, the founder of Philadelphia, was in some ways a very remarkable man. He was immensely rich, and grudged nothing that led to the fulfilment of his desires. His chief hobby was collecting manuscripts, his ambition being, according to Josephus, to get together "all the books that were in the habitable earth." In this laudable effort he was ably seconded by his librarian, Demetrius, who once suggested that he might have the Jewish books of the law, which were written in their own dialect, translated. The King had just asked him how many tens of thousands of books he had in his library and the librarian had replied that there were about twenty times ten thousand on the shelves then but that there would soon be fifty times ten thousand. The reply pleased the King, who wanted quantity as well as quality, and he approved the idea of having the books of the Jewish law translated to add to the number.

It was then suggested to Ptolemy that it would be most unsuitable to study the laws which, his Greek informers had learned "by particular enquiry," had been made by God Himself—the God they too adored, although they called him Zeus—when so many Jews were still in captivity in Egypt. The King, with a cheerful and joyous countenance, asked how many captives there were, and when he heard that there were "a few more than ten times ten thousand" he published a decree setting them free, and himself paid their ransom to their masters. In this way one hundred and twenty thousand Jews were repatriated who had been made prisoners by Ptolemy I and others. The number sounds as if it might be overstated, but it agrees with the numbers given elsewhere.

Demetrius then wrote out a long memorandum setting forth the advantages of the affair, and he suggested the letter that the King was to write to the Jewish High Priest, which Ptolemy duly signed and sent off with the most wonderful presents, including an immense quantity of jewels and a golden altar. The High Priest was naturally delighted to hear that so many Jews were to be set free and to receive such rich gifts in this unexpected manner; he made a suitable reply, and sent the men who were to make the translations—six elders from each tribe, skilled in the law—according to Ptolemy's request.

When these learned men arrived at Alexandria they were received by the King, and feasted with him; Ptolemy even sent away the sacred herald and forbade the usual sacrifices to be made, merely asking the chief elder, Eleazer, to say grace. Eleazer complied, calling down a blessing on the generous King, and Ptolemy, amid the applause of the company, shed tears of joy. The Jews made the translation and were sent back loaded with presents, Eleazer having ten beds with silver feet, and furniture to match, besides rich garments, a crown, linen, dishes, and two golden cisterns that were to be dedicated to God.

Not only did Ptolemy do all this to enrich his library, but he spent twelve evenings in succession discussing the Jewish books with his guests, and his wide-minded and liberal outlook may be contrasted favourably with the intolerance of the Jews when they got possession of the Greek cities. It was only another evidence of his conciliatory spirit that prompted him to give his daughter in marriage to his hereditary enemy, Antiochus II, with what unhappy results we have seen.

There is a story told of Ptolemy III which I cannot help thinking really belongs to his enterprising father. Either Ptolemy II or Ptolemy III borrowed from Athens a copy that had been made, by order of the Government,

THE EMPEROR'S BOX, AMMAN THEATRE

of the plays of Æschylus, Sophocles and Euripides ; it was an authoritative edition rendered necessary by the manner in which the producers treated the original manuscript, taking out passages and putting in others according as it suited their taste. Ptolemy had to leave fifteen talents as a surety, and he forfeited them because he returned, not the copy sent to him, but his own transcript of that copy. No doubt it was Philadelphus, and he must have been delighted to add it to his tens of thousands of books in his library in Alexandria.

Although the theatre at Amman has been adapted to Roman fashion, it is evidently the Greek theatre cut out of the living rock by the order of the Macedonian, and very much Hellenised, King of Egypt.

To begin with, all the early Greek theatres were excavated in the hollow of a hill ; they were, of course, built originally with a round space in the middle for the dancers. The religious ceremonies in connection with the rites of Dionysus took place here at his festivals, the chorus dancing round the altar which continued to be placed in the middle of the space, called the orchestra, long after the festival took on a more essentially dramatic character. As the dramatic idea developed, one actor recited from the altar, sometimes mounted on a sacrificial table by its side, and exchanged a conversation with the chorus. He was dressed in a peculiar long dress, mounted on thick-soled shoes, and wore the traditional masks, which he changed according to the character that he assumed.

The orchestra was given up to the chorus, and as time went on the Greeks took off a portion of the orchestra and made a high and narrow stage on it for the actors ; in time again, the booth or tent in which the actors changed their masks and dresses became a building such as we now see at Amman, a few paces off the theatre, to which it was connected by a colonnade.

The skene, a word that came from the tent, was used in time to mean the back cloth and the scene of action among other things, a word that we still preserve, as we do the pro-skenion and the para-skenion. But, in spite of evolution, the Greeks remained simple in their architecture and details, and their theatres remained, to the end, on the lines of that primitive wooden edifice that first supplanted the precincts of the temple of the god.

At the risk of being tedious, it seems necessary to refresh our memories of those first Greek plays in order to place the provincial theatre of Amman in its proper light.

There were various festivals devoted to Dionysus, the god of wine and fertility—the most important took place in the spring, when Athens was crowded with strangers as well as its own citizens, when the Ambassadors of foreign powers and other Hellenic States, and those bent on commercial enterprise, found themselves in the city. It was then that the great competitions took place, at what was called the City Dionysia. These were the contests of the tragedians; the comedians had their contests in the winter at the Lenæa festival, which was a much quieter affair. Comedies were not considered in the same category with tragedies, and the glory of obtaining a prize at the Lenæa was nothing as compared to that of gaining the laurel crown at the City Dionysia. Between the years 499 B.C., when the first mention of a tragedy by Æschylus is mentioned, to the death of Sophocles in 405 B.C., was the golden age of Greek drama, when immortal poets presented three tragedies and one satyric drama for the annual contest. The picture has often been drawn. The great theatre filled with eager spectators to the number of eighteen to twenty thousand, sitting there from sunrise to sunset for six consecutive days, must have presented a wonderful sight. The Athenian audience has been called the most sensitive and appreciative audience in the world, and there is no doubt that the Athenians adored their theatre and made the most of the opportunity of hearing the new plays produced at the contests. From the first procession in the early morning to the last great excitement of seeing the urns opened and the names of the successful poet-playwrights read out the great audience remained deeply interested. They cannot have been comfortable, sitting on the bare stone without a back to lean against, but some of them would have brought cushions to sit upon, which suggests to the mind the Spanish audience in the bull ring, though their seance is far shorter.

The third festival at which plays were heard was the Rural Dionysia, held in country places ; at these gatherings old plays were given, and there was consequently no contest. I conclude that the provincial Dionysia were of the same nature and that at the great dramatic performances in the theatre of Philadelphia some of the famous Greek tragedies were presented, which had first been heard at the City Dionysia at Athens.

In Greece a theatre was a necessity ; it was part of the religious and public life. The Romans never had the same love of the pure dramatic art, and the theatre never spoke to them in the same way. What really appealed to them was a vast amphitheatre in which they could gloat over the bloody contests of men and wild beasts or of men with each other. When it came to a theatrical performance they preferred pantomimes and pyrrhic ballets to one of the old tragedies setting forth the awful consequences of some primeval sin. But, of course, they did, with their practical genius, revolutionize stage machinery, and Greece took up the new ideas to a certain extent.

In the late A. E. Haigh's " Attic Theatre " there is a good deal of interesting information concerning the improvements made by the Romans, which are too technical to enter into here ; the stage gradually encroached on the orchestra and became less high ; the chorus declined in importance and the actors became more prominent. Vitruvius has many interesting details to tell concerning the development of the great reconstruction of stage effects in the time of Nero, who had a passion for the theatre. There was then an elaborate architectural façade for the proscenium and one with columns and an entablature erected at the back of the stage; mechanical contrivances were brought up to date.

From the foundation of Philadelphia and the probable construction of the theatre, to the days when Nero set fire (if indeed he did) to Rome for the pleasure of building it up again, is a matter of over three hundred years. The theatre must have been completely Hellenic in its early days; indeed up to the time of Pompey in 63 B.C., there would have been little chance of novelties from Rome coming to that remote spot. And it is very unlikely that they did even then, for it has been often remarked that the theatres of Asia Minor showed very little Roman influence, many of them retaining their primitive Greek character. It is evident that, at Amman, a stage had been erected across the orchestra, and the odeion, now full of rubbish and difficult to reconstruct mentally, was a quite up-to-date small theatre to seat about four hundred people. In these little theatres there used to be what we should call rehearsals, but which were, in reality, more, for in them the poets who were going to compete appeared with their actors and choregi, and with the rich citizen who was going to pay for the performance of his plays. It was a full-dress show of great brilliance, and no doubt all playgoers were anxious to assist. Recitations of rhapsodists and contests of harp-playing were also held here.

It is quite clear that, even so late as the time of Nero, the Greeks still held the palm for the theatre. That extraordinary mortal, the Emperor Nero, who thought that he excelled as singer and reciter as well as charioteer, went to the Greek cities in 67 A.D., and competed at all the contests, being given the crown at

all, for evident reasons. He evidently looked on Athens as the theatrical Mecca, and returned in the best of spirits. When he committed suicide in the following year it will be remembered that his last words were :—
" What an artist is lost in me ! "

Ptolemy Philadelphus was no such lunatic; he may have had a less marked love of the drama, on and off the stage, than Nero, but it does not seem to be stretching the point too far to suggest that the book lover, and the man who stole the plays of the Greek poet-dramatists, took an interest in his theatre at Philadelphia, and that he may have even been present at some great event there. Whether the Emperor's box is an addition at a later date, as seems probable, or whether it was part of the original structure, is for the archæologists to decide. It is certainly distinctly Roman in character.

One would like to know what plays were given here, and what use the theatre was put to after the Greco-Roman power fell. Whether, for instance, the Moslems, who appear to have lived here for a considerable time, ever used it for their functions. Probably not; but the tired pilgrims coming here on their way to Mecca, for it is very little off the Haj route, may have rested here or even slept in the roomy boxes off the main corridors, where now the Arabs' horses walk up and down. A family of Circassians did take up their abode in the Emperor's box when first they came to Amman, but now it seems given up to form stables for the Arab steeds.

Once more we are on the site of a vanished city, of which this theatre and a few columns are the only visible signs; empires have risen and have fallen, battles have been fought with first one side victorious and then another. Greece and Rome and Persia have fallen, the great Arab civilization that lit up dark ages has gone, though we hope it is reviving now on a more solid basis. Amman, the new capital of a new state, has risen from the ashes of Rabboth Ammon and Philadelphia. Half the population have come from far-off Circassia, refugees from their country, and set here to keep the Bedawin in check; the other half are the descendants of the old race, how much mixed with past civilizations we know not, and out beyond are the desert Arabs, as nomadic and as liable to raid the settled population as they ever were in the days of Ishmael.

Amman is the only one of the vanished cities that has really a stir of life over the past ashes. Madeba has a quiet life, Kerak has one that seems somehow not to have emerged out of the time of the Crusades; Petra has none. Here, though the straggling village street has none of the dignity of a capital city, yet there is a noisy bubbling life that speaks of the present rather than of the future. Cars rattle over the stones and hoot ceaselessly, hoping to clear a way through the crowd. Men sit by the roadside smoking narghillies, boys drive flocks of sheep and black goats to the fountain that stands where two roads meet; veiled women shop, and unveiled Arabs from the desert trail their long garments after them in the dust. The wonderful colour of it all delights the eye, the animation that prevails is cheerful. Tall powerful negroes, tall thin Arabs, looking taller as they swing along in their petticoats, middle-class men in the universal tarbush, ancient doubled-up beggar-men, there are some of all sorts. Little, black-eyed, impudent children roll in the dust and are miraculously saved from the hoofs of the donkeys and the little Arab horses by some dispensation of Providence. And some men of the Arab Legion or the police force are sure to be riding by to see that all is well.

It is only of late years that Amman has arisen again from a long period of neglect. For many years it was merely used as a dumping ground for passing nomads, and was described by a traveller in the last century as being extremely dirty and neglected, so much so that it was disagreeable if not dangerous to stay there. The

THE KASR EN-NUEIJIS, AMMAN

late Turkish Government allowed a colony of Circassians to settle in various places in Trans-Jordan, and the refugees had a very difficult time at the beginning. The Arabs naturally resented the intrusion, but the newcomers were hard-working, self-contained people, who had nothing to call them away from their city of refuge, and they gradually made their way among the Arabs, who settled in Amman in greater numbers when there was a competition. The Circassians are very clean and thrifty; after many years they keep their national characteristics and their national dress, and are never mistaken for the race among which they have come to dwell. In only two ways do they seem to assimilate themselves to the Arabs, and that is in their religion and in their instinct for hospitality. As far as the former goes, it was, of course, on account of their strict Mohammedanism that the Turks encouraged them to settle in what were then their dominions; the hospitality is perhaps a native virtue.

In leaving Amman I feel that so much remains unsaid; but it is impossible, without encroaching on the preserve of the Guide Book, to do justice to all that is to be seen in these intensely interesting towns with their histories reaching back into the dim ages. Luckily I can again rely on the masterly sketches of Major Fletcher, which give a true and faithful rendering of some of the points of interest of which I have endeavoured to speak.

CHAPTER XX
THE NABATÆANS AGAIN

CHAPTER XX

THE NABATÆANS AGAIN

TWENTY centuries before Christ the people who occupied the Hauran were wealthy enough to attract the unwelcome attentions of Chedorlaomer, a prince from the head of the Persian Gulf, as we may read in Genesis. Taking a leap to comparatively modern times, we come to a cuneiform inscription of the time of Shalmanezer II (859-824 B.C.), which runs: " to the mountains of Hauran I went; cities without number I pulled down, destroyed, in the fire I burned; their spoil, without number, I carried off."

It seems a wonder that new generations had the courage to build again, but it is the old story—wanton destruction followed by laborious rebuilding, until such time as the attempt is given up as hopeless or the district has been swept clear of men.

The Nabatæans, who began their dominion in the south, and who became great at Petra, got possession of much land in the Hauran as well as of Damascus; their talent as stone-cutters and builders had a peculiar development in the land of black basalt. It has been said that the Hauran is the cradle of Byzantine architecture, and it is here that the Nabatæans evolved a style that mingled the Orient with the classic architecture hitherto prevalent in Syria. " It is the Hauran," writes that great authority, M. de Vogüé, " that will give us the key and furnish the history of these curious attempts."

He describes the remains of the temples of Si and Siwada. Si was built during the reigns of the two Agrippas; it is strange in style, a combination of Greek and Oriental. " The necessity of placing a cupola on a square plan," he writes, " led the architects to discover the form of ' spherical sconce,' a special characteristic of the style called Byzantine ; but being unable to arrive at this at once they approached it by a series of tentative methods which it is interesting to study. . . .

" It was under the early Roman empire and for the needs of a pagan society that this fruitful and original movement had its birth : when that society and the empire itself had become Christian, the movement, far from being arrested, was continued and developed. Not only were the sanctuaries of paganism transformed into Christian sanctuaries, but new churches were erected adapted to the new worship ; houses, palaces, and tombs were built, even entire cities were founded."

M. de Vogüé then reminds us that the classic system insisted on a formula that varied very little whatever might be the size of the monument or the character of the material employed. The plan of a small temple, for instance, would serve for a larger one by increasing the scale. " The Greco-Syrian architects proceeded in a different manner. While adopting the elements of Greco-Roman orders, they employed them with a grand logic, retrenching the useless members, and no longer subordinating their dimensions to a uniform rule of proportion, but to the dimension and to the nature of the material placed at their disposal and to the design which they wished to carry out. Wishing to use only monoliths, they never exceeded a certain height, and gave to their openings almost invariable dimensions, whatever might be otherwise the size of the edifice."

The only material that was really at hand for these early architects, working out a new style, was hard black basalt. They had learned how to make a cupola from Mesopotamia via Persia, and also possibly through the Arabs of Hira, who were under Persian influence and situated in Irak. They applied their ingenuity in fashioning doors studded with nails, wheel-shaped windows, or square windows with lintels cut in basalt ; the hinges of the doors, even the knockers, were all of

VIEW IN THE MOUNTAINS NEAR AMMAN

The Nabatæans Again

the same material. The houses seem to have been built on Greek models, but modified to the new developments and to the exigencies of the material. They had series of columns in their rooms, supporting arches on which slabs of basalt were placed for the ceiling. Where the space was too large to be covered in this way they placed a cupola.

The temple of Sia, where so many interesting remains have been found is at the gates of Kannawat, one of the cities of the Decapolis; a fact that shows clearly how the interlinked properties of that League were mixed up with the domains of the Arabs.

The Hauran, which answers, more or less, to the land that the Hebrews knew as Bashan, was divided by the Romans into five provinces: Ituria, Gaulanitis, Batanea, Trachonitis and Auranitis. It included the fertile land of extinct volcanoes, the strange plateau of the Lejah, a mass of lava stream petrified, and the range of the Hauran mountains, now called the Jebel-ed-Druze, because the Druses have migrated there in numbers from the Lebanon district. Within the Hauran were various noted cities, such as Der'aa, Kanatha, and Bosra, the capital city which became specially important in the early days of Christianity.

Part of this country was colonized by the enterprising Nabatæans, and there are many inscriptions in their language, as well as those in rather bad Greek, which abound in all the district. From these we learn a good deal about their pantheon, and discover that they introduced the worship of " Allah " to the Mahommedans, while Allat, the mother of the gods, was Hellenised and became Pallas Athene. M. René Dussaud publishes in his study of " Les Arabes en Syrie avant l'Islam," a reproduction of the door of a sanctuary of Allat-Athena, discovered in the Lejah. It is a square-cut opening, with the lintel and door-posts carved with a bold design of grapes and leaves; the head of the goddess, which was over the door, is missing or defaced, but the dedicatory inscription is still in its place. The temple at Sia is said to have been designed on the same plan as the temple at Jerusalem, having a central portico flanked by two towers. It had a statue of Herod the Great inside, which reminds us that this country was handed over to Herod at one time by his friends the Romans, the gift even including two of the cities of the Decapolis. Although this may appear arbitrary, as it certainly was, both the district and the cities profited by his being overlord. He managed to get some sort of law and order in the wild district of Trachonitis, where the robbers lived who attacked the caravans on their way to Damascus; and he was in sympathy with the Greek culture, as a good Roman citizen should be. With the Nabatæans he was always at war, and it must be allowed that they did treat him rather badly over that affair of the brigands who were given shelter in Nabatæan dominions by the ambitious Minister of Obodas II.

It was no doubt partly owing to the colonies in the Hàuran that the Nabatæans wanted to make a second capital of Madeba, a sort of half-way house between Petra and Damascus. The Hauran lands were very useful to them; besides their fertility and the profit to be derived from their cultivation, they must have made the protection of their caravans a comparatively easy affair. They were, moreover, very suitable people for colonizing this arid land, with its tracts of arable country, for they were both agriculturists and builders with a genius for stone-cutting, as can be seen by examining the remains of their monuments. Another account of this phase of architecture is given in the interesting report of the Princetown Expedition, by H. C. Butler. As it agrees fundamentally with that already quoted, it may be as well to read over this one after having just considered the other :—

"There are remains of pre-Roman, though not pre-Hellenistic, architecture in Syria that offer a comparatively new field to the student—the remarkable style called the Nabatæan—discovered by de Vogüé in the temples of Si and Suweda. The southern parts of the Hauran are strewn with this civilization. Fragments, remains, inscriptions, architectural details, temples built in a peculiar style that borrowed little from classical art and represents a distinct racial, if not national, life. It is oriental in sentiment and expression, new and original. As builders the Nabatæans are unrivalled in the art of stone cutting and dressing; as architects they show an extraordinary ability in planning large schemes, in arranging masses, and in accommodating buildings or groups of structures to given sites. The ornament is rich yet reserved, adapted to hard black basalt, free from neighbouring influence. The architecture has a style of its own, a style that strongly influenced the succeeding styles of Roman and Christian periods in Syria, not only in principles of construction, but in decoration."

I make no apology for quoting these two considered opinions at some length, for they give such a clear idea of what this curious and interesting architectural development was. There is no doubt that Roman architects or Syrian architects, under Roman authority, had a far freer way of treating the classic orders; this freedom, far from spoiling the beauty of the design, often improved it because the taste of these artists was unerring. Trajan's great architect, Apollodorus, came from Damascus, the Romans learned from the Syrians, who had been under the artistic influence of Greece for centuries before they ever came under that of Rome. With roots firmly planted in the classic tradition the Syrian architects, with their oriental training, arrived at great effects of mass, of light and shade, as well as of attention to detail. They had inventive genius and enough tradition of the best sort to keep them from extravagance.

The chief building material in the Hauran, as we have seen, was basalt; whole villages built of these flat, black slabs may yet be seen in all that district. They also used, occasionally, sun-dried bricks, and are said to have been addicted to small conical domes, such as we still see in the villages. Both the Seleucids and the Ptolemies, however much they sinned in destroying whole towns and ravaging the countryside, were fine builders, and employed great architects. It was an age of expansion and development, in spite of being also an age of destruction.

It is important to realize that in the Hauran were two civilizations—the Greco-Roman and the Arab. The Hollow Land was, of course, a great plain, stretching from Hermon to the Yarmuk, two thousand feet above sea level. Towards the Jaulan and the Lejah it rose up in a series of terraces, ending in the land of frozen lava. In the plain itself were very fertile fields, where the corn grew in profusion, the grain being carried off on the backs of strings of camels or heaped up in " grain boats " when it got to the seashore at Acre or one of the coast cities.

The Romans never really occupied the Hauran. In 25 B.C. Trachonitis and the Hauran were under the nominal rule of Zenodorus, who had leased also part of the Iturian domains on the slopes of Hermon. As he did not restrain the bands of robbers that infested the place, but seemed rather to sin in that way himself, Augustus ordered him to be replaced by Herod, who was already master of Gadara and Hippos.

Herod built fortresses in the wild regions of Trachonitis and garrisoned them with Idumæan mercenaries; whatever his faults, and they were many, he was the pioneer of civilization in that region.

When he died this portion of his dominions went to the best of his sons, the Tetrarch Philip, who ruled till he died, when it was taken into the province of Syria, but in 37 A.D. Caligula gave it to Herod Agrippa, the grandson of Herod the Great, so that the Hauran has many associations with the Herodian dynasty.

The Nabatæans Again

The Nabatæans, meanwhile, were pushed down by the Romans south of the Hauran, though they still kept their cities of Basra and Salkhat, until, in 106, Cornelius Palma, the Governor of Syria, at last succeeded in bringing the whole Nabatæan kingdom into the Roman province. The Nabatæans of the Hauran held out even after Petra had fallen, but they had to give in finally.

It was after this date that the Romans began the fine series of public works that they always accomplished in the countries that they incorporated within the empire. Aqueducts and palaces, fortresses and baths, roads and bridges testified to the engineering powers and the enterprise of these remarkable people. The roads for the matter of that, were usually laid on the foundations of the old caravan routes or camel tracks, for in countries where valleys so often wound among hill-tops there was only one way to take; over the desert the Romans made their roads straight as a die, according to their usual plan.

Herod Agrippa was very much upset by people who, like the inhabitants of Edrei, the modern Der'aa, lived underground. That marvellous subterranean world, with its market places, its public squares and its houses and shops, had been excavated out of the rock for purposes of safety, for those were days when whole cities were sacked and pillaged in a day or a night and the place knew them no more. But Herod Agrippa thought that the time had come when public safety was protected, and he published an edict in 41 A.D. to the effect that the inhabitants of the Hauran ought to leave off their beast-like habits of living in caves and build themselves houses.

They certainly followed his advice, for many pre-Islamic houses are still inhabited by the Druzes to-day. A house described with some detail by M. de Vogüé, of which the remains are still standing, must have had a square court, with the house built round three sides. To right was a tower, very characteristic of the Hauran villages, with three stories and a porter's lodge on the ground floor. A large hall rose to the height of the two stories of which the house was composed, and there were bedrooms with an alcove for the bed, and dressing-rooms with recesses in which to put clothing. There was an outer staircase, offices and a stable for eleven horses with a manger. That was, of course, the house of a well-to-do Sheikh, but there were others more modest but comfortable and very stable.

The Nabatæans brought with them from Petra the worship of Dusares and that of Allat, the mother of the Gods; the temple of Si was dedicated to Ba'al Samin, as a Nabatæan inscription relates: "To the good memory of Malikat, the son of Ausou, the son of Mo'ayyirou, who have built in honour of Ba'al Semin the interior temple and the exterior temple of this and the towers... From the year 280 to the year 311 ... in peace."

This inscription is pieced together, and some of the words—for example, the towers—are not quite certainly exact, but the main point is there telling of those who built the temple. The inner and the outer appear to refer to the double naos, and the year, which is given in the calendar of the Seleucids, is 32 B.C.

As for Herod's life-size statue, for whatever cause it was introduced into a Nabatæan temple, whether in gratitude for benefits received or to flatter the enemy of their country, we cannot say; the Christians smashed it to atoms, and there is nothing left of it but one foot, still attached to the pedestal, and some undistinguishable fragments.

What happened to the Nabatæans after they were chased away from their houses of black basalt? Probably some of them became nomads and went eastward to the desert; they may be the ancestors of some Bedawin tribe of to-day. But many must have stayed to cultivate the land under new masters; and one can almost imagine that they drifted into the great cities of

The Nabatæans Again

the Decapolis, where they could carry on the trade that had always been a national asset. If their caravans were taken from them they might surely work in some shop or stationary camp where goods were received ; as to the field labourers, they were too useful to be discarded. The word Nabatæan came to signify field labourer.

The two principal cities of this vanished people were Bosra, the capital, and Salchad ; the importance of both of them shows clearly the wealth and position of their owners ; Bosra remained the capital after the Romans annexed the Hauran, and it became a very important Christian centre under the Byzantine empire. It is still one of the very interesting places of eastern Palestine, and has extensive ruins both of Roman and Byzantine periods. And it was there that an insignificant Arab made love to a rich widow, whom he married ; in the intervals of his courtship he studied this question of the Christian religion, so much of which was to be included in the new faith by means of which he was destined to move the world. Among all the many associations that cling to Bosra, from Old Testament times onwards, this one of Mohammed studying Christianity is the one that remains in the mind an emblem of the irony of Fate.

CHAPTER XXI
Jerash

CHAPTER XXI

JERASH

JERASH, the ancient Gerasa of the Decapolis, lies basking in the sunshine. It is early spring, yet it is quite hot; it is quite early in the morning, but the sun's rays have an appreciable amount of heat, with a promise of more to come. The sky is blue, the nearer hills have a blue haze over their spring green, the farther hills are a soft violet. Near by the Triumphal Gate, the Bab-Amman, the corn stands a foot high, the tender green contrasting with the wild flowers that are sprinkled about the ground, splashes of wild mustard, poppies, charlock and the wild acanthus that grows at the feet of columns bearing its glorified and decorative semblance on their capitals.

It is a very peaceful scene, the ruins stand among quiet country far from noisy towns; the Circassian village on the left bank of the river is too far from the heart of the old town to interfere with its noble peace. There is none of the bustle and clamour of Amman round the ruins of Philadelphia; Jerash is a dead city, or perhaps a sleeping city dreaming of the past. It is absorbed in the past with no thought of the present, because it has remained a fossilized Roman town, with no additions of a later age to disturb the harmony of the whole.

That is the charm of Jerash; it is an almost unique example of a Roman town—for Roman it undoubtedly is, although, in spirit, the citizens retained much of their original Greek character, a certain something of culture and point of view that outlasted for centuries the brief period of Greek power.

Jerash is situated in a basin surrounded by hills; through this basin of cultivated land a shallow valley runs in which a stream—the Chrysorrhoas, the Golden River of the Romans—rushes over the stones, finally emptying itself two thousand feet down into the Zerka. It is a lively stream, always full of water, which makes the site of Jerash an ideal one. Its banks show a mass of foliage, willow and oleander and poplar predominating, although there were fruit trees and, not far off, figs and olives.

One of the first impressions that you get as you stand by the Bab-Amman, is of the great extent of the field of ruins. The great gate with its triple arch, the mass of columns still standing within what were the city walls, much of which still remains—the ellipse of the forum, the upstanding columns of the great temple of Artemis and other principal features of the city, would be enough in themselves to interest the most greedy archæologist, but there, almost as far as eye can reach, are little groups of columns standing out on the hillside, lonely evidences of some past habitation. And the second impression will certainly be the quiet beauty of the setting. If you come from Petra, the contrast in colouring as well as in all the characteristics of the scene, will not fail to strike you ; Petra a rosy flame in a desert of rock, Jerash all golden stone set in green fields.

It is a good plan to get a snapshot view of the geography of Jerash before considering it in detail.

The Bab-Amman stands on the Roman road going south to Amman, at a short distance from the city walls ; to the left is a filled-in space where was once a naumachia for sham sea-fights and water pageants and beyond it was a circus. The south gate set in the wall of the city appears to have been rather like the outer gate, but very little of it remains. Inside the walls, a little to the left of the gate, the ruins of a peripteral temple stand on an artificial terrace on a sudden hillock ; the southern wall of the cella and some columns of the Corinthian order are still to be seen and are called by the Arabs the " Beit et-Tei." Near to this temple is the southern theatre. On the right is the graceful ellipse of

THE TRIUMPHAL GATE, JERASH

the forum, columns of the Ionic order with the entablature so much in place that it scarcely leaves room for regret that the oval is not complete.

The great street of columns begins to the north-east of the forum and continues for about half a mile ; two roads intersect this main street which are also colonnaded and which have each a tetrapylon at the crossing. Between these, nearer to the further street, stood the great propylæa of the temple of Artemis, which stood up on a terrace on rising ground, dominating the city. Remains of the cella and a fine group of columns of the Corinthian order that once adorned the portico are a striking feature of the general view. Near to the temple were various churches built of the old material ; one of these is a fine basilica of the Byzantine period.

The further colonnaded street was the street of the theatre ; to the left was the northern theatre, which seems to have been intended for gladiatoral shows and other performances dear to the heart of the Roman soldier ; to the right the road ran down to the river where there was once a bridge. On this road were some magnificent baths. The road which led to the temple was quite a short one ; it was continued down to the river passing the site of a later Byzantine church. The first cross-road, which is much the longest, ran from one of the eastern gates to a steep flight of steps that led down to another bridge over the river. Outside the gates, north and south, were sarcophagi ; one large mausoleum, that of Es-Samuri, has a fine portal and some columns of the Corinthian order. Outside the northern gate is the ruin of a basilica that was built on the site and with the materials, of the pagan sanctuary of Nemesis.

That, in a few words, is the skeleton of the town ; to give an idea of its beauty is luckily not necessary, as that is admirably given by the sketches. The street of columns is particularly impressive, as some seventy-five columns are still standing out of the great number differently estimated that formed the original street.

There are some remains of an inner line of columns and it has been suggested that the colonnade that was so typical of Greco-Roman towns was surmounted by an open arcade on a level with the first story of the houses. We know from Libanius how important these colonnades were; they were brought into fashion in Syria after the building of Antioch. As that amusing writer explains, in his account of the many attractions of the city by the sea, you need never stay indoors because of bad weather when you had an arcade under which to shelter yourself from rain and wind. It speedily became a necessity to the growingly luxurious Greco-Syrians and, no doubt, also to the Romans.

In this bird's-eye view of Gerasa, there seems no great space where a Roman legion could have been accommodated; there seems no site where a fort could have stood in Crusading days. Was the legion in camp outside the walls? As to the fort, we have it on the authority of the Arab geographer Yakut, although he never visited Jerash in the course of his wanderings. He says that in the twelfth century the King of Damascus built a strong fort here, and that in 1122 Baldwin II took it and rased it to the ground. Now Yakut was born about 1179, so that he might have talked to older men who had been alive at the time and on whose testimony he might have relied, but it seems as if his informant had made a mistake of the place. Yakut spent some years in Hama as a slave before he was freed; he was established in Baghdad later and he died in Aleppo in 1229. It is certain that the Crusaders never tried to keep the place as no remains of that period are to be found. Yakut, as early as the latter part of the twelfth century, speaks of Jerash as being completely deserted.

After admiring the extensive view from the Triple Gate, and after taking in the sun-steeped golden hue of the limestone that furnished material for nearly all the buildings here, the gate itself claims attention.

It stood apparently without any connection with an

outer wall; it was just a triumphal gate through which people had to pass on their way to Gerasa. The suggested date is that of the arch of Trajan at Rome to which it bears some likeness, but some of the details seem to be against this theory.

The gate is built of the limestone from the neighbouring mountains; it consists of a central arch with lesser openings on either side over which are square spaces evidently intended for sculptured decorations or busts. The central arch is supported by engaged pillars with capitals of the Corinthian order, but the most interesting feature of the whole building is the calyx of boldly sculptured acanthus leaves from which the shaft of the columns rise that stand on either side of these. The only column with a base ornamented in this fashion that I can recall at the moment is one that is spoken of in Anderson and Spiers' "Architecture of Greece and Rome." Concerning the cotive column that was found at Delphi, the authors write: "In the acanthus column found at Delphi and dating from the same period, viz., the last quarter of the fifth century B.C., the lower part of the shaft rises from a calyx of three acanthus leaves, and from the upper portion of the shaft spring three other acanthus leaves which support caryatid figures carrying a tripod. The great projection of these acanthus leaves, and the vigour shown in the carving, testify that as a decorative feature the foliage of this plant must have been adopted from a very early period."

I cannot now remember, and cannot find it mentioned in books concerning Jerash, if there were found the capitals belonging to these columns. It might be possible that they, too, supported figures, which would have increased the importance of the processional entrance to the city. At any rate, these pillars are interesting on account of these unusual bases.

Seen from the other side, the arches of the side entrances, which have fallen on the exterior, are shown; that on the right having a double arch, but the whole interior is heaped up with stones and bits of fallen masonry, which spoils the view of the gate as a whole.

By the time that the gate has been examined and the general view taken in, the sun is high in the heavens and beats down on the stone until the heat is like that of summer. It is good dry heat and not at all overpowering, but it is quite hot enough to make you feel inclined to take things in a leisurely manner. A stroll down to the poor remains of the south gate is the first effort to make; I say effort because walking is not easy in Jerash, that is to say it is rather tiring. Picking your way over stones, climbing up and down banks, you are either on very rough ground or on bare rock; if you want to see anything at all, you are bound to have something of a scramble.

The oval space that was once enclosed by columns of the Ionic order, is supposed, and with some degree of assurance, to have been the forum. If it were, it must have resembled the Greek agora, which was often simpler than the Roman forum became with its temples and public buildings and statues. This forum might well have been an open place surrounded by columns, as they always were, perhaps with the shops under arcades that developed as commerce itself developed. The middle space would certainly have served as an exercising ground for horses, which was utilized in this way in some more primitive market places. But the authors just quoted merely say:—

"The main street of Gerasa was 1,800 feet long, of which one portion, about 1,300 feet, had a range of columns of the Corinthian order twenty-five feet high on each side, and the remaining portion, columns of the Ionic order, twenty feet high. This latter terminated in an immense circular piazza, apparently to change the line of axis to an important temple beyond."

The temple in question is, of course, the exquisite "Beit et-Tei" and the colonnaded oval space—for it is not circular—may just have been a great piazza, though

STREET OF COLUMNS, JERASH

Jerash

it seems curiously placed, just within the walls. This would, on the other hand, have been a very convenient position for the farmers and husbandmen to bring in their flocks and the produce of their fields, especially as, in a Roman city, wheeled traffic, and indeed any other traffic but that of the ruling class, was forbidden during the daytime and only allowed at night. That is one of the points that Libanius makes when relating the perfections of Antioch—the perfect quiet of the day when nothing was allowed in the streets but the litters of the great or an occasional chariot. By night, he admitted, heavy traffic was allowed, but as the happy citizens of that pleasure-loving city were accustomed to turn night into day, that did not signify. It was evidently not considered a grievance by anyone.

As it stands, the forum, or whatever it may be, of Jerash is one of the most picturesque subjects for the artist's pencil. The curve of the entablature that connects the columns makes a fine sky line, through the spaces between the columns the broken groups of the opposite side of the semi-circle are seen and the ground is covered with grass and wild flowers. All about, dotted among the slopes of the near hills, columns appear, singly or two together ; right ahead the imposing group of the columns of the portico of the temple of Artemis rises up against a pure sky.

There is too much to be seen in Jerash, too many fragments attract the attention, besides those important buildings that must be studied. In the street of columns alone you may pass days and yet leave much unseen. The columns in the middle of the town are the finest and are all of the Corinthian order, which, indeed, is the prevailing order here as it usually was when the Romans built. It suited their taste for the ornate and the magnificent, far better than the austere Doric and the simple Ionian. The drums of these fine columns are often shaken by earthquakes ; they are always plain and never once fluted. The capitals were of the Roman development of the Greek acanthus, but were probably executed by Greek artists, as was usually the case in Syria. Almost every base of the columns that once lined the main street is in place and enough of the columns are standing to give a very good idea of what it must have looked like when the town was occupied. Much of the Roman pavement is still in place, but it is covered up in the rubbish and the broken stone that cumber the ground. At the tetrapylon the bases are in place but the columns and the statues that stood on them are gone. Those erections at the crossing of the street added greatly to the general effect. Whatever was done in a Greco-Roman city was done with a view to the vista and the composition; the cramped and casual arrangement of modern towns would have offended the Greek sense of the æsthetic order of a well-arranged mass of buildings.

The propylæa of the temple of Artemis is unfortunately in a very ruined condition. The architrave of the great portal has fallen but there are two window niches with richly decorated pediments. On the west side are some well-preserved sculptures.

Jerash has been said to be second only to Palmyra in size and importance and second only to Baalbek in beauty of architecture. It is well worth a visit and will repay any trouble taken to make the necessary arrangements for a stay of, at any rate, some days.

CHAPTER XXII
THE STORY OF GERASA

CHAPTER XXII

THE STORY OF GERASA

GERASA, which saw its rise and fall within four centuries, is said to be almost without a history. To that apex of happiness, however, it can hardly aspire. The " almost " perhaps meets the case, considering the far more thrilling histories of other towns, but enough is there to make it worth while to endeavour to place that story in the setting of the complicated history of those four centuries.

Another assertion that is frequently made, appears rather arbitrary, namely, that Gerasa was built on a fresh site. It is very unlikely that such an excellent site, by running water, a site of all others to attract people living in a waterless land, should have remained unoccupied; there are various theories concerning a former city here, but as there are no remains of pre-Roman buildings it is a question that need not detain us.

Reland, after pointing out various mistakes that have been made, such as confusing Gerasa with Gadara, mentions that the Arabs called it Galaad and describes its origin as a Grecian city to the " old men who made war under Alexander and who, being unable to follow his camps longer, settled here." That is, of course, the usual story. The veterans founded here a city that was to be a Greek city-state, like those that were planted all over the country by that nation of colonists. It was ruled by Greek laws, and the gods worshipped there were exclusively Greek. Even Dusares-Bacchus and Allat-Athene do not appear to have been admitted and, what is more strange, the Roman hierarchy was also excluded.

When Gerasa was built there were already various

Greek towns in the neighbourhood; the city of Gadara lay off the central of the three roads that led from the Jordan to the desert and Damascus, Pella being on the south and Hippos on the north or Damascus road. Their territories touched, and they commanded the tableland east of Jordan. From Pella a road went southeast over the hills of Gilead, which has been traced out by means of the Roman milestones discovered from time to time. Eusebius calls this road, on which were situated Dion, Gerasa and Philadelphia, the Onomasticon.

From the first, therefore, Gerasa, which was not one of the first to come, was in communication with other cities with which there was even then some league of defence. Each of these cities had suburbs and lands round that owned their suzerainty; each was built on the usual scheme of a great colonnaded street with others, not so important, crossing it at intervals; each had great public buildings, temples, forums, theatres and private houses, with the baths that were indispensable to the Romans. For a time Greece and Rome gave civilization to the country that had already received the same boon from so many different sources.

At first Rome was a great benefactress. Roads were made, those fine paved roads with boundaries and milestones on which you come sometimes without realizing it, except for a sudden hard metallic sound under your horse's hooves; aqueducts brought water from a distance, brooks were spanned by bridges, towns sprang up, complete and beautiful, from the smoking ashes of those that were destroyed. And with it all, there was a largeness of view as long as the religious sentiments and the laws and customs of the conquered people were concerned; where the shoe pinched was in the exactions of a nation that was always wanting money to carry out schemes of conquest and expansion, and that had to maintain huge armies of mercenaries in so many countries. Sometimes these exactions took the form of

AT THE CROSS ROADS, JERASH

making some kinglet pay the whole cost of the warfare in which he had been worsted; we have seen how the Herods bought the friendship of Rome with hard cash.

The first that is heard of Gerasa in history is the capture and sack of the town by Alexander Jannæus. Alexander was, of course, only following the fashion of the day when he changed his Hebraic name for a Greco-Roman one, but it really gives one rather a shock when his family history is remembered. His great-grandfather was that fine old fighter Matathias, the priest, who with his five sons engineered a Jewish rising for independence when the tyranny of Antiochus IV became intolerable. Judas Maccabæus the Hammer, or the Hammerer, turned out such a good soldier and able organizer that, by 166 B.C. the Jews had recovered from the taking of Jerusalem by Antiochus and his consequent exactions; the King then made an attempt to weaken the power of the new party, and indeed set out with the purpose of extirpating the race and putting a new one in its place. But the war ended in a compromise, and a period began when the Jews had peace and prosperity under first Judas, then Simon, who was proclaimed Ethnark and High Priest, and practically ruler, after the rest of the family had been murdered according to the practice of the day. Simon himself suffered the same fate, but his son, John Hyrcanus, fled to Jerusalem, where he took up the office of High Priest and ruler. We do not know why he called himself Hyrcanus, any more than we know why his sons were known as Aristobolus, Antigonus and Alexander. The only explanation is that the Jews, like the Syrians, were Hellenised to such a degree that they changed their names; the women did the same, changing a family name like Salome to Alexandra. In the family of the anti-Greek and patriotically Jewish family of the Maccabees, it is hardly to be expected.

The Hasmonian family were always at war with

each other, brother against brother; they turned a time of prosperity, inaugurated by their forebears, into one of disaster, which ended in the Roman dominion. Simon, who founded the dynasty, and John Hyrcanus, who ruled well for many years, were the last of the great figures that made the race remarkable; after them degeneration set in, and Alexander was the most degenerate of his family. He was hated alike by Jews and Gentiles; his cruelty was so terrible that many of his acts could not be surpassed by those of Nero.

Antiochus VII, who succeeded his brother Demetrius, who had given great privileges to the Jews, ratified them all when he wanted their goodwill, and went back on his promises when he found that he could do without them, with the result that the wars all began again. The wars of the Maccabees could be understood after the capture of Jerusalem by Antiochus IV, and his behaviour on that occasion; but there seemed no adequate reason for the endless fighting that went on in the reign of Alexander Jannæus. The capture and sack of Gerasa are said to have been undertaken as an act of revenge, but Josephus expressly says that it was owing to the fact that Theodorus, son of Zeno, the tyrant of Philadelphia, had put his treasure there. This brings us into touch with Philadelphia again, which was then a Greek city of the Decapolis, ruled over by a Greek, or by a Syrian with a Greek name; most likely the former. It does not appear why Theodorus placed his treasure in Gerasa, but a good deal of fighting had been going on around Philadelphia, and perhaps he thought it farther from the great highway between Egypt and Syria.

Alexander took Pella, and then he built a triple wall round Gerasa and took the place by force. We can only imagine that he made off with the treasure, but he did not long enjoy it, because death came to him soon after; he had reigned twenty-seven years. His widow, Alexandra, reigned after him, and proved a much better ruler than he had been; her two sons, another Aristobulus and another Hycranus, carried on the family feud.

The Hasmonian princes took away the rights of the Greek cities, and exacted tribute from them; they were also exposed to the inroads of the desert Arabs, and the years that followed were difficult. Then came another catastrophe for Gerasa. Vespasian, having taken Jerusalem, sent a large force of cavalry and infantry over Jordan to Gerasa, under Lucius Annius, who took the city at the first onslaught. It was a foregone conclusion, as the fortifications were much weakened after the assault by Alexander, and the garrison appears to have fled at the approach of the Romans, as we learn that Annius put to the sword all those who had not escaped. The Roman commander allowed his soldiers to loot the town, and he took all the non-combatants prisoners. He then burnt the place down. So perished the Greek city of which no vestige remains.

The demolition seems to have been complete, yet, within half a century, Gerasa had arisen again from her ashes; the Romans who had destroyed her built a new city, and a season of great prosperity arose. With the privileges restored by Pompey, the League of the Decapolis began its civic life in earnest. It became one of the favourite colonies of the Romans, it was under Roman rule far longer than it had ever been under the Greek, yet the older character remained and the language spoken was Greek, as is that of the inscriptions found. In what way did the Romans modify the life that they lived in common with the Greeks and Syrians? One thing is pretty certain, and that is the amusements provided. The theatre is on the improved Roman model, and there is one evidently devoted to gladiatorial shows. Bilingual edicts began to be published as time went on and other signs of a hybrid civilization slowly appeared. Excessive taxation was the greatest burden that the Gerasenes had to bear; as it ensured them from the attacks of weaker powers, and a period of comparative tranquillity set in, it was not money thrown away, whatever may have been thought at the time by those who suffered.

Gerasa was not one of the towns that were, quite arbitrarily and without a scrap of right, given to Herod; neither was it handed over by Mark Antony to Cleopatra, that remarkable personality that lit up the dying embers of the Macedonian dynasty of Egypt.

It remained a city of importance and one in which, though not so much of a metropolis as Antioch, the learning and the luxury of the age made an agreeable place in which to pass the time. Up and down those colonnaded streets the provincial Greco-Syrians must have walked, discussing the news of the day; Romans, fresh from the Eternal City, or, half orientalized, coming from Byzantium, mingled with the original population of Macedonian Greeks. Intermarriages were frequent, and the type of both Roman and Greek became very much modified and, in time, degraded. The old warlike spirit died out, and the army of Syria became a shadow of the Roman legions that had done such doughty deeds when they had first carried their standards over Jordan.

At Bosra, then a great Greek centre, where a legion was always quartered, there were circuses and theatres erected largely in the interest of the troops, for whose amusement gladiatorial shows and performances by travelling mimes were given. Although it was not usual to make the Decapolis cities garrison towns for the Romans, it being the custom merely to make their own garrison into a reserve to be called out if necessary, both Ammianus Marcellus, in 353 A.D., and later, Eusebius, speak of the 3rd Cyrennian legion as being quartered at Gerasa. As the Roman camps had their altars where the troops from different parts of the world could worship, as well as the perfunctory worship of the Emperor and the Standard, it is difficult to imagine one within the walls of a city where the gods were more exclusive than the mortals.

However that may have been, no doubt the legionaries did come here, and must have enjoyed the contests in the northern theatre, perhaps preferring them to the tragedies that, from time to time, were performed in the southern theatre. Both of these theatres were quite Roman and up to date; racers and boxers were in great request, while chariot races excited much interest. Musicians, troops of mimes, dancing girls who played on the flute, and jesters of all sorts contrived to brighten life in Gerasa.

And then there were the shops along the arcaded streets, where anyone could while away an hour or so, or perhaps there would be an assembly up on the terrace in the temple enclosure, where, maybe, the markets were held instead of in the oval space we call the forum.

It was a life full of interest, yet one that made little real progress. The very rich were luxurious and idle, the poor were slaves. Yet the temperament of the Greco-Syrian population was lively and happy, and there was much intelligence among the cultivated classes.

As the years went on a great change came with the adoption of Christianity; it was gradual at first, and for a long time the pagan spirit predominated, but it had to yield in the end.

The early Christian period was one of great prosperity for Gerasa, which became the seat of a bishopric. In everything it is the same; one civilization overlapping another, one nation conquering and mingling with another; and now the religion of Christ gradually taking the place of paganism after Constantine the Great declared himself a Christian. Byzantium was still thronged with Greeks, and they were the same eager argumentative people that they were of old; they argued about the mysteries of the new religion until various sects arose and heresies were rife. It was to settle the question of the nature of Christ that the famous Council of Chalcedon was called to assemble in the city opposite Byzantium on the shores of the Bosphorus. Bishops came from all over Syria to discuss this important point of doctrine which they finally declared to be that there were in Christ two natures that could not be intermixed, but were not in entire separation, thus avoiding the heresies of both the Nestorians and the Monophysites.

Gerasa sent a bishop to this conference; we can imagine him setting forth in state from the great white pagan city with its newly added basilicas, to accomplish this long journey; also we learn from Reland that a bishop went from Madeba to represent his see, which was a very illustrious one. The number of bishops present was six hundred, and no doubt they visited Byzantium and were received by the Emperor Marcian, who had ordered the assembly to take place.

The Roman empire fell in the West long before it succumbed to the attacks of the Turks in the fifteenth century in the East. But the Eastern empire was not strong enough to protect the cities of the Decapolis, which fell, one after another, as the hordes of savages ravaged the country. The Moslem Arabs destroyed much, the horrible Mongols passed, like a plague of locusts, over the land, and the once populous region occupied by the linked properties of the Greek cities became a desert.

Gerasa, the modern Jerash, lay uncared for and deserted for a thousand years and more, before a new population was settled on the right bank of the river, among some of the ruins but away from the most important. These were the Circassians, flying, as those who made Amman their home, from troubles in their own country. They were posted there by the Turks to act as a barrier to prevent the Bedawins from raiding the neighbourhood, and for that reason, and also because it is never a popular move to introduce a new element into an old country, the first coming was not all joy to the settlers. They had to be armed against tribes who had found the ruins of Jerash a convenient place for their camps when on the march, or for flocks moving from one pasture to another. Little by little, the Circassians arranged their lives in this new setting, for which only their fervent Mohammedanism fitted them. There would have been no harm done had they not found in the ruins a convenient quarry from which to take stone to build their houses. They blew up some of the standing buildings with gunpowder, according to report; they certainly took much from the ruins, as anyone can see who takes the trouble to inspect their houses. Luckily there is now no further pilfering, as the ruins are protected, but the mischief is done.

Before the Circassians settled on the right bank of the river the scene must have been much wilder, and the dangers run by early explorers were not imaginary. As usual, the Arabs were convinced that, somewhere hidden among the refuse of fallen stone, was a buried treasure. It was protected in this instance by a peculiarly awesome bird. The late J. S. Buckingham, who visited Jerash in 1916, was incautious enough to take a moonlight walk after wickedly writing his name in the inner wall of the thermæ, where he was camping that night. The Arabs were sure that he had marked the place because he had discovered that hidden treasure, and they further imagined that he had gone out to make incantations before digging it up.

Most authors dwell on the many difficulties that met them at every turn, cutting short their visits and interrupting their studies. The authors of " Travels in Syria " were particularly unfortunate. They spent their time and their money in bribing the Bedawin tribes to take them to the places of interest that they wanted to visit. After just missing Lady Hester Stanhope, who was away from the deserted convent which she usually inhabited, they came to Jerash, but failed to get an escort to go on to Amman and Petra. At last they got some of the Beni Sakhr tribe to come, and the description of the arrival of some mounted men, headed by a " young prince," who fired pistols as they galloped downhill, is quite romantic. They evidently meant to overawe the travellers, but the only comment made by them is: " They made a curious and interesting appearance."

In contrast to all the unpleasant adventures experienced by pioneer travellers in this region, we are now guarded by the local police and by the ever-helpful Arab Legion, so that we may say that after all the advance of civilization has done something to secure for us the peaceful enjoyment of the monuments of the past.

CHAPTER XXIII
THE TEMPLE OF ARTEMIS

CHAPTER XXIII

The Temple of Artemis

THERE is no more charming place to wander about in than Jerash. Sitting up on the terrace upon which the temple stood, you can look up at a column that has lost its architrave and the stone acanthus leaves of the capital stand out boldly against the blue sky. At your feet, among the usual litter of fallen masonry, the humble wild plant of the acanthus shows what art can fashion out of the suggestion of Nature. You can look down over the field of ruins, noting the many columns that stand as sentinels marking out a road that once must have been gay with the colours of the Orientals' draperies and imposing with the toga of a Roman or the glint of the helmet of one of the legionaries. There is no discordant note.

The temple itself is worth careful study, and much might be written about it by those who have the technical knowledge. As a wanderer intent rather on the impression of the moment, as it is inspired by the passing scene, and without that inner knowledge which alone makes a treatise on architecture worth reading, I must deal lightly with the details. It is enough to note that all Syrian temples were built on large terraced enclosures —this one is said to be five hundred and twenty-seven feet long by three hundred and forty-four feet wide. That gives one an idea of space. The temple is built on a podium eight feet high ; the great portal was once approached by a flight of steps that have since disappeared. It was erected in the early part of the second century A.D., and is consequently rather earlier than the street of columns.

The temple of Artemis, which used to be called the Temple of the Sun, was a peripteral temple of great size and splendour. All that now remains is a part of the cella, which has a chamber at the end which was probably the sanctuary, and niches in the walls where statues must have stood. The remaining columns of the portico, of which there are eleven, make a group that is the most arresting feature of the whole of the field of ruins; they are of the Corinthian order.

Looking down from this terrace in the days that are past, the view must have been very effective, for the Greeks and the Greco-Romans after them made a point of attending to the composition of a town as a whole, and were specially anxious to beautify the vistas. Their work as architects was as different to that of the modern planners of cities as the art of the landscape gardener is to the careless planting out of the uneducated amateur.

From this point of vantage the old inhabitant of Gerasa looked down a noble flight of steps to the richly decorated propylæa and on to a road or small piazza which bordered the river. Looking up from the river, the temple with its portico, in which were two hundred and sixty columns of golden sun-soaked stone, closed the vista superbly. The two cross-roads were both colonnaded, and at their intersection they had one a tetrapylon and the other a tetrakionion. The former had four columns on high bases surmounted by statues, the latter a domed roof springing from four columns. The vista in each case, when looking up or down the street, was carefully thought out.

The temple was supposed to be dedicated to the sun because of an inscription that was found in the propylæa, but there seems no doubt that the right attribution is that of Artemis. "Artemis of the Gerasenes" was as much a phrase in common use as "the good fortune of the Philadelphians" was, as applied to Herakles and Pallas in Philadelphia. Pella worshipped Pallas, Gadara Zeus; each city had a civic patron among the gods.

The cities that could build so lavishly were presumably rich, owing not only to any property that they might

THE PORTICO OF THE TEMPLE OF ARTEMIS, JERASH

own around, but also principally to the money made by means of commerce. If Gerasa stood on a road that led to Philadelphia and the south on one hand and to the Jordan on the other, that was only the beginning of the long route that led to India and Egypt and China, or to the Mediterranean Sea that carried merchandise all round its shores. Besides passing on the produce of other nations, Syria had many industries of her own. Glass-making, silk-weaving, purple dyeing, besides all those products like balm, spices, corn, oil, were a source of income to the Gerasenes and the inhabitants of other cities; the Romans got taxes out of the profits, and some of the public buildings were paid for out of this source of revenue.

There are two statements made in an article in the " Town Planning Review " that are interesting to note here. Speaking of the forum and the Greek agora which suggested it to the Romans, the writer says: " The areas that really corresponded to the vast enclosed market places of Hellenic towns are the great colonnaded courts of the Syrian temples, such as Jerash." So that we may be sitting where the crowds collected to buy and sell, to gossip and to glean the news, over a thousand years ago.

The other statement is concerned with the loss of importance of the agora in these towns; but it is suggested that the Syrian towns were not without public places, as their colonnaded streets sometimes ended in expanding " as at Jerash, into a piazza." We may be content to leave the question of the forum, about which authorities differ, unsolved.

There are many questions that suggest themselves in this sanctuary of Artemis; why was the Greek tradition so strong? Was it because the scattered colonies were really linked up with Greece by stronger ties than they ever were with Rome, in spite of the long period of the Roman dominion? Rome ruled, and her customs were imitated, but the heart of the people was

Greek. All their sympathies seem to have been rooted in Greece, and they looked to Byzantium for inspiration far sooner than to Rome.

Looking down on the ruins of the Byzantine church the pagan world gives way to the dawn of Christianity, and one can but remember a very famous son of the Decapolis, who may have come here in the course of his wanderings.

St. Joannes Chrysostomus, the most famous of the Greek fathers, was born at Antioch on the Orontes, of a noble family, about 345 A.D. He was a pupil of Libanius, the great pagan teacher, who moulded the minds of many clever men in those times. Libanius says that his promising pupil's mother snatched him away from his studies in order to convert him to her own faith, which she succeeded in doing. Joannes was baptized by Bishop Meletius of Antioch, and went, like the greatest of the teachers, into the desert, where he stayed for ten years. He was thirty-four when he returned to his native city, where he became famous as a preacher and where he rose by degrees to the position of Archbishop of Constantinople. He was always ascetic and was always thundering from his pulpit against the vice of the day; he declared against luxuries, much as Savonarola did, centuries afterwards, in Florence. For this reason he became a marked man and had many enemies, especially in Constantinople, where he preached publicly against the great ones, even including the Empress. He said that the men spent too much in eating and drinking at their perpetual feasts and that the women spent too much on dress, for which they would certainly be eternally punished. The ladies, however, only smiled and said that they had never heard of a woman being so punished for a little thing like that, and they continued to paint their faces and clothe themselves in tissue of gold until the bishop said that they could hardly be distinguished from the courtezans.

In his writings we get a glimpse of the life of the

gay world on the shores of the Bosphorus, for he describes the semi-circular tables covered with costly cloths, the great golden flagons that the servants, who were always young and handsome, took from the storerooms, the dresses of the guests. He resents the jewellery worn by the women, and says that there is nothing a woman will not do for a fine pair of ear-rings. No wonder that, in spite of an immense and devoted following, he was exiled, though he was soon afterwards brought back because of the anger of his adherents. He continued to preach against lax morals, especially divorce, and was a supporter of women's rights, influenced perhaps by love of his talented and pious mother, to whom he was devoted. He loved the poor and hated, not riches, but the bad use of them that so many made; he finally offended the Court to such a degree that he was exiled, and this time it was for ever. During his captivity Joannes Chrysostomus died, helped, so report ran, by the guards, who were given orders from headquarters to the effect that the inconvenient apostle of purity and asceticism was not to return alive.

Up here, in the portico of the temple of Artemis, the mind reverts to the strange revival of paganism that must have lit up once more the fires on the altars of the old gods. Julian the Apostate! What an inconceivable figure he makes trying to push back a force that was already too strong for any such puny effort. Yet, when one tries to understand the circumstances, to realize the environment of a weak youth, enamoured of beauty, influenced by clever and brilliant men who perverted his judgment, it is not hard to realize the temptation that beset him.

As a boy Julian was a scholar, drinking in all the beautiful old heroic stories of Greek legend and the religion of nature worship that was, after all, at the root of their belief. He was flattered by stronger-minded pagan teachers, repulsed by the asceticism of much of the early Christianity, and no doubt he believed that he would be doing a service to the world by harking back to the old dead gods of Hellas. He failed, mercifully, and the short-lived resurrection of Hellenistic ritual died down again; yet looking at the pagan ideals dispassionately one can but acknowledge that there was a great deal that was good in them, much that was even comprehensible.

The Macedonian Greeks brought with them from their native land the special worship of Dionysus, that has been described by the late Walter Pater in his " Greek Studies " as the worship of people who had lived among vines, but a worship that became a cycle that covered the whole of life.

It is easy enough to think of bacchanals in a fine frenzy, under the influence of the god, chanting their frenzied choral songs with their faces stained with the lees of the wine, but that was the lesser and ignoble development—one of the main features of the personality of Dionysus was that he had something of everything; he represented life, like the sap in the stem of the vine, he was akin to all growing things. He was dual in his nature, as representing summer and winter; in winter he was the mad, wild creature, the werwolf—he wanted the blood of human sacrifice; in spring he became the gentle and beautiful god that showed the other side of his nature.

Dionysus was twice born : child of Zeus, the open sky, and a mortal mother, he was born of the lightning and the dew; his cup of wine was symbolic, like the sacramental cup. In his circle he completed the whole of life. He was the soul of the vine, and so of life and growth; from him descended the three sisters who could turn all to corn, oil and wine.

The worship of Dionysus was originally a sort of free worship, and he is connected with all the nature spirits, with the sun and the water, with the nymphs that inhabited the silver poplars, with the satyrs even, half-human, half-animal, and with Pan who cuts his pipe among the reeds that grow in the domain of the god. And so he reigns over music, even as Apollo did, by virtue of the pipes of Pan. Pan, followed by the little goat-footed children, always ends up the procession made in honour of Bacchus.

"He comes at last," we read in the "Greek Studies." "To have a soul equal to that of Demeter, a realm as wide and mysterious as hers; the whole productive power of the earth is in him and the explanation of its annual changes. As some embody their intentions of that power in corn, so others in wine. He is the dispenser of the earth's hidden wealth, giver of riches through the wine as Demeter through grain."

It is easy to see here how this cult of Dionysus fitted in with that Dusares, who was also, in a lesser degree, a nature god, and whose first shrine was always by running water. Dionysus transformed the water into wine.

"He is the soul of the individual vine first, and afterwards the soul of the whole species, the spirit of fire and dew, alive and leaping in a thousand vines; as the higher intelligence, brooding more deeply over things, pursues, in thought, the generation of sweetness and strength in the veins of the tree, the transformation of water into wine, little by little; noting all the influences upon it of the heavens above and the earth beneath and shadowing forth, in each pause of the process, an intervening person. What is to us but the chemistry of nature being to them the mediation of living spirits. So they passed on to think of Dionysus (naming him at last from the brightness of the sky and the moisture of the earth) not merely as the soul of the vine, but of all that life in flowing things of which the vine is the symbol, because the most emphatic example."

The Ba'al worship of the Moabites was partly a nature worship too, as the many shrines in some oases in the desert testify; but it was a religion that demanded victims far more imperiously than did the Greeks; their

Molochs and Ba'als were cruel, inhuman monsters. The Nabatæan Dusares may have been some form of Ba'al, and victims were sacrificed at his shrine, but in some ways the cult of Dusares was higher and purer than other Asiatic cults, and he was certainly worshipped as a supreme god, not as one of a hierarchy.

Perhaps the simple peasants who continued to till the soil, and were often slaves of the Greek colonists, felt near the religion that came from the forces of nature amongst which they lived. There was something for everyone—gods of war, of love, of abundance, of health; a little lyric translated by Sir Rennel Rodd, from the Greek Anthology, must find a place here on the steps of the great temple that must have been so magnificent in its day, because it shows the other side of the Greek religion: the side that would appeal to a field labourer, just as the religion of Dionysus appealed to the labourers in the vineyard. It is by Perses, written in the 4th century B.C.

A Rustic Shrine.

I am the God of the little things,
  In whom you will surely find,
If you call upon me in season,
  A little god who is kind;
You must not ask me great things,
  But what is in my control,
I, Tychon, God of the humble,
  May grant to a simple soul.

CHAPTER XXIV
The Theatre

CHAPTER XXIV
THE THEATRE

I Thespis am, dramatic song who fram'd
And new delights to village folk proclaim'd
When Bacchus brought the triple choir whose prize
A goat or crate of Attic figs supplies.
New heads new changes make, many and fine
The marvels in Time's womb—but these were mine!
Thespis was its inventor. What he spoke,
In wild wood revel and in rustic joke,
Did Æschylus exalt. Not smooth nor fine
But like a winter torrent, his strong line
Renew'd the theatre. O matchless tongue!
From ancient demi-gods which doubtless sprang.
               " DIOSCORIDES."
   (*Translated by Major R. Guthrie MacGregor.*)

THE remains of the theatres in Jerash have been so minutely described by those writing with authority that it seems useless to repeat what has been told already with so much detail.

Let us then briefly turn up the few facts concerning them that will enable us to get as clear an idea as may be of the performances that used to take place there during the first few centuries of our era.

These theatres are excavated out of the sides of the hills on the old Greek plan which the Romans are said to have adopted in Syria because it minimized expense and labour. It is, however, likely that the original Greek cities had them already, as no Hellenic city was complete without one or more theatres; they were part of the national life and were connected with the older worship of Dionysus. We have no records of what took place before Pompey restored the rights of the cities in 63 B.C.; their civic life began then, and their greatest season of prosperity came after that date. The Macedonians, who had founded Jerash after 333 B.C.

had no national tragic drama of their own; we know that because when Euripides went into exile there towards the end of his life, he reverted to the older form of choral drama, writing for the chorus rather than for the soloists. "'The Bacchæ,' one of his latest plays," writes Professor Gilbert Murray in his "Literature of Ancient Greece," "has a large choral element, and no monodies. Why? Because when Euripides wrote he had migrated to Macedonia and apparently had not taken his operatic actors with him. Macedonia has no drama; but it had living dithyramb with professional performers, and it was they who sang in 'The Bacchæ.'

"This upward movement of the satyr song," (he is referring to the development of the Attic drama), "was due to various causes—to the spiritual crises that ennobled the Athenian people; to the need for some new form of art to replace the dying epos as a vehicle for the heroic Saga; to the demand made by Dionysus—worship for that intensity of emotion which is almost of necessity tragic. The expropriated satyrs were consigned, with their quaint old-world buffoonery, to a private corner at the end of the three tragedies, and the comic element was left to develop itself in a separate form of art."

It is with this comic element that we have to take stock, because it is evident that, although, no doubt, the great old tragedies of the golden age of Greek literature were performed still at the great festivals, the standard was lower than it had been in old days. The audience was not so brilliant as it used to be in Athens, though it was appreciative and clever enough in its own way. The dark tragedies of Æschylus, intent on showing the effect that some awful catastrophe, some overwhelming fate, had on weak human beings, the deep character study and the development of will power shown by Sophocles, which was even more realistically brought forth by Euripides, were no longer part of the very life of the people. Hundreds of years had passed since they

COLUMNS OF THE IONIC ORDER IN THE FORUM, JERASH

had, in successive years, held Athenian audiences spellbound, and the world had changed, the audience was of mixed race in spite of Hellenic sympathies. It is therefore more than likely that the Gerasenes, like other people of that era, took more interest in comedy.

Comedy appears to have had its origin in a different way, but from much the same source as tragedy. Thespis, who belonged to the village of Icaria, was a Dorian, as Æschylus was, who was born in Eleusis, the City of Mysteries; accustomed to the choral chantings in honour of Dionysus and to the strange mimic rites of the Mysteries, he evolved the idea of tragedy. It was he who made the leader of the chorus carry on a dialogue with the rest of the body, he taking the part of leader himself. From this beginning the whole vast fabric of tragedy arose, as is well known; we must, however, part with one illusion that I confess to have cherished. Thespis never went round the villages with a travelling company of mimes; he was a poet and an actor, and a person of far too great importance to cater for rustics. Æschylus, as we may remember, was accused of revealing the Eleusynian Mysteries, and went, perhaps for that very reason, into exile in Sicily; he, too, was influenced by the Dionysus worship, which had such a strong hold on the early theatre. Euripides ended his life in exile in Macedonia, also a vine country, where the same rites were observed, and there he wrote his last great work, the astounding " Bacchæ," in which we see the awful effects of the disbelief of Pentheus, who attempts to put down the worship of the god who is here represented as a beautiful wild thing, luring the women up into the mountains to perform mad orgies. It is the mad side of the worship, drunken with the wine from the cup that once was sacramental.

Comedy came from the worship of Bacchus, but in a humble manner. At the country festivals in his honour, when the potters had their fair, and the country people assembled at the time of the bottling of the wine, the usual dances and processions and songs were performed, but they were of a homely character. The mimes that performed later to whom unlimited licence of free speech was given, were born of these village jollifications, mingled, as in the Middle Ages, with religious rites. The early comedies were "monstrously indecent," women and boys were excluded, ribaldry ran riot, extemporary chaff which might be considered libellous in these days, was flung at great and small alike. But the Old Comedy, when it came to be written and learned by heart, instead of trusting to the inspiration of the moment, had the salt of wit as well as the inherited coarseness of the original mummers. Then came the Middle Comedy, that is said to lack the wit of the Old and the polish of the later development, but which had its great moment; the New Comedy began its career after the death of Alexander the Great, and consequently just before the period, about which we know anything, began for Jerash. The great days were over for Greece and the literary centre of the Greek spirit was rather to be found in Alexandria than in Athens.

Aristophanes was the great exponent of the art of Comedy in the Middle Period, verging on the New development, where no name so great as his own was to be found. In his days Comedy had come into her own and was performed at the City Dionysia after the tragedies that still had first place. The New Comedy, of which Menander was the best-known exponent, suffers because so much of the works of the writers has been lost and only lives again for us in the comedies of Plautus and Terence, who acknowledge to have taken much from these sources. The Latins owed so much to the genius of Greece that the original inspiration can nearly always be traced back. Look at the source and you will nearly always find Greece. It is not that they did not make beautiful works of art which may even have surpassed the inspiration that called them forth; it is simply that the Romans found in Greek art a base for nearly all that they afterwards executed.

The New Comedy found talented exponents among the Syrians. In the works that they and others produced, the old characters came up again. The cook—why was he always such a butt?—the sycophant, the courtezan, the clown, the charlatan, the slave, the parasite and the procuress are some of the amiable characters that were part and parcel of the New, as they had been of the Old Comedy.

The tremendous licence of the primitive type had gone, the personal abuse, showered so liberally on anyone who chanced to be unpopular, or merely to have a bald head or other personal peculiarity, had given place to topical songs and political allusions. Love had not very much place in these works, and no comedy of manners was possible in a society in which women had so little part. For female characters the writer had to go to the courtezan, or to some innocent girl who had been stolen from her belongings or sold by them. Marriage was a misfortune that you preferred to be the lot of your enemy rather than yourself; sentiment was often absent from Greek drama, though the New Comedy showed a decided advance in the matter of love stories. What shadows they are to us, these people of another era, although they continue into our own and live side by side with Christian development!

" Lights in their hands, old music on their lips,
    Wild honey and the East and loveliness."

In spite of all that has been written about them, they pass like phantoms half-seen at night-time, and disappear into the mist before the day breaks. Do we really know anything about them? Do we not take certain characteristics as giving us the key to the whole nature of a people? Were the men in Gerasa always feasting, and did the loud sound of the lyre offend the ears of the serious-minded wherever you went? Sounds of revelry, garlanded heads, roses on the table, hours spent in the talk that never failed and that was often witty if immoral, this is the picture that is called up by books old and new. The army in Syria succumbed to this oriental love of luxury and ease, and the soldiers could hardly bear the weight of their armour when called to put it on. Rome, that had idolized Greece and all that was Greek, very soon found out that the orientalized Greek was becoming a poor thing, lazy and luxurious. So there is some truth in the picture, but perhaps there was another side.

Byzantium, the centre of the civilized world, was an overcrowded city in which there was something of everything. The Court was cultivated yet gay; religion was pompous and ascetic at the same time; men and women were good and bad, as they might be anywhere, but there was a good deal of crime. Adventure was in the air, fortune raised up and threw down her votaries with surprising quickness. As for the bodies that were cast into the blue waters of the Bosphorus, their number was something fabulous. There was plenty of material for a comedy in the capital of the eastern empire.

But the writers of comedy were not so much out to study the manners and customs of their own day, though they were ready enough to bring in some topical or political reference into the warp and woof of the story. They seem to have been singularly conservative in their methods, and any change came gradually.

As it seems difficult to place a comedy in the theatre of Jerash without considering what was being written and how some of the playwrights were connected with the Decapolis, we must journey to Alexandria, where some of them were produced.

According to the late Professor Mahaffy, the Greek classic period closes with Menander; and the works of this polished dramatist were much studied at Alexandria when the writers of the New Comedy were producing their earliest works. One of the chief points was the simplicity of the language. An old grammarian notices this fact when speaking of the poets of the Middle Period: "They did not attempt to use a poetic style, but employ the language of ordinary life, they had the excellencies of prose." This famous passage, from a Latin play derived from a Greek one, shows the flatterer who lives on his rich patron and who despises him while doing so. " There are some men who wish to be first in everything, but who are not. To these men I attach myself. I do not come to them in order to make them laugh, but I laugh with them of my own accord, and at the same time I admire their cleverness. Whatever they say, I praise it; if they say just the opposite, I also praise it; if they say no, I say no; if they say yes, I say yes; in a word, I have made it a rule to praise everything. This is by far the most profitable business nowadays."

The dramatists of the later periods were many and their output was enormous. We hear no more of a man producing one trilogy a year and so presenting the world with a masterpiece. Horace has some biting things to say about them in his "Satires." He talks of Lucilius, who would dictate a hundred verses as though it were a mighty exploit, standing on one foot. " As he flowed on like a muddy stream, one would have been glad to remove a good deal; a verbose author, too lazy to endure the labour of writing, correct writing, I mean, for as to quantity, I do not regard that."

Another author, who is abominably prolific, challenges him to a contest.

" See, here is Crispinus, he challenges me, giving me long odds. 'Take,' says he, ' if you please, writing tablets, so will I; name your place, hour, umpires; let us see which of us two can compose most.' ' No,' say I, ' I thank Heaven for having given me a poor and humble genius, that speaks but seldom and very little; whilst do you, if so you please, imitate the air enclosed in bellows of goat skin, puffing hard till the fire softens the iron. . . . '"

Time has its revenge on those who so misuse its gifts; who that has ever heard of literature has not heard of Horace? and how many, even fairly well versed in such knowledge, have heard of Crispinus?

There are many little hits at the playwrights of the day in the writings of Horace, with, incidentally, criticism of the drama. He blames the roughness of the verses of Lucilius, though the world says that he has rubbed the city down with Attic salt. "However, though I allow this, I am not prepared to allow the other points—for so I should admire even Laberius's farces as though they were fine poems. For it is not enough to make the hearer's jaw open wide with laughter; although there is a certain merit even in this; but conciseness is required, that the thoughts may run on unembarrassed by words loading the wearied ears: we need, too, language sometimes severe, often gay, maintaining the character—sometimes of an orator or poet, then awhile of a polished wit, who puts not forth his strength, but husbands it on purpose. A joke often decides weighty matters more powerfully and better than does severity. Those famous writers of the Old Comedy took their stand on this point, in this are worthy of all imitation; though that coxcomb, Hermogenes, never reads them, nor that monkey whose only skill is in singing the verses of Calvus and Catullus."

Could anything be truer? He also objects to the mixture of Latin and Greek affected by Lucilius, and is quite unconvinced by those who say that it is as charming to mix languages as it is to mix a cask of Falernian with one of Chian wine.

What a comedy of manners Horace might have written, giving his characters the brisk dialogue that comes out in his "Letters" and "Satires"! But he says that he is no poet, and that Satire, the daughter of Comedy, as well as Comedy herself, canot be dignified with the name of poetry.

We have come to Rome after all, because the only

writer of farce who made a name for himself coming from the Decapolis tried his fortune in the Eternal City. This was Publilius, who had a troop of mummers with which he travelled about the world. He was well known in Rome; Cicero and Atticus mention him in their letters to each other. His great rival was the Laberius whose farces were not appreciated by Horace, and who was not half so popular with the Romans as the clever Greco-Syrian.

Publilius was a native of Antioch, who was taken to Rome as a slave and attracted the attention of his master's guests by his wit; after he was freed he became a comic actor, and was head of a party of mimes, who seem to have enjoyed popularity with the lower classes, though people of all sorts went to laugh at their jokes. Publilius invented his own plays in which he took part; some of the dialogue was improvised, but there was a written script. Cicero was present at the games held in honour of Cæsar during which Publilius carried away the prize in competition with Liberius, both apparently improvising.

The mimes seems to have given rather a rough-and-tumble performance, quite amusing and often witty, and, in the case of Publilius, expressed in elegant metre. But it was far from the definition of Aristotle in which he stated that comedy ran parallel with tragedy; one purified our nature by tears and the other by laughter.

When all is said and done, the stage was progressing. The disappearance of the chorus was a great step towards more realistic comedy, the acting became more realistic also, and less just a matter of gesture and a resounding voice. Cratinus invented the political play. Menander, whose patriotism made him reject an offer to perform at the Court of Ptolemy, was an Athenian who liked to stay in his own country. But there were many who did go to Syria, and the mimes of Alexandria were famous.

Menander and Philemon were the finest of the later

playwrights; they preferred the glory of taking the prize in the classic home of the theatre and, no doubt, as has been suggested, were more at home with the clever, emotional, alive audience of Athens than they would have been elsewhere. It was partly the lowering of the tone of the audiences that dragged down the playwright, who had now to write to please the world instead of making the world more highly developed because of his writing.

Philemon went to Alexandria eventually, where he produced many plays; he was a native of Syracuse, and so was not so wedded to the soil of Athens as was his greater rival, Menander, but with all the dramatists the hall-mark of fame was only to be acquired on Greek soil.

Many of the Syrians found a successful career in the theatre; they were not wanting in wit and were immensely prolific, just as they were good at improvising and indefatigable talkers. As to their fondness for the theatre, they certainly came up to the Attic standard and they had far more opportunities of indulging in their passion than the Athenians had in the early days of the Dionysian festivals. In these later times, any excuse seemed good enough to have games, accompanied by chariot-racing, variety entertainments and theatrical performances.

The open air theatre of Greek and Roman times sounds romantic, but it had its disadvantages. Not only a sudden shower of rain which drove the audience to seek shelter in one of the buildings or porticos, but the glare of the sun might make the mind wander. If the theatre, large as it was, was going to be full to overflowing, it was wise to secure a place overnight. The performance began at dawn and went on, apparently without a break, till dark. One play succeeded another; the audience, having had a good meal before it began, had no opportunity of refreshing themselves except by picnicking during the duller parts of the play. But the opportunity was always seized, people sat spellbound, as on the celebrated occasion when a character on the stage remarked that the Persians were coming, merely repeating a stage cue which was taken up by the real Persians appearing on the highest rank of the theatre, which they had climbed unnoticed by the intent audience.

This note on the Athenian audience from A. E. Haigh's " Attic Theatre," is probably a true picture of the Greek and Syrian audiences in any theatre in the Decapolis :—

"The Athenians were a lively audience, and gave expression to their feelings in the most unmistakable manner. The noise and uproar produced by an excited crowd of twenty thousand persons must have been of a deafening character, and is described in the most uncomplimentary language by Plato. It was exceedingly difficult for the judges to resist such demonstrations and to vote in accordance with their own private judgment. The ordinary modes of signifying pleasure or disgust were much the same in ancient as in modern times, and consisted of hisses and groans on the one hand and of shouts and clapping of hands on the other. The Athenians had also a peculiar way of marking their disapproval of a performance by kicking with the heels of their sandals against the front of the stone benches on which they were sitting. Stones were occasionally thrown by an irate audience. Æschines was hissed off the stage and " almost stoned to death," in the course of his theatrical career. There is an allusion to the practice in the story of the second-rate musician, who borrowed a supply of stone from a friend in order to build a house, and promised to repay him with the stones he collected from his next performance in public. Country audiences in the Attic demes used figs and olives, and similar missiles, for pelting unpopular actors. On the other hand, encores were not unknown, if particular passages took the fancy of the audience. Socrates is said to have encored the first few lines of the ' Orestes ' of Euripides."

CHAPTER XXV
THE SILVER AGE

CHAPTER XXV

THE SILVER AGE

THE first centuries of the Christian era were, as we have seen, centuries of unrest; it is unnecessary to say this again, when the fact itself is so obvious, but without remembering it, one is apt to miss the keynote of this later intellectual output.

The great nations were losing power, the old ideas were losing weight, civilization and religions were overlapping; the future looked dark and confused, as well it might.

The chief period of prosperity for Gerasa coincided with these centuries when different strains flowed side by side without mingling, when people of varying race and creed still lived under the banner of Rome on Hellenistic ideals, striving to hold up a state of society that they must have realized was doomed to fall.

The centres of civilization were, besides the still vital claims of Rome and even of Athens, Alexandria, Byzantium, Damascus, Baghdad, Antioch and some other cities in Asia Minor. The Decapolis cities, on the high road between Egypt or Damascus and the coast, and thence to Greece or Rome, were very much in the literary movement and themselves supplied some of the men who rose to fame. Antioch, Gadara and Pella are the cities which seem to have been the most important literary centres and a good many distinguished Greco-Syrians were born there. Gerasa has three illustrious sons given her by Stephanus Byzantinus, but there does not seem to be any authority for the attribution. The three names given are Plato, who we know was born in Ægina, where his father had a property, Ariston, the Christian apologist, who is always said to have been born in Pella, where he lived; and Kerykos, whose birthplace I have not traced.

Whether or no Gerasa had any literary offspring, there is no doubt that there was a keen interest felt in the development of any new movement by the Gerasenes, who were probably as eager and argumentative as others of their race. We can imagine the arrival of travelling lecturers, men who had journeyed all over the vast Roman empire, and their reception in the white city; a welcome given with all the enthusiasm that characterized a people who loved learning as much as they loved luxury and who were specially interested in fine speaking. And it was an age when, in spite of the difficulties of travel and the time that it took getting from one place to another, the literary man wandered far and wide in search of patrons or merely desiring to see the world and give a course of lectures. Before the times of which we are speaking various great men had left Syria and other countries to try their luck in Athens and Rome, and not a few of them had turned up from time to time in the Decapolis. The great Aristotle, of Stagiros in Chalcidice, born in the first half of the fourth century, went to Pella in Macedon, invited by Philip of Macedon to be tutor to the young Alexander. After the death of Philip and the beginning of Alexander's campaigns, he returned to Athens and founded a school of philosophy.

Timon, the sceptic, philosopher and poet, used to lecture in Chalcedon; he was a correspondent of Ptolemy Philadelphus. Literary patrons were a necessity in those days and we find that Apollodorus, a pupil of Diogenes, was not above dedicating his metrical chronography of principal events from the taking of Troy down to his own times, to the same king; a fact that Scymus of Chios notes in his dedication of his own work to another sovereign prince. This book was a metrical geography based on the compendium of an earlier writer, which was expressly written for the convenience of people in a hurry, for those who had no time, and perhaps little inclination, to study other than superficially.

THE ROMAN BATHS, JERASH

The Silver Age

Scymus suggests in his letter that the King will derive fame if he accepts the dedication and that the writer will see what the sovereign is really like and will be able to talk about it afterwards. A delightful touch that! As a probably unique specimen of its kind, it is worth a quotation. He is speaking of Apollordorus and his chronology :—

" He expounded a period of over 1,040 years, recounting the taking of cities, the expeditions of armies, the wanderings of nations, the incursions of barbarians, the course of naval operations, public games, treaties, battles, the acts of kings and other celebrated men, the removal of tyrants—an epitome of all that is told diffusely; and he preferred to set it forth in metre and chose the comic for the sake of clearness and seeing that it would thus be most easily committed to memory. He takes an illustration from life. If a man wants to carry a number of logs, he could not do so unless he tied them together; so a metrical story has its advantages over prose. He then, having gathered the chronicle of time into this summary, paid the compliment of dedicating it to King Ptolemy, which, becoming known all over the world, conferred immortal glory on that Attalas whose name appeared in the dedication."

Who could not accept a dedication that offered so much glory at the cost of so small an act of graciousness?

In the third century B.C. a great writer was born at Gadara. Menippus, whose prose and verse have unfortunately been lost, though his influence on other writers is well attested, was a slave who became a freedman and made money enough to become a moneylender; perhaps those past experiences were accountable for his cynical and satiric outlook on life. He attacked all classes, including the philosophers, and had a pretty knack of treating serious subjects wittily. Only fragments of his works remain, but there is one treatise under the name of Lucian, who studied his works and copied his style, which may have been from the pen of the ex-moneylender who became a philosopher. Personally, I can never think of Menippus without a vision of a full-length portrait of a man that hangs in the great Valazquez rooms in the Prado; it represents a tall old man wrapped in a black cloak who peers out from under a wide-brimmed hat with an expression of malevolent misery. Why did the great Spaniard paint Menippus of Gadara? —and why in the guise of a Spanish beggar?

The greatest imitators of Menippus, whose curious fate it is to be remembered through the works of others, were Meleager, the epigrammatist, also of Gadara, and the celebrated Lucian. Witty and polished, an admirer of Plato and one who had studied the best Greek writers, Lucian has come down to us as a classic. He was born at Samosata on the Euphrates, about A.D. 120, was apprenticed to an uncle who was a statuary, disgraced himself by breaking a marble slab for which he was well beaten, and then started off on his wanderings. He went to Antioch to study, like so many others and it was probably there that he studied the works of Menippus. He has been called the Aristophanes of prose.

Meleager, who was born about 135 B.C., was well educated; he knew Greek—not the common talk of Grecian Syria, but the cultivated language of Greek literature; he knew also Aramaic and Phœnician. He seems to have gone to Tyre where he wrote epigrams and charites, based on Menippus, besides an anthology. A little poem of his which shows his love and appreciation of nature that comes from the "Anthologia Palatina" may find a place here :—

"Snowdrops and mountain lilies bloom again
 And the narcissus, lover of the rain,
  Zenophule, the fair, persuasive rose,
  The perfect flower in lovers' eyes, now blows.
 Why vaunt ye then, your bright attire, ye fields,
  Since to no fragrant breath her beauty yields?"*

---

* Also quoted in Mr. E. S. Bouchier's "Syria as a Roman Province," in which many interesting details concerning the Syrian writers are to be found.

The Silver Age

Here is another charming lyric from the "Anthology":—

> "Chirping Cicada! drunk with drops of dew,
> Muse of the fields, the desert prattling thro'
> With jagged feet, on petals perched aloft,
> Striking from dusky body, music soft,
> Come, pleasant friend! to Pan responsive sing,
> And to the wood nymphs some new carol bring,
> That, fleeing love, I noon-tide rest may find
> Here underneath a shady pine reclined."

Meleager eventually settled at Kos. Lucian, who was one of the travelling lecturers, must have visited Gerasa often; he went all over the Roman empire and finally settled at Athens. His restless nature, or the offer of an appointment in Egypt, took him to Alexandria where he probably died, as no more is heard of him.

Before, however, getting to the age of the Antonines, there is another son of Gadara whose adventurous career offers some interesting and amusing details. Philodemus, who came after Meleager and after a still earlier poet Antipater, also a Gadarene, was an Epicurean and a *bon viveur*. He went to Italy, where he secured as patron that Lucius Piso against whom Cicero thundered the resounding periods of his eloquence, even bringing the attendant poet into the oration. "Est quidam græcus," the great orator said, speaking of Philodemus as of a man of talent but one whose talent was debased.

Cicero had spent six months in Athens in his youth; he admired and studied Greek literature and was fully alive to the great artistic quality of the Greeks. But, as individuals, he had no great opinion of them. He speaks more than once of their laziness and their love of luxury; as to their performances in the witness-box, he mentions a Greek proverb which says "Lend me your evidence," implying that the speakers evidence would be given in return when required. Here is his unbiased opinion of the Greeks of his day, spoken in the defence of Flacceus:—

"I will say this of the whole of the Greeks : I grant their literary genius, I grant them skill in various accomplishments, I do not deny them eloquence in conversations, acuteness of intellect, fluent oratory ; to any other high qualities they may claim I make no objections, but the sacred obligation that lies upon a witness to speak the truth is what that nation has never regarded."

Cicero's advice to another governor, his own brother, who fulfilled that sometimes pleasant and profitable post in Asia, shows how the Roman governors "collected" objects of art for their palaces, and is interesting as showing something of the spirit of the intercourse between Rome and her colonies. This particular one was of much the same character as that of Syria ; the population was composed, besides the Asiatics, of old Greek colonists with a large Roman element of merchants and bankers and moneylenders, and the whole crowd of people out to make a little fortune in a short time. Cicero writes :—

"You will find little trouble in holding your subordinates in check, if you can but keep a check upon yourself. So long as you resist gain, and pleasure, and all other temptations, as I am sure you do, I cannot fancy there will be any danger of your not being able to check a dishonest merchant or an extortionate collector. For even the Greeks, when they see you living thus, will look upon you as some hero from their old annals, or some supernatural being from heaven, come down into their province.

"I write thus, not to urge you so to act, but that you may congratulate yourself upon having so acted, now and heretofore. For it is a glorious thing for a man to have held a government for three years in Asia, in such sort that neither statue, nor painting, nor work of art of any kind, nor any temptations of wealth or beauty (in all which temptations your province abounds) could draw you from the strictest integrity and self-control : that your official progresses should have been no cause

The Silver Age

of dread to the inhabitants, that none should be impoverished by your requisitions, none terrified at the news of your approach ; but that you should have brought with you, wherever you came, the most hearty rejoicings, public and private, inasmuch as every town saw in you a protector and not a tyrant—every family received you as a guest, not as a plunderer.''

After recommending a strong course of justice, he suggests that mercy is a quality that will bring its own reward :—

'' If such moderation be popular at Rome, where there is so much self-assertion, such unbridled freedom, so much licence allowed to all men ; where there are so many courts of appeal open, so many means of help, where the people have so much power and the Senate so much authority ; how grateful beyond measure will moderation be in the Governor of Asia, a province where all that vast number of our fellow-citizens and subjects, all those numerous states and cities, hang upon one man's nod ! Where there is no appeal to the tribune, no remedy at law, no Senate, no popular assembly. Wherefore it should be the aim of a great man, and one noble by nature and trained by education and liberal studies, so to behave himself in the exercise of that absolute power, as that they over whom he presides should never have cause to wish for any authority other than his.''

But to return to Philodemus. He was a merry fellow, a sarcastic writer who would fire off an epigram on a bald head or on the age of a courtezan, and who satirized himself more mildly in a poem in which he said that he was growing old, but that in his insatiate heart the old fire burned—which one can well believe, for he was of the type that keeps a young spirit up to the very end. A little poem that gives an amusing picture of an impromptu supper party provided by a group of friends is translated by Major Guthrie MacGregor :—

> " Artemidorus gives of greens a dish
> And Aristarchus brings us pickled fish,
> With onions Aristagorus adds part
> And Philodemus sends a dainty heart,
> From Apollophanes two ribs of meat,
> Three saved from yesterday—our meal complete,
> Eggs, garlands, sandals, take from us and myrrh,
> At the tenth hour my presence I'll confer."

No doubt much time and money was wasted in these feasts, which were not all so simple as the one just described. Posidonius of Apamea, who was born about 135 B.C. and who died in Rome 57 B.C., was the author of a work that continued the history of Polybius down to his own times. He describes the clubs in the Greek cities in terms that make us believe in all the old stories of overeating and drinking, of rose-crowned heads and golden hours spent in recovering from the effects of the feast. Even Cæsar, when he went to stay with Cicero, we may remember, ate a very good dinner, as his host noted in a letter to Atticus, having prudently taken an emetic beforehand. So we must receive the picture that Posidonius draws as being a true one of the clubs of his day; one that would make the members of the staid and stately palaces in Pall Mall feel, perhaps, just a shade of regret for " the good old times " of the pagan world.

" There are many clubs in which they amused themselves continuously, using the gymnasia as baths, anointing themselves with expensive oils and unguents, and using the *schools*, for so they called the dining-halls of the members, as if they were their own houses, stuffing themselves there for the greater part of the day with wines and food, and even carrying off much besides, amidst the sound of noisy lyres which made whole cities ring with the uproar."

Philodemus, who must have assisted at many of these gatherings with his patron Lucius Piso, met Horace in Roman society, and is mentioned by that delightful individual in one of the " Satires."

" We all dwell in a city which has no bulwarks

against death, and everything is full of what will bring it about," Philodemus wrote in one of his philosophical homilies, in which he laughs at poor, finite mankind planting cypresses, or letting himself be hanged for two farthings, or laying the foundations of buildings that cannot be completed for a thousand years. Just as if a glass vessel could remain unbroken when in perpetual contact with iron pots! Where he ended his days does not appear. He scoffed at the idea of immortality, and indeed it was a doctrine out of fashion in his day, though there were exceptions, and the new trend of thought towards Neo-Platonism did much to bring it into men's minds as a possibility. These two epitaphs show the pagan idea in its evolution; both are translated from the Greek by Sir Rennell Rodd :—

MELEAGER'S EPITAPH.

" Tread softly, ye that pass, for here
  The old man rests his head,
And sleeps the sleep that all men must
  Among the hallowed dead.

Meleager, son of Eucrates
  Who linked the joyous train
Of Graces and of Muses
  With love's delicious pain.

From Gadara, the sacred land,
  I came, and God-built Tyre,
But Meropis and pleasant Cos
  Consoled life's waning fire.

If thou be Syrian, say Salaam,
  All Hail! if Greek thou be,
Say Naidiol, if Phœnician born,
  For all are one to me.

MACEDONIUS—6TH CENTURY, A.D.

Spirit of birth, that gave me life,
  Earth that received my clay,
Farewell, for I have travelled
  The stage that 'twixt you lay.
I go, and have no knowledge
  From whence I came to you,
Nor whither I shall journey
  Nor whose I am, nor who.

The far wider outlook, the enquiring spirit of the later poem, shows the progressive nature of thought. There is no answer to the question that the poet asks, but he is convinced that there is a future, although he cannot fathom what it will be.

We have already met Libanius, but he must have a few words here, as he was one of the men who made a mark in what has been called the Silver Age of Greek literature. He was born at Antioch in 314 A.D., and was brought up in the country; from his earliest youth he showed a studious mind and an inclination to teach. He went to Athens to complete his studies, and then set up the Rhetorical School in Byzantium, which he had to abandon because of the jealousy of the professional teachers, in whose ranks he appears not to have been. At the age of forty he settled in Antioch, where his school was attended by all the best talent of that city, and of many others. People flocked to hear Libanius lecture, as they also flocked to the preaching of his great pupil St. Joannes Chrysostomus.

Libanius was a thorough pagan. He did not understand Christianity, and wrote against what he conceived to be its doctrines. He was an admirer of Julian the Apostate, and wrote a eulogium on him after his death. He adored Greek and despised Latin, and even upheld the characters of the Seleucid Kings. His description of the burning of the temple of Apollo at Daphne during the last visit of Julian to Antioch is most pathetic; we seem to see the old gods fleeing sadly away from a world in which they have no more place.

" The wayfarer cried out as the blaze rose up, and the loved dweller in Daphne, the priestess of the god, lamented. Beatings of breasts and bitter cries speeding through the bosky groves penetrated to the city amidst terror and dismay. The eyes of the emperor were but just tasting sleep, but he leaped from his bed with accents of grief and hurried on in frenzy, as though on the winged sandals of Hermes. He

The Silver Age

advanced to seek the cause of the evil, blazing within no less than without the temple, while the beams swept down bearing flame with them, consuming all that stood nearest ; first Apollo, who rose almost to the roof, then other things too : the beautiful figures of the Muses, the founders' statues, flashing jewels, noble columns. The throng of men stood round lamenting, unable to give succour, like those who look on a shipwreck from land, whose only help is to weep at what befalls. Verily the nymphs, starting from their founts, raised a great lamentation ; great too, was that of Zeus, enthroned hard by, on seeing the honour of his son thus overthrown ; great that of the countless company of deities that dwell in the grove. Nor less a wailing did Calliope raise in the midst of Antioch, when the chorus-leader of the Muses was violated by the flames.''

It is only after reading the lives of the men who made the history of the Greek cities in Syria, and after studying what fragments of their work remains, that we can re-people the silent streets of Gerasa. The temple of Artemis was once glorious within, the shrines of the gods were decked with gold and jewels ; one can imagine the ghost of Libanius wandering up and down its desecrated precincts and lamenting its desolation. And down by the river are the fine remains of the baths which were, of course, equivalent to the clubs of which we have just read. They contain even now, many interesting features and a dome structure that has aroused the interest and the admiration of architects.

CHAPTER XXVI
The Neo-Platonists

CHAPTER XXVI
THE NEO-PLATONISTS

" Je ne pense pas qu'il y ait dans le monde une seule ville, Rome comprise, qui recueille et concentre des souvenirs si nombreux et si divers."

J. AMPÈRE

ALEXANDRIA, one of the beautiful cities of the world, must have presented a marvellous appearance to the throng of learned men who congregated there as well as to the touts in quest of a soft job. The marble city lay along the quays washed by the shores of the Mediterranean; right through the middle the Canopic Street cut the town in two halves and in front of it was the island of Pharos on which Ptolemy Philadelphus had built what has been called one of the marvels of the world. This was the lighthouse, built of gleaming white marble which was square at the bottom, octagon-shaped in the middle and round at the top. It might have been taken for some mighty mausoleum, had there not been a light at the summit to guide the ships to the entrance of the harbour, reflected by means of a gigantic mirror designed by a Chinese workman. The monster lighthouse is said by old writers to have contained three hundred rooms, in which you could easily lose yourself, and a staircase so gently graded that beasts of burden could walk up to the top of the building. It took twelve years to build and Ptolemy II, who had spent vast sums of money on it and on the island generally with its fortresses at either end, must have looked at it with satisfaction when it was completed.

The King lived in the quarter known as Bruchëium, where was the library in which he took so much interest. The great harbour was always astir with ships going and coming, the quays were like a hive of bees, the whole city with its great palaces and its shops and its Jewish quarter, was very much alive.

Strabo describes Alexandria as having spacious streets through which horses and chariots passed freely, fine temples and public buildings and many royal palaces built by each successive King. "Part of the palace," he says, "is called the museum. It has corridors, a court, and a very large mansion in which is the banqueting-room of those learned men who belong to it. This society has a public treasury and is superintended by a president, one of the priesthood, whose office, having been established by the Ptolemies, continues under Cæsar."

It appears by this account that the King provided a club for his literary lights, and we can imagine the meetings that took place there. The eagerness of the learned to develop their theories and to write their books under the protection of so magnificent a patron can be imagined; and then, besides the glamour of the riches and the luxury of Ptolemy's Court, they had also the patronage of a true " man of letters," as our forefathers would have called him. It was no mere whim of Ptolemy Philadelphus making his Court a centre of learning; it was a real love of the beautiful and interesting things of life, a really passionate curiosity impelling him to seek out knowledge and to aid those who were capable of advancing it, to gain their ends.

One of the most interesting developments of spiritual enquiry took place in this very palace, under the direct personal supervision of the King. This was no other than that curious blending of the occult doctrines of ancient Egypt with the more mystic side of Greek mythology, the cult of "Thrice Greatest Hermes." Mr. G. S. Mead, the translator of the Trismegistic literature, gives an account of the movement before passing on to his translation of the Hermetic dialogues and discourses, which contain much of the garnered wisdom of the Egyptian priests. The company of

THE FORUM, WITH VIEW OF THE BEIT ET-TEI, JERASH

mystics who gathered together in the Royal Museum talked of Thoth, the Master of Wisdom, the heart and tongue of Ra the Supreme, the Logos through whom the divine knowledge was to reach mankind. His word had resulted in the creation, his name was the creative word. He taught Isis the words that enabled her to bring to life the dead body of Osiris, referring presumably to the resurrection from the dead. Osiris had to die before he could be raised immaculate; Horus, the child of Isis and Osiris, had to die before he could be raised by baptism to the purer life.

Thoth was the Supreme Master of Wisdom, the Logos of God; those who studied the wisdom had to become initiates in the Mysteries, for Thoth was the initiator. Into this extremely mystic theosophy, the cult of Hermes entered. I quote from " Thrice Greatest Hermes " :—

" The more intimate contact of Greek thought and philosophy with Egyptian lore and mystic tradition began immediately with the brilliant era of the Lagides, who gradually made Alexandria the intellectual and religious, philosophic and scientific centre of the Hellenistic world."

Thoth-Hermes had been for ages the teacher of hidden things in Egypt, where his statue bears the feather of truth on his head or the papyrus roll in his hand, symbols of Thoth in his dual character as revealer and scribe.

Greek fragments concerning these matters have also been preserved, dating from before the end of the second century B.C. Petosiris wrote on comparative Greek and Egyptian theology, astrology and the Egyptian mysteries : " Vettius, writing in the first half of the first century, A.D., laments that he did not live in those days of initiate kings and rulers and sages who occupied themselves with the sacred science, when the clear æther spoke face to face with them without disguise, or holding back aught, in answer to their deep scrutiny of holy things. In those days so great was their love of holy mysteries, so high their virtue that they left the earth below them, and in their deathless souls became ' heaven-walkers ' and knowers of things divine."

Ptolemy Philadelphus, then, was an initiate who was in intimate communion with Manetho, the priest of Heliopolis, who was the most learned man in Alexandria. The Ptolemies had made Alexandria the centre of all sorts of learning by founding this museum, together with libraries and schools of philosophy and rhetoric. One of the great activities there was the translating of the records of other nations into Greek, and we have seen how the Jews came to Alexandria at the invitation of the King, and lived there while they translated their ancient books for his library. Manetho wrote on history as well as mysticism, and was a great student of Greek literature. As to Egyptian sources, he is said to have gleaned his knowledge from priestly records in the temples, and from hieroglyphic inscriptions there; unluckily his great works have been lost, and only quotations from other writers show what the loss must be to those interested in such subjects.

One of these fragments, preserved from Manetho's "Book of Sothis," is addressed to the King :—

" The letter of Manetho, the Sebennyte, to Ptolemy Philadelphus.

" To the great King Ptolemy Philadelphus the Venerable : I, Manetho high priest and scribe of the holy fanes in Egypt, citizen of Heliopolis, but by birth a Sebennyte, to my master Ptolemy send greeting.

" We must make calculations concerning all the points which you may wish us to examine into, to answer your questions concerning what will happen to the world. According to your commands, the sacred books, written by our forefather Thrice Greatest Hermes, which I study, shall be shown to you. My lord and king, farewell."

By which it will be perceived that Ptolemy's curiosity

extended into the future and that, like other people of that age, he asked the oracle for an answer to his questions.

Whatever may be our views concerning the doctrine of the Hermetic philosophy, it cannot be denied that there was really an intense desire on the part of the many students of higher things to arrive at the heart of religion. Their endeavour was to attain to a higher state of consciousness, to be "heaven-walkers." We are reminded of Saint Paul, who was caught up to heaven: "Whether in the body, I cannot tell; or whether out of the body I cannot tell." Greek mystics leading the ascetic life pursued their search for the hidden wisdom, learned Jews, under Hellenistic influences developed theories that were to find an exponent later in Philo; Christians studied the old scripts and endeavoured, like Clement and Origen, to reconcile Christ and Hermes. All these students were vowed to the ascetic life, because the body had to be subject to the soul.

A visitor to the Court of Ptolemy who did not at first find recognition was Theocritus, who wrote three of his idylls here after his return as a celebrated writer with a distinct claim to immortality. In an age of imitation he struck out an original note that he is said to have derived from the piping of the shepherds in Sicily. These pastorals were quite a new departure, for the earlier Greek poems were all about city life, and the adventures of men and the active side of human affairs. The picturesque was only lightly touched on, if at all, as in the Homeric Hymn to Pan.

Theocritus was born either at Kos or Syracuse; he was a good deal in Sicily before he came to Alexandria, where he wrote the fourteenth, fifteenth and seventeenth idylls about the year 259 B.C. His bucolic and mimic poems touch the highest note of his genius.

Having failed to receive recognition at the Court, probably on account of the number of suppliants, Theocritus had left for Sicily, where he studied the Mimes of

Sophron and developed his style. This time he was more fortunate, meeting with the reception that his beautiful pastorals and poetic gifts generally entitled him to expect. The fifteenth idyll is concerned with a scene in Alexandria, describing the conversation of two women and their maids, who are going to the ceremony of the laying out of Adonis: anything more modern, more intensely and wittily descriptive of the actual talk of two women it would be difficult to imagine. If the dramatists of the day had given us dialogue like that we should know more of the intimate everyday life of ordinary people. I quote from it here, in spite of the fact that it is so well known, because it does really give a picture of life in Alexandria and the casual talk of two ordinary women, who are neither courtezans nor adventuresses. The translation is by Mr. James Henry Hallard.

GORGO AND PRAXINOE.

Gorgo (*to Slave Girl*): Is your mistress in?
Prax: Oh, there you are at last,
Dear Gorgo! Yes, I'm in. I'm quite surprised
To see you here at all. Quick, Eunoe, fetch
A chair for her, and put a cushion on it.
Gorgo: Nay, leave it as it is.
Prax: Well, sit you down.
Gorgo: How out of breath I am! I hardly got
To your house alive out of the dreadful crowd
Of carriages and people. Soldiers' boots
And cloaks here, there, and everywhere—I thought
The way would never end. Your house, my dear,
Is really much too far away from ours.
Prax: My madcap husband's fault. He came and took
At world's end here a beast's hole, not a house,
Merely to keep us apart, the jealous wretch!
And all for spite, as usual.
Gorgo: Hush, my dear!
Don't rail at Dinon so before the child.
Look, woman, how he eyes you. Never mind,
Zopyrian dear, sweet boy, it's not papa
That mother talks of.
Prax: By our Lady Goddess,
The baby understands us!
Gorgo: Pretty papa!

The Neo-Platonists

How fresh it all is, after the lapse of so many centuries! And the talk goes on in the same happy-go-lucky way, expressed with the same simple yet subtle art. Praxinoe's oaf of a husband goes out to buy soda and rouge, and comes back with salt; Gorgo's spendthrift spouse wastes his money on trash. Praxinoe puts on her gown and mantle, and Gorgo immediately asks her the price; and then they go off to see the show in Ptolemy's palace, and get hustled in the crowd.

> *Prax:* Oh heavens, what a crowd!
> How shall we elbow through it all? They're like
> A swarm of countless ants. O Ptolemy,
> Many the noble deeds that thou hast done
> Since that thy sire was numbered with the gods!
> No rascal now skulks up, Egyptianwise,
> To maul the passer-by, as once they did,
> The lumps of villainy, the knavish tricksters,
> All birds of a feather, scoundrels every one.
> O Gorgo, dear, what *will* become of us?
> Here are the King's own chargers. My good man,
> Don't trample me—his roan is rearing—see
> How fierce it is! O Eunoe, run, you hussy,
> Run, it will kill its leader. What a blessing
> The babe's at home!"

And they struggle on among the crowd; Praxinoe's mantle is torn, but at last they get in, and are rewarded by the fine things that they see and by the singing of the Argive girl. And the Argive girl sings of the mysteries of Adonis brought from the deep, and Gorgo, who certainly has not listened to a word, says:—

> "What can be wiser than a woman's wit?"

When Neo-Platonism arose in Alexandria, the change that had taken place in that city must have been vast; yet the old literary and mystic tradition still lived. The Lagide dynasty had come to a tragic end with Cleopatra VII, whom we have come to look on as the only Cleopatra, supreme type of beauty and fascination, the woman, the shape of whose nose, as a French writer wittily said, changed the fate of nations. The nose, so it appears, was aquiline, the eyes were very large, the chin was rather long; her power lay rather in fascination and in her master spirit than in actual beauty. However that may be, one of the greatest love dramas in all history was lived through in Alexandria and the dynasty of the Ptolemies perished in the general upheaval that followed on the suicide of Cleopatra.

Centuries passed; great Roman buildings of the familiar form rose in the marble city; its magnificence and its commercial importance were well sustained. Hadrian visited it on one of his journeys, as did most of the Roman emperors; that particular journey was made memorable by the death of the young and beautiful Antinous, drowned in the Nile, either by accident or as a voluntary victim, suffering to protect his royal master from the stings of ill-fortune, from some fate that may have menaced him. The story is obscure and seems never to have been really understood. The emperor wept over his lost favourite, perhaps they were tears of repentance; who shall say? He called a city of Egypt after his name and went his way, leaving to the artists of the future a subject that has fascinated the imagination. The perfect form, the face that is mindless and yet has an expression of sadness given by the downcast eyes, all these familiar details strike us as we enter almost any gallery in Europe. Antinous stands there, a type of bodily perfection, looking down, perhaps, in the endeavour to conceal the secret of his sacrifice, if sacrifice it were, loyal to the end. There is something half animal in his nature that is infinitely touching, suggesting an undeveloped soul or a beautiful body that has been without the final touch of the spirit.

Ammonius Saccas lived in Alexandria in the third century A.D. He was the inspirer of Neo-Platonism, but, like Socrates, he wrote nothing himself; his pupil, Plotinus the Egyptian, acted for him as Plato did for Socrates. Porphyry of Tyre and later Iamblichus of Chalcis, two Greco-Syrians, carried on the torch.

The Alexandria of Saccas and Plotinus was still very beautiful; the great Pharos still stood on its island, not yet destroyed by successive earthquakes and the destructive hand of man. The museum and the libraries—the latter had been added to by Cleopatra who inherited the tastes of her family—were available. But the once intellectual race of the Lagides, which had become so degraded as time went on, was no longer there to act as patron of the learned and supporter of art.

Plotinus must have marvelled at this city when he roamed about it looking for a master whom he could not find. The masses of palaces, set up by each king in turn in the royal quarter, the Acropolis with the second superb library, must have struck him as magnificent, even after Rome and Athens. Perhaps he mounted the hundred steps to the Serapeum, the vast temple erected by Ptolemy Soter I, and walked about on the terrace where the three hundred marble pillars of the portico made it a feature of the whole city that was seen from afar off. Here, too, was the colossal figure of the god Serapis, given to Ptolemy Philadelphus by the King of Pontus; at a certain moment the sun touched his features and played about his mouth making him look like a god of fire, endowed with life. He must have walked about Alexandria while he was looking for a school in which to study, noting the temples, theatres, the Hippodrome and the great baths that still acted as the rich man's club.

In his search for a teacher Plotinus was disappointed, and he was just leaving Alexandria in despair when chance, or fate, took him to the class held by Ammonius Saccus. The revelation was instantaneous. He had found the man, the master that he sought, and he lost no time in enrolling himself as a disciple.

Saccus may have derived his name from the fact that he wore a garment made of sacking; but it is more likely that he started life as a porter. In this case his education might not have fitted him to be a writer, and the opportune arrival of a cultivated man like Plotinus was a godsend. Plotinus went to Rome eventually, where he developed his own theory, which was spread all over the Roman empire by Porphyry and Iamblichus after his death. He was a good Grecian scholar, but always sent his manuscripts to Porphyry to edit before he gave them to the world, even after the disciple had left Rome and was living in Sicily. Plotinus is not a good subject for a personal memoir; he told Porphyry that " he was ashamed that his soul should be in his body " and that is about all the information his friend gleaned of the family history of the master.

Plotinus was twenty-seven years old when he went to Alexandria and he remained there for eleven years, then he followed the Emperor Gordian who was fighting against the Persians, apparently because he wanted to study in Ctesiphon, and thought that it was one way of getting there. The Emperor, however, died, his forces were dispersed, and Plotinus fled to Antioch, afterwards passing on to Rome.

When Porphyry left Grecian Syria for Rome he went with the express purpose of studying under Plotinus, whose writings were known to him. The master was then fifty-nine years old; he received his earnest, argumentative, imaginative disciple with great kindness, and the two spent six years together. When Porphyry used to keep back the swift course of some scholastic discussion and the other pupils got impatient, Plotinus used to say that it was no use trying to go on until he was satisfied and had clearly understood the point at issue.

Porphyry's real name was Malchus; his nickname of " Clothed in Purple " was given him by his first master at Antioch, probably as a skit on his name, which was derived from the Arabic Melek—a king. He made a great discourse on the occasion of the anniversary of Plato's birth, that was held in Rome; it was ridiculed by some, but Plotinus said warmly, " You have shown yourself at once a poet, a philosopher, and a hierophant."

Porphyry seems to have had a fit of melancholia at one time, and to have even contemplated releasing his soul from its mortal envelope, but Plotinus persuaded him to go to Sicily to change his ideas, a course which proved successful. He edited there his master's works, reducing a number of sections into the six Enneads in which form we know them, and he maintained his affection for the great man unimpaired, describing him as one who was "worthy and mild and gentle and endearing."

Up to the end the greatest of the Neo-Platonists remained aloof from the life of the body. When he was near to death he put off the last moment in order to see a friend who did not hurry as he might have done had he realized that the case was serious. Plotinus reproved him gently :—

"As yet I have expected you, and now I endeavour that my divine part may return to that divine nature which flourishes throughout the universe."

Iamblichus of Chalcis returned to his native city after studying under Porphyry; he went a long way towards manifestation and magic, and developed the Neo-Platonic doctrines in that direction. He wrote on Pythagoreanism, saying that it was the root of the newer development, on philosophy, on Plato, and on the magic significance of numbers.

In Alexandria the various schools persisted for a time, especially those of the Gnostics, but after the death of Julian the Apostate they were persecuted by the Christians. Hypatia, Kingsley's beautiful heroine, was one of the most distinguished of the later Neo-Platonists, whose end will be remembered by all readers of romance. And then the priceless books and the statues and the jewels and all the accumulated riches of the Ptolemies were swept into the gulf into which disappeared so much that was irreplaceable.

Gerasa, which we seem to have left for an unconscionable length of time, was influenced by the men going to and from Alexandria, as well as by those whose business or whose pleasure took them to Byzantium, Antioch, Rome or Athens. In this way it was that the life in these cities kept their vigour and their freshness.

It is far more difficult to enter into the lives of the women than into those of the men. A great courtezan stands out in the limelight; a learned lady, like some of those at Byzantium, may become famous; but the majority of women seem to have led a quiet existence, taking little part in public life, never going out unless attended. They went to the theatre when the festivals were on, they attended worship in the temple, some of them were priestesses. They did not travel about, though it is remarked that the original settlers from Macedon brought their wives with them, a fact that is brought out in the accounts of the Greek colonists who settled some four hundred miles up the Nile. These ex-soldiers of Alexander's army were given land, sometimes as much as an Egyptian acre, that was reclaimed from the river; they had every advantage, as the Greek settlers had in the days of the Ptolemies, when they were exempt from military service and from taxes. In those days it was said that Alexandria was very much Greek, partly Jewish and hardly at all Egyptian.

CHAPTER XXVII
Arab Geographers and Christian Pilgrims.

CHAPTER XXVII

Arab Geographers and Christian Pilgrims.

ALTHOUGH it is altogether outside the history of the various towns that we have considered, with the exception of Kerak and Amman, it may not be quite out of place to devote a few pages to the Arab and his literature as well as to a few of those pilgrims whose notes throw light on the subsequent history of the ruins.

The Arabs had a very fine pre-Islamic School of Poetry which the post-Islamic writers dubbed the Age of Ignorance; all their early works were in verse, even their historic records. Right back to the days of Yemen and to the desert tribes of the earliest time, poetic inspiration came naturally to a people who had imagination and facility of expression. These poems were handed on by the reciters and were never written down until after the Hejira. But it has been pointed out that even the earliest of these poems have not the character of primitive art; they bear the impress of a long training and an earlier tradition. One of the Seven Golden Odes of Pagan Arabia, freely rendered by Lady Anne and Wilfred Scawen Blunt, that is often omitted on account of not being from the pen of one of the most celebrated poets of the time, gives an idea of the Bedawin and his desert steed. It is by the satiric poet Tarafa ibn al-Abd, who was always in hot water on account of this unlucky gift which caused his death in the end. The poem is one that is included in the collection known as the Mu'allaqat, the so-called suspended poems, a name that is interpreted differently. The old story that the seven poems were suspended in the Ka'aba on account of being prize-winners and were afterwards inscribed in gold on Egyptian linen, is clearly a romance, as there is no authority for such a suggestion. It is now considered that the word merely refers to a precious thing, or to something that is hung up because it is precious. The poem shows us Tarafa as he must have been; impulsive, wild, but not, in this case, sarcastic. He has just bidden farewell to his dark-lipped love the maid of the topazes, hardly yet grown a woman; he turns away from her with a new enthusiasm to his beloved and long-limbed camel that will bear him quickly over the sandy stretches of the desert.

> "Enough! New joys now claim me. Ay, mount and away from her!
> Here on my swift-footed camel I laugh at love's bitterness.
> Ship-strong is she, my naga, my stout-timbered road-goer,
> Footing the long-lined pathway—a striped cloak—in front of us.
> Steel-tempered are her sinews. She runs like an ostrich-hen,
> One which has fled, defying the ash-plumed proud lord of her.
> Outpaces she the best born, shank still on shank following,
> Threading the mazes lightly. Ah! what foot shall follow her?"

The rise of Islam made the most enormous difference all over the East, and even as far as Spain the followers of the Prophet arrived and changed the face of the country. In less than a century this formidable force invaded countries, changed religions, imposed customs, destroyed the most beautiful works of art in an apparent iconoclastic fury, and then proceeded to build up, on the smoking ashes of the past, their own wonderful mosques and fortresses and palaces. It was a new world starting up on the ruins of the Roman provinces, as far as Syria and Palestine were concerned. The new regime wanted the goods of this world, they had no uncomfortable ideals about austerity; one of the first points to notice in the Moslem world was its culture, so remarkable when Europe was passing through dark years; the second was the luxury with which the leading families surrounded themselves. The oriental taste for magnificence was to the fore, their taste in art was admirable. If their inspiration was not original, if it took from the conquered nations and differed in Spain to what it showed in Egypt, or Syria, it had certain invariable features, derived, some of them, from Persia and Mesopotamia it is true, but making a homogeneous art that has been the delight of subsequent generations.

In literature, of course, they were pre-eminent. The great physician and philosopher Abu'Ali ibn Sina, better known as Avicenna, the man who sowed the seeds of the European Renaissance, was summoned to Bukhara towards the end of the tenth century. He describes the library of King Nuh II in these words:—

" I found there many rooms filled with books which were arranged in cases row upon row. One room was allotted to works on Arabic philology and poetry; another to jurisprudence, and so forth, the books on each particular science having a room to themselves. I inspected the catalogue of ancient Greek authors and looked for the books which I required; I saw in this collection books of which few people have heard even the names, and which I myself have never seen before or since."

One wonders what has happened to the library of King Nuh II and if he was a patron of literary lights.

One of the greatest of these poets was al-Mutanabbi, so called because he once pretended to have a gift of prophecy, but whose real name was Abu'Tayyib Ahmad ibn Husayn; he was the son of a water-carrier who was sent to Damascus to be educated. He lived among the Bedawin tribes for a long time and completely mastered their customs and learned Arabic, which was not his native tongue. He found a royal patron, and once handed him a couplet in which were fourteen imperatives, each asking for some benefit. The Prince was so much amused that he granted them all.

But it is the geographers rather than the poets that must be considered here. It is a fascinating theme that has been treated by a good many writers, and some few —too few—of the works of these enterprising people have been translated. The best-known is Al-Muqaddasi, "the native of the Holy City," who was born at Jerusalem in 946 A.D. Writing about geography was an adventure in those days, when you had to go to see the places you were to write about; just as commerce was an adventure in times when travel was difficult and dangerous.

Another geographer, the greatest perhaps, was Yakut, born 1179 and died in 1229 A.D. He was a Greek by birth, sold as a slave to a merchant of Baghdad, who had him educated and sent him to trade in the Persian Gulf. He quarrelled with his benefactor, was freed, and supported himself for some time by copying manuscripts. He got into trouble, was captured by the Tartars, and, in his own words, "fled as naked as when he shall be raised from the dust of the grave on the Day of Resurrection." (Translation by Guy Le Strange.)

Yakut describes Gerasa as "a great city, now a ruin, through which runs a stream used for turning many mills. It lies among hills that are covered with villages and hamlets, and the district is known as under the name of the Jerash Mountain."

Al-Muqaddasi spent twenty years travelling about the region that he was to describe in his book; Yakut also travelled much while composing his Geographical Dictionary.

The Moslem dynasties succeeded each other, the Crusaders came and went, leaving the followers of the Prophet omnipotent in the East. And then the Christian pilgrims came to visit the shrines, and there are little bits of information scattered about in their often diffuse writings. As they wrote for the information of the pious who were unable to make the long and difficult journey themselves, it was important to leave nothing undescribed that might interest those left at home.

THE FORUM, JERASH

Arab Geographers and Pilgrims

Several of these pilgrims have been noticed in the course of this vagrant study; Brother Felix Fabri, who came to the Holy Land about 1480-83, has not found a place, because his wanderings were on the western side of Jordan. He did, however, visit the Dead Sea, which he describes as having smoke rising up from the waters, and Engadi, from which point of vantage he looks about and makes a fine confusion as to the various "Stones of the Desert." He could have seen Kerak had he looked almost directly east over the waters of the Salt Sea, but he looks south towards Petra, while all the time he appears to be talking of Shobek, which he could not possibly have seen.

"We turned our eyes away from the east to the south," he writes, "far beyond the Dead Sea, where we saw the land of the wilderness of Petra, but Petra in the wilderness we could not see." That sounds correct, but he goes on to say: "This Petra in the wilderness was, in days of old, an exceedingly strong castle in the land of Moab, where was born Ruth, the virtuous Moabitess. This strong city was fenced by Baldwin II, who put three walls round it, and it never would have been taken if it had not been for the treachery of disloyal Christians. The 'Soldan' took it and placed his eldest son there and all his treasure, and at this day it is the treasure chamber of the Soldans, Kings of Egypt." He then explains that the Latins called it Petra of the Wilderness, the Saracens "Krach," and the Greeks, who surely never took it or had any interest in it, "Schabat."

It is very natural that he should mix up the story of the three Stones of the Desert, Petra, Kerak and Shobek, but his evidence as to Ruth the Moabitess coming from any of them seems to rest on the smallest foundation.

Brother Felix suffered a great deal, as did all the pilgrims, from the enmity of the Saracens, a dislike that was returned with interest. On one occasion he says that a black and half-naked Saracen stopped a band of noble pilgrims from proceeding on their way by throwing stones at them. One would think that it was a game that two could play at, but perhaps the pilgrims were not allowed to show fight. Brother Felix is naturally indignant and his comment is amusing:—

"Oh," thought I, "if you were thus to stand in the road unarmed in our part of the world, and stop the way of one of the least of these nobles, how quickly would you have a sword or an arrow in your side. But in these Eastern parts it is not so; for the Easterns are men of different kind to us, or rather, our rules of life are not like theirs; they have other passions, other ways of thinking, other ideas; their bodies are of a different complexion; they are influenced by other stars and a different climate."

Nearly all the pilgrims are too much occupied with Jerusalem and places of interest in the New Testament to spend much time on the other side of Jordan; it was, moreover, far more dangerous than western Palestine. The people who undertook to take charge of pilgrims were always unwilling to take them further than Jericho. The ruined cities of the Decapolis did not interest them, for they were real pilgrims who had come for the sole interest of the religious idea and had not the intention of visiting anything that was not connected with their ostensible object.

In the works of the Moslem geographers there are many interesting things to be found, facts that throw some light too on the Moslem Renaissance, which made the reign of Mamun and some of the Caliphs so remarkable. Science now began to make progress, translations from the classics and other tongues disseminated learning and later set the fashion in Europe. The Crusaders had returned home before the European Renaissance began to show signs of life in the schools of Moslem Cordova; the inception of the new learning started, like most other mental and spiritual schools of thought, from the East.

East of Jordan life must have been very sluggish, for the cities that had been destroyed had not been replaced. Great stretches of desert land alternated with mountain range and with the cornfields and olive groves that were cultivated, it is true, but always under the fear of an incursion from the desert. Brother Felix says that the Bedawin could easily have taken cities and villages had they wanted them, but they declared that they were the nobles who lived on pillage, and that it was beneath them to own places in which they had to do any work.

Walking about among the splendid remains of the past at Jerash, the mind naturally wanders to the condition of the world when all the golden stone pillars were upright and the temples dominated all the scene, and the whole town was surrounded by walls flanked with towers, and the people of another epoch lived their lives in the sunshine and under the blue skies of what we now call Trans-Jordan. As Brother Felix remarked, we live under other stars and our ideas are different too, but, after all, human nature is much the same all the world over and the differences are mostly superficial. If only Theocritus had written one of his inimitable dialogues about the inhabitants of a town that he surely must have visited during his travels; if only he had described the sylvan scene as he alone could do, borrowing the pipes of the shepherd in order to reproduce his music, how much richer we should be and how much more vividly the life of the dead past would come before our eyes.

Jerash remains in the memory as a mass of grouped columns set in a sea of waving corn, under a bright blue sky against which the warm tint of the age-worn stone shows conspicuously.

CHAPTER XXVIII
Sunset

CHAPTER XXVIII
Sunset

TO journey from dawn at Petra to sunset at Jerash, from the dawn of history to the dusk of the destruction of the vanished cities, is a pilgrimage that can only be accomplished by those who have patience and curiosity. Curiosity is, of course, one of the virtues that should be carefully taught and explained to the rising generation, for it implies keen and intense desire for information. Was not the Queen of Sheba moved by philosophical curiosity when she set off with her train of richly laden camels to visit King Solomon? Whether she derived much advantage from hearing the answers to the riddles that she asked, we do not know, but the motive that prompted her pilgrimage, the curiosity and the thirst for knowledge that she displayed, are surely most commendable.

To those who have had patience and curiosity enough to read this book, I can only apologize that the way has not been made more exciting. My own pilgrimage was well worth the trouble involved, the long journeys and the endeavour to learn what could be assimilated; but it is one thing to see the world and quite another to describe it in comprehensible terms to another.

At first the subject seemed well defined within certain limits; while leaving aside those celebrated cities of northern Syria, Baalbek and Palmyra, about which so much has been written, the less well-known cities of Edom and Moab and the Decapolis presented a study that had many attractions. The field was comparatively fresh and had been rendered interesting by the recent explorations of archæologists and explorers. Books, old and new, were ransacked in search of information concerning the subject, books that, alas! proved only too fascinating, opening doors on to all sorts of unexpected prospects, suggesting side issues, luring the curiously minded to explore along side tracks, almost forgetting the main road that ran along ahead, like those few and winding roads in Palestine that look like a white ribbon and lose themselves in the misty distance. The temptation to linger too long by the wayside was almost irresistible, and if I have incurred this reproach, I can only apologize to those who have followed so far, and assure them that they would probably have done the same. The object that I have really had in view was to endeavour to tell the story of these vanished cities, and to people the deserted sites where once they lived, with those who made the history of their times. If I have succeeded, even in a degree, to accomplish this object, I am satisfied.

We have covered thousands of years in our pilgrimage, and have seen the rise and downfall of nations and of dynasties. Mysterious Egypt appears early in the story and remains in it until nearly the end ; Assyria, Babylon, Amurru, that yet to be clearly defined empire ; Persia, with her art and her imagination that influenced the Jews in captivity as well as the Syrians ; Greece the all-pervading, Rome the masterful, Byzantium the great Christianised pagan city, occupy the stage, and then ! . . . annihilation.

After the few poor hundreds of years of prosperity that the Romans brought, came the rise of Islam and the Moslems, who built such glorious buildings and battered down the temples for religion's sake ; after the defeat of the Byzantines on the Yarmuk, the Arabs overran Syria. Three hundred years of constant fighting follow, and then the Fatimites take Egypt and Syria, followed by inroads of the Seljuk Turks, who take again Damascus and Antioch. During the Crusaders' period, though they fought all round the country, Kerak and Petra were the only cities of all those we have visited that suffered much. Saladin's bloody battle of Hattin was on the other side of Jordan ; after Richard Cœur de Lion took Acre there was a truce, but the wild hordes were soon out again. The Kharezmians ravaged

THE END OF THE DAY

Syria and then, in the thirteenth century, came the horrible Mongols. This invasion, accompanied by cruelty and wanton destruction, has been painted in eloquent colours by M. Mouradja D'Ohsson in his " Les peuples du Caucase." I translate literally from the French.

"The conquests of the Mongols," he writes, "changed the face of Asia. Great empires collapse, ancient dynasties perish, some nations disappear, others are almost annihilated; everywhere, on the traces of the Mongols, one sees nothing but ruins and human bones. Surpassing in cruelty the most barbarous people, they cut the throats of men, women and children in the conquered towns; they burn cities and villages, destroy the harvest, transform flourishing countries into deserts; and yet they are not inspired by hatred or revenge. They scarcely know the names of the people they exterminate."

A terrible picture, and one not overdrawn. One wonders, after reading of the barbarities of these ruthless hordes, how anything escaped. Farther than that we need not go in the unhappy history of eastern Palestine, for by that time all the harm had been done, and the smoking ruins were all that were left after the Mongols had gone.

As the sun sets on the wonderful land beyond Jordan the experiences of the past few weeks pass before the mind like a pageant. It shines on the rosy peaks, on the boulders and the fantastic spires of Petra, recalling that curious city of the dead, where no dead rest; I see again the basin through which the stony river course is overhung by oleander and the steep red cliffs honeycombed with tombs and rock dwellings. The setting sun brings out the most unimaginable colours out of the sandstone, ranging from pale flame to crimson; it seems to give a life of its own to the rock city, which changes though it does not end when the sun disappears behind some boulder sharply outlined against the paling sky.

The true history of Petra may yet be buried under the scrub and the tamarisk bushes that cover the ground that lies over successive towns—towns of the Romans and the Greeks and the Nabataeans—perhaps even of the Edomites. It is curious, in a place where all is curious, that the great solitude is really peopled with the ghosts of those who once walked up and down the steep steps that lead up to their houses, or passed along the streets in the plain the traces of which are just apparent. They are very human, the men and women about whom we know such little scraps of their personal history; it is not difficult to get into touch with them. And in spite of the strangeness of Petra, in spite of the almost forbidding grandeur of the gorge that ends so suddenly with the vision of the Treasure House of Pharaoh, it is a place that grows upon you and one that you are loath to leave.

Leaving Petra the mind dwells on the desert, where the lengthening shadows and the long, slanting rays of the departing sun give it a more impressive appearance than it can attain in daylight. The camels walking along in single file have all the appearance of a procession, the shepherd standing in the midst of his flock really looks as if he might need the rifle that is slung from his shoulders, so desolate the scene all around him looks. We pass the great tank and the Arab fort at Qutrani, which used to be garrisoned from Kerak, and can imagine that it still is fortified against the assault of the enemy. The bushes of white broom sprinkle their light branches across the track which was once a Roman road and a caravan route before that; the spaces appear larger, the hills loom mysteriously, Bedawin Arabs smile as you pass, showing a gleam of white teeth in brown faces, almost featureless against the failing light, and their white garments take a lower tone in the gradual decline of the daylight. Even the Hijaz railway, that looks the picture of desolation in daytime, gains a shade of romance as the setting sun gilds the line.

All these memories are connected with the sunset,

and there are others that are equally insistent. It typifies so much in a land where greatness is a thing of the past ; perhaps that is why it seems to affect one more here than in most places.

Madeba is another memory that always comes quite free from tragic thoughts, although it had its history of blood and rapine too ; it suggests a fertile plain and a peaceful and prosperous town in which is the celebrated mosaic map, and in which, in some outhouse, a mop and a pail of water bring to view a pavement of mosaic that would grace a museum. Birds and beasts and human heads and arabesques, they appear gradually as the hay and other rubbish is swept off. And the many and interesting remains of basilicas stamp Madeba as a Christian stronghold, as indeed it was before it, too, vanished.

One of the unforgettable memories is that of the Dead Sea—the stinking sea, as Yakut elegantly called it ; at no time did that freak of nature look more beautiful than when the sun shone down like copper on its translucent green waters, turning to gold the white crystals that lay on the ruffled surface. The Dead Sea takes one back to the very early days when the great upheaval changed the whole aspect of all that deep depression, which originated, so they say, in a fault in the earth's crust. What a sight it must have been ! One can imagine but faintly the terrific explosion of all that bituminous and volcanic eruption that threw up the range of hills on either side and lowered the level of the salt sea, leaving the old sea bottom of the tertiary period to remain there to this day. Did the thunder growl and the lightning fork over the wild scene, and did the sunset, at last, flood the seething waters with a copper radiance just as it did when last I saw it at the close of a perfect spring day ?

In Amman the sunset is most effective when it catches the tiers of stone seats in the theatre, or when seen from the citadel hill, from which extensive views of the country round are obtained. Again, it plays among the reds and yellows and tawny browns of the Arabs' robes in the Suk, and catches the ripples on the stream as some rider throws up the water from his horse's hoofs.

A whole procession of people spring to the mind when the vision of Ammon and, later, of Philadelphia suggests itself. The fierce old tribe of Ammon that succeeded the race of giants and perhaps conquered them, keeping watch in their high fort, treating David's messengers with contumely and fighting his forces to the bitter end when attacked—these and David himself, and Uriah the Hittite, and the jewel from the King of the Ammonites' crown that David wore in his own afterwards, crowd the canvas. And then Herod, called the Great, and Herod Antipas and the daughter of Aretas of Petra come and play their part in the drama, with a dim vision of John the Baptist in the dungeon of Machærus.

Philadelphia gives us less of personal interest, beyond suggesting the silhouette of King Ptolemy Philadelphus of Egypt and his cultured Court or the endless battles of the other Macedonian sovereign Antiochus III, who eventually took the citadel by stopping up the water supply. Of the government of the city of the Decapolis by Tyrants we know little, of the sojourn of the Moslems still less. But the admirable Arab geographer Muqaddasi tells us a little about it in his pleasant book, which makes one regret that the Arabs and their culture have no part in this story of vanished cities, with the solitary exception of the Nabatæans, whose development was, of course, pre-Islamic.

There is something rather attractive in the idea of a whole people of nomads, especially when one comes from the contemplation of all the stored-up wealth and possessions that have been engulfed in the wars. How simple existence must be in those black goats'-hair tents which can be struck and pitched again with so little trouble! And how little you want when existence is simplified. A Damascene coffee-pot, a vessel to make lemman in, a few blankets, some pots and pans, a spindle to prepare the goats' hair and a simple machine for weaving it when spun, and—yes, certainly, a narghilly. Outside, some flocks of goats and sheep or camels, perhaps a horse or two, and the household arrangements are complete. And yet, if you see a camp on the trek, there seems to be a good deal of luggage, so perhaps the simple life in the desert is not so simple as it appears.

The last place on which to throw the light of the sunset is the city of a thousand columns that we have just left. Sunset at Jerash is a very decorative affair; the monoliths loom large against a golden glow and throw exaggerated shadows; a great peace descends on the field of ruins. The oval of the piazza, or the forum, whichever it is, outlined by the pillars with rude Ionic capitals, takes on the appearance of a fairy circle, the birds twitter, little rocksparrows who make their home among the Corinthian capitals of the columns in the portico of the temple of Artemis.

In Jerash it is far more the memories of the artistic beauty of it all than of the human interest that lingers in the memory. And yet in the linked cities of the League of the Decapolis, many names of note appear. They suggest the Greek culture of the late pagan and the early Christian period, when Byzantium was the centre of civilization and when all the wit and the gaiety of a polished society had its little day before it, too, vanished into the evil times. But the wits and the scholastics did not vanish completely, for they lived in their works when they were saved from the general destruction. Yet they had their day and perhaps the Arab poet, Malik ibn Harim, was right when he sang somewhat sadly and cynically :—

> " Yea, knowledge I have of Time, the best of all counsellors, the passing of days that brings to light wealth of hidden lore :
>
> I know how the rich is served by riches, how fair the praise they gather with cunning hands, whatso be the blame his due;

> And how lacking wastes and wears a man though his heart be high—yea, sharper the thing thereof than falling of untanned scourge!
> He looks on the steps of Fame—the steps he can never tread—and sits in the midst of men in silence without a word."

To sit in silence was certainly not the usual practice of the Greco-Syrian, whether he were able to mount the steps of fame or not; the poem, that is pre-Islamic, shows the power of riches in those days. And, indeed, in all ages, " lacking " has wasted and worn many a man who might have risen to fame had he been given the opportunity.

Lucian the satirist, Menippus the author, who lives though his books are lost, Meleager the epigrammatist, and all the rest of the brilliant writers and lecturers that were natives of the Greek cities, give a lustre to their country. They were nearly all wanderers; some of them became the friends of emperors and one was the tutor of Tiberius, while Cicero owned another as collaborator. When the sun sets on the ruins of Gerasa there are many pleasant memories that remain behind.

The last picture in this book is a very striking view of the Dead Sea from the Mount of Olives, and as it represents the scene bathed in the rays of the setting sun it seems a good point of vantage from which to take our last look at the country that we have just left.

One of the most beautiful views to be obtained from Jerusalem is that of the Dead Sea seen from this particular spot. The pool of turquoise blue is shot through with the sun's rays, the rose-red haze is over the intense blue of the mountains of Moab, that long straight range that makes such a superb skyline and that is one of the most arresting visions when seen from almost any eastward-looking part of the Holy City.

With this picture of the sunset we may well leave this record of wanderings among the vanished cities of Arabia.

THE END.